Northwestern
Fights and Fighters

Chief Joseph

From the collection of J. W. Redington

Northwestern Fights and Fighters

BY

CYRUS TOWNSEND BRADY

University of Nebraska Press
Lincoln and London

TO THE

Peace loving, hard working, honor seeking, duty following,
never failing, hard fighting
ARMY OF THE UNITED STATES

Foreword copyright © 1979 by the University of Nebraska Press
Copyright, 1907, by The McClure Company
Copyright renewed 1934 by Katharine M. Brady

First Bison Book printing: 1979

Most recent printing indicated by first digit below:
1   2   3   4   5   6   7   8   9   10

Library of Congress Cataloging in Publication Data

Brady, Cyrus Townsend, 1861–1920, comp.
  Northwestern fights and fighters.

  Reprint of the ed. issued in the author's American fights and fighters series; with new foreword.
  Includes index.
  1. Indians of North America—Wars, 1866–1895. 2. Nez Percé Indians—Wars, 1877. 3. Modoc Indians—Wars, 1873. 4. Little Big Horn, Battle of, 1876. I. Title. II. Series: Brady, Cyrus Townsend, 1861–1920. American fights and fighters series.
E83.866.B82   1979   973.8   79–15171
ISBN 0–8032–1156–2
ISBN 0–8032–6053–9 pbk.

Manufactured in the United States of America

FOREWORD TO THE BISON
BOOK EDITION

First published in 1907, *Northwestern Fights and Fighters* is a collection of accounts of army operations in the Nez Perce War and the Modoc War. Nearly all the accounts are, as the author says, "contributions from participants in the various undertakings," and he has contented himself "with writing a general and comprehensive description of each of the two wars considered, leaving to the actors themselves the telling in full of the detailed story."

Although most of these eye-witness accounts were written by army officers, Part I, on the Nez Perce War, includes "Chief Joseph's Own Story," first published in 1879 in the *North American Review,* with comments on Chief Joseph's narrative by his opponent, Major General O. O. Howard. Also in Part I are chapters devoted to the Battle of White-bird Canyon, the Salmon River Expedition, and the battles of Clearwater, Big Hole, and Camas Meadows. In Part II the scene shifts to Oregon and the Modoc War of 1872–73, which Brady calls "the most costly war in which the United States ever engaged, considering the number of opponents." His overview of the campaign is fleshed out by the reminiscences of eight officers who fought against the Modoc leader, Kientpoos, commonly known as Captain Jack. Since it was written at Brady's request, this material is almost impossible to find elsewhere.

Foreword

The Appendix consists of letters from army officers who were moved to take pen in hand by Brady's 1904 book, *Indian Fights and Fighters* (BB 538), much of which dealt with that never-ending source of controversy, Custer's Little Bighorn Campaign, and memoranda from Yellowstone Kelly on the 1877 Wolf Mountain Campaign in Montana, also treated in the earlier companion volume.

Born in Allegheny, Pennsylvania, Cyrus Townsend Brady (1861–1920) attended the United States Naval Academy at Annapolis, from which he graduated in 1883. After three years in the navy, he and his wife and their young family moved to Omaha, Nebraska, where he worked for the Missouri Pacific and Union Pacific railroads. While in Omaha Brady joined the Episcopal Church and studied for the priesthood, being ordained a deacon in 1889 and a priest in 1890. Shortly thereafter he volunteered for missionary work and during the next five years his duties carried him into five western states. Returning east, from 1895 to 1902 he served first as archdeacon of Pennsylvania and then as rector of St. Paul's Church in Philadelphia. During the Spanish-American War he was chaplain of the First Pennsylvania Volunteer Infantry.

Brady's career as a writer began in 1898 with the publication of *For Love of Country,* a historical novel; it was followed by a long series of romantic novels, popular in their day but of ephemeral interest. In 1902 Brady resigned his post at St. Paul's to devote himself entirely to writing, turning out histories as well as fiction. Although he twice returned to active church work, he concentrated primarily on writing; eventually he wrote motion picture scenarios in addition to three or four novels a year. Of his enormous literary output, only his histories are remembered today, and of the histories the two best are *Indian Fights and Fighters* (1904) and the present work.

PREFACE

IT will be noticed that this book differs from others of the AMERICAN FIGHTS AND FIGHTERS SERIES, and especially its immediate predecessor, "Indian Fights and Fighters," in that I am not the author of all or most of it. In the former volume I declared my intention to devote its successor to the Modoc, Nez Percé, and other wars. In furtherance of this design, I asked contributions from participants in the various undertakings. The response was so immediate and so adequate; the papers submitted were of such high value, not only from an historic but from a literary point of view as well, that I had not the presumption to rewrite them myself — not even the proverbial assurance of the historian would warrant that.

Therefore, I have contented myself with writing a general and comprehensive account of each of the two wars considered, leaving to the actors themselves the telling in full of the detailed story of the splendid achievements in which they were making history. I can affirm, therefore, that never before has there been included in a single volume such a remarkable and interesting collection of personal experiences in our Indian Wars as in this book.

And as I admire the doers of the deeds so, also, do I admire the tellers of the tales. Their modesty, their restraint, their habit of relating adventures which stir

the blood and thrill the soul as a mere matter of course,
—"all in the day's work"— enkindles my enthusiasm.
And how graphically these old soldiers wield their
pens! What good story tellers they are!

And what different sorts and conditions of men are
here represented! Major-generals and scouts, captains
and sergeants, frontiersmen and troopers, soldiers and
civilians, to say nothing of an Indian chief and a bishop,
have all said their say in their own way. The reader will
be glad, I know, that I have permitted these men, like
Paul, to speak for themselves.

The whole book constitutes a trumpet call to American manhood, and honor, and courage, and that I believe
to be true of the whole series.

The Army of the United States is sometimes slandered.
A case in point is now in mind. The chief official of a
city of no little prominence, who is also an author and a
publicist of national repute, has recently put forth a
bitter diatribe against our soldiers. Such a book as this
refutes these unfounded accusations. The Army is not
perfect — neither is the Church! — but not only man
for man, but also as an organization it is the equal of
any, and the superior of most, of the armies of the world!
And I am sure that no one can get a much better training
for the battle of life than he gets in the peace loving,
hard working, honor seeking, duty following, never
failing, hard fighting service of the United States —
on sea or shore. I have been in both, worn the Army and
also the Navy blue, and I know. We all deprecate the
necessity for armies, but if we must have them, let us
thank God for an army like that of our beloved country.
I am glad to express this my deliberate and matured
conviction, begot of much study, wide observation,
and ripe experience.

ACKNOWLEDGMENT

Thanks for valuable contributions and assistance in the preparation of this book are due, and are hereby most gratefully expressed by the author, to the following:

Major-General O. O. Howard; Brigadier-Generals David Perry, H. C. Hasbrouck, Theodore F. Rodenbough, C. A. Coolidge, W. S. Edgerly and E. S. Godfrey; Colonels John Green, James Jackson, W. R. Parnell and D. L. Brainard; Lieutenant-Colonel W. H. C. Bowen; Majors J. G. Trimble, James Biddle, F. A. Boutelle and H. L. Bailey; and Captain R. H. Fletcher, all officers of the United States Army; the Right Reverend W. H. Hare, D.D., LL.D., Bishop of South Dakota; Chief Joseph of the Nez Percés; Lieutenant-Colonel Theodore Ewert, Illinois National Guard; Messrs. E. S. Farrow, J. W. Redington, G. O. Shields, H. J. Davis, I. D. Applegate, L. S. Kelly, and Theodore W. Goldin; *McClure's Magazine,* the *Metropolitan Magazine,* the *North American Review,* the *Century Magazine, Sunset Magazine,* the *United Service Magazine,* Harper & Brothers, Rand, McNally & Co., the New York *Sun,* and the Klamath Falls *Express;* together with the War Department of the United States and the Department of the Interior.

C. T. B.

ix

CONTENTS

PART I

THE NEZ PERCÉ WAR

Contents

❧

PART II

THE MODOC WAR

Contents

APPENDIX

LIST OF ILLUSTRATIONS

XV

MAPS AND PLANS

PART I
The Nez Percé War

CHAPTER ONE

The Epic of the Nez Percés

By Dr. Brady

XENOPHON has chronicled the retreat of the ten thousand; De Quincey has romanced about the migration of the Tartars; a thousand pens have recorded the annihilation of the Grand Army of Napoleon: the story of Joseph and his Nez Percés is my theme — the story of the bitterest injustice toward a weak but independent people to which the United States ever set its hand. And at the outset let me confess that I am the *advocatus diaboli* — the friend of the Indian, at least in this instance!

In 1855, Governor Isaac I. Stevens of Washington Territory negotiated an equitable, even a liberal treaty by which the Nez Percés were confirmed in their undoubted title by immemorial occupancy to the vast region in Idaho, Oregon, and Washington, including the valleys of the Snake, the Salmon, the Clearwater, and the Grande Ronde Rivers.

The scope of the Stevens treaty was so extensive and its provisions so fair, that it is probable no question would ever have arisen had not the convention been abrogated in 1863 by a new treaty which materially diminished the Nez Percé Reservation. This treaty was signed by a majority of the Indian tribes and has been loyally kept by them to this day. Old Joseph and other chiefs declined to sign it, refused to live on the proposed reservation, and continued to occupy the fertile valleys of the Wallowa and Imnaha, tributaries of the Grande Ronde and the Snake respectively. They also refused even to stay on the lands they claimed except when it suited them.

As the majority of the Nez Percés had signed the treaty, the United States, pressed thereto by the settlers, took the position that the action of the majority was binding upon the minority. The Nez Percé Nation was made up of a number of small tribes more or less independent of one another. The lower Nez Percés of whom Old Joseph was the recognized head, who had refused to sign the treaty, recognized no power in the majority to constrain them to acquiescence. To the non-treaty Nez Percés their position was absolutely impregnable. They were the original owners of the land. From time immemorial they had been absolutely free men, as free to go where they pleased as any people on earth.

Old Joseph died in 1872, bequeathing to his son and successor, Young Joseph, called in his own language Im-mut-too-yah-lat-lat,* which means Thunder-rolling-in-the-mountains, the policy of ignoring the treaty and retaining the land. Young Joseph thus records the eloquent dying speech of his aged father:

My son, my body is returning to my mother earth, and my spirit is going very soon to see the Great Spirit Chief. When I am gone, think of your country. You are the chief of these people. They look to you to guide them. Always remember that your father never sold his country. You must stop your ears whenever you are asked to sign

* The reader will notice that many of these Nez Percé names are spelled differently by different writers in this series of papers. Inasmuch as most of the names are phonetically presented I have not striven for uniformity, but have let each man spell for himself as he pleased.—C. T. B.

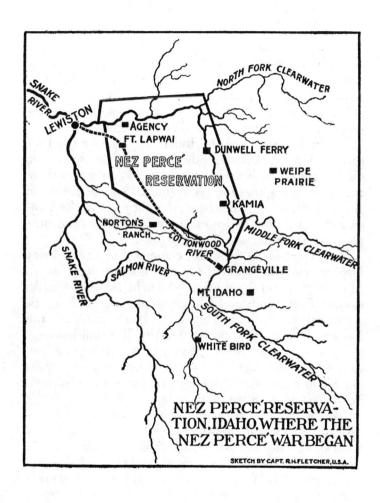

NEZ PERCE RESERVA-
TION, IDAHO, WHERE THE
NEZ PERCE WAR BEGAN

SKETCH BY CAPT. R.H.FLETCHER, U.S.A.

a treaty selling your home. A few years more, and white men will be all around you. They have their eyes on this land. My son, never forget my dying words. This country holds your father's body. Never sell the bones of your father and your mother.

In 1873, further to complicate matters, the United States gave the Indians temporary permission to remain in the Wallowa Valley. This valley is admirably adapted for grazing and agricultural purposes. Settlers, pouring into the Northwest, recognizing no right of proprietorship among the Indians, occupied it.

The white man and the Indian have never lived together in peace. Among other Indians less forbearing there would have been instant outbreak. As it was there was a growing friction. A commission, appointed in 1876, decided — in defiance of right — that the non-treaty Nez Percés had no standing and that they must go upon the reservation of 1863.

Maj.-Gen. O. O. Howard, commanding the Military Department, was ordered to carry out the decision. In May, 1877, several councils were held in quick succession at Fort Lapwai, Idaho. Joseph, attended by his young brother Ollicut, White Bird, Hush-hush-cute and Looking Glass, sub-chiefs, and by Too-hul-hul-sote, the priest, or *too-at*, of a peculiar religious organization called the "Dreamers" to which Joseph and the others belonged, which had evidently risen out of the disputes in connection with the land, were present.

"Joseph at this time must have been about thirty-seven or thirty-eight years old. He is tall, straight and handsome, with a mouth and chin not unlike that of Napoleon I. He was, in council, at first probably not so influential as White Bird and the group of chiefs that sustained him, but from first to last he was preëminently their 'war chief.' Such was the testimony of his followers after his surrender, and such seems to be the evidence of the campaign itself." *

The proceedings were dramatic but not happy. Old Too-hul-hul-sote, the Indian orator, who was remarkable for the inveteracy of his hatred of the white men, was summarily placed under arrest to keep him quiet. Joseph secured his release and the council adjourned on May 7th, Joseph agreeing for himself and the rest to obey the order of the commission and go upon the reservation. He did this most reluctantly, and only because he felt that it would be better to submit to injustice rather than to provoke a war in which he was wise enough to see that he and his people would be the chief sufferers.

A certain time was given him to collect his people and move to the reservation. His pacific intentions were not shared by his younger warriors. Among them were three whose fathers or brothers had been killed by white settlers some time before; a fourth had been beaten by a white man. Some perfunctory investigations had been made; but as they were carried on by the white men, nothing was done to punish the offenders and pacify the enraged Indians. It is certain that the first act of aggression was committed and the first blood was shed by the white men.

Joseph and White Bird had withdrawn to the Salmon River and were engaged in preparing for the removal. The three young Nez Percés mentioned, with a few other reckless braves, resolved to take matters in their hands and, if they could, force the issue. On June 13th, they assumed the offensive. On that and the next day several settlers were murdered. Other warriors joined the first aggressors. The alarm spread through the

* Quotation from Colonel Wood's *Century* article.—C. T. B.

surrounding ranches and little settlements. From the Norton House at Cottonwood Falls, half-way between Fort Lapwai and the little town of Mount Idaho, the settlers started for the latter place to escape the savages. The party was pursued and overcome. Two men and some children were killed, two others mortally wounded, the women outrageously treated, although Joseph afterward denied this. It is a matter of record that Joseph had no personal knowledge of this affair. He was not there, he had not ordered it, he could not have prevented it. The young men rode into the camp of White Bird waving scalps and other booty, and succeeded in stampeding the camp.

Too-hul-hul-sote welcomed the diversion and incited the men with all the power he possessed. Every voice was for war, resistance to unjust decree, vengeance upon the white men. When Joseph reached his camp he found his band was committed to war against the United States. Hostilities had begun. He protested, but in vain. Matters had gone too far. From his point of view there was nothing left for him but to cast in his lot with the rest. Joseph had not provoked the outbreak. He had done his best to keep the peace: but now the outbreak had come he would do his part to make it formidable.

Joseph was at this time about thirty-seven years old. The Nez Percés had been at peace with everybody for years. Joseph had done no fighting whatsoever. What his capacities as a soldier were no one knew. The first test came quickly. Messengers from Mount Idaho were sent speeding to Fort Lapwai with the news of the murder of the settlers and piteous appeals for help. General Howard acted with commendable promptness. There were two skeleton troops of the First Cavalry at the post.

The garrison numbered a little over one hundred and twenty men. Ninety of them, under Captains Perry and Trimble, with Lieutenant Parnell of the First Cavalry and Lieutenant Theller of the Twenty-first Infantry, were despatched to protect the settlers. Nobody believed that the Indians would fight and it was expected that Perry's force would be adequate to secure the criminals and bring the rest to the reservation. Nevertheless, to be prepared for any contingency, Howard ordered an immediate concentration of the available troops in his Department at Fort Lapwai. It was well that he did so.

Perry marched rapidly, making eighty miles in about thirty hours over execrable country for the most part. He was joined by ten volunteers from Grangeville, and on the 17th of June, very early in the morning, came in contact with Joseph in White Bird Cañon. So soon as Joseph recognized that hostilities were inevitable, he had concentrated his and White Bird's bands on the banks of the Salmon River, a tortuous torrential stream, just where White Bird Creek empties into it.

The country is mountainous and broken. Some distance back from the river there is a high rugged table-land. The tributaries of the river take their rise in this table-land and run through precipitous and gloomy cañons until they reach the valley. The cañon, at first very narrow, grew wider as it approached the river several miles below. Between the entrance of the cañon and the bank of the river was a stretch of rolling ground several hundred yards in width. The entrance was covered by buttes and rocky ravines, forming a natural defense. At intervals on either side of the cañon extended lateral cañons, short and steep, but through which the soldiers, if hard pressed, might escape to the upper levels. The banks of the rushing brook, the White

Bird, were slightly timbered, the valley of the Salmon bare of trees.

Arriving while it was yet dark at the source of White Bird Creek, Perry waited until dawn, giving his men and horses a much-needed rest. In the gray of the morning, when he could see the gleam of the river far below him, he took up the march down through the wild gap in the mountains.

In the open valley with his back to the Salmon River, his front toward White Bird Cañon, Joseph had pitched his camp. It was concealed from Perry by the inequalities of the ground. Only the smoke from the camp-fires, rising in the still air of the spring morning, indicated its position. Silhouetted against the sky in the light of the rising sun, illuminating the west side of White Bird Creek, keen eyes in Joseph's camp discovered horsemen at the head of the cañon. A field-glass revealed the soldiers.

As Joseph watched them the descent began. For an instant all was confusion in the Indian camp. Something like a panic began to develop.

"Let us cross over the river with the women and children and abandon the camp," urged Ollicut. "The soldiers will not be able to get at us there."

White Bird, too, thought the advice was good, but Joseph was in no mood for retreat. He resolved to remain and give battle. With quick military instinct, he sent the women and children with the spare horses down the river behind the bluffs. He divided his two hundred warriors into two bodies. One moiety he gave to White Bird with instructions to move to the right, taking position just at the mouth of the cañon behind the ample cover afforded by ridges and ravines. With his own men, he lined the buttes covering the space where the cañon debouched in the valley. His dispositions were admirable. He had set a trap for the soldiers.

The cañon widened sufficiently as it descended to permit the soldiers to approach in a column of fours. No precaution was neglected. One hundred yards in advance rode Lieutenant Theller with eight troopers. Captain Perry with the volunteers and his own men followed, and some fifty yards after this party, Trimble with his troop.

Not an Indian was to be seen, but every man was on the alert and ready. Suddenly, the buttes were lined with Indians. Rifle-shots rang out; several bodies of mounted Indians galloped between the buttes and charged toward the approaching column, yelling and firing. The trap was sprung. From an elevated point Captain Perry discovered that the level ground back of the buttes was filled with Indians. Lieutenant Theller, upon whom the first attack fell, deployed his squad of men and, by putting up a bold front, kept the Indians in check until Captain Perry's company came up at a gallop. The volunteers seized the most commanding position on the field, a hillock to the left. They at once dismounted and opened fire. Perry dismounted and deployed his company in a slight depression on the right of the volunteers, backing up Theller who retreated on the main body in good order. On the right of Perry, Trimble's company galloped into line.

The soldiers were cool and determined. The firing was fast and furious for a few moments. Several of the troopers were hit; but there were no serious casualties. The cañon was filled with smoke. The Indians galloping to and fro, those on foot scarcely exposing themselves at all, escaped with little loss. As the exciting moments fled away, White Bird gained his appointed position and suddenly appeared in force opposite the left flank of the soldiers. At the same time, Joseph extended his line on the right flank. To prevent his right from being turned Perry detached Sergeant McCarthy with six men to take position on the slope of the cañon and hold it. White Bird instantly attacked on the left and was completely successful. The volunteers, losing two men, fled, leaving the flank of Perry's company in the air. Joseph seized the abandoned butte, the key to the position. There were moments of confusion and alarm, but the officers kept their men in hand. The troopers sprang to their horses and slowly retreated up the cañon, seeking another ridge upon which to reform, fighting every foot of the way.

They were furiously pressed by the Indians. In the confusion, Trimble's troop gave back, leaving McCarthy's band isolated and surrounded. Trimble rallied them and charged the Indians; they were checked and the retreat of the soldiers halted for the time being. But they had lost their position and in a short time the whole body was forced back for the second time. Again brave McCarthy and his desperate six, who had been grimly holding their place among the rocks, were abandoned.

Lieutenant Parnell with a platoon of Trimble's troop made a gallant charge to rescue them. The party was brought off except two who were shot from their horses and killed. Parnell and his men streamed up the cañon in a wild gallop after the flying main body. The officer kept his head, however, and succeeded in rescuing another wounded man on the way. For these two exhibitions of distinguished gallantry he received a medal of honor, as did McCarthy, the heroic sergeant.

There is no disguising the fact that the troops were

now panic-stricken. They had not looked for such fighting, such generalship. The officers displayed splendid heroism, but unavailingly. Lieutenant Theller brought up the rear. The Indians, by taking to ravines and intersecting cañons, were able to intercept a number of the soldiers who were pressed so hard that they had retreated into one of the lateral cañons. The rear-guard was thus cut off. Unfortunately they retreated into a cul-de-sac and were killed to the last man. Only the speed of their horses saved the rest of the men from annihilation; as it was, Theller and thirty-six men were killed and two desperately wounded. It was not until they got out of the cañon and the pursuit was abandoned that Perry was able to bring them to a stand. The total casualties among the troops were nearly forty per cent!

The first blow in the grim little game had been struck and all the honors were with Joseph. He had displayed in this battle all the qualities of a soldier. He had demonstrated in force along the enemy's lines and had suddenly attacked him heavily on the left flank. When the enemy had retreated he had made use of his topographical knowledge to intercept his rear-guard and cut it to pieces. Throughout the battle he had been in the very thick of the fighting. He had exposed himself to every possible danger without hesitation. During this battle Joseph's wife gave birth to a daughter. When he finally gave up the struggle in Montana this was the only child left him. And the baby was with him all through the long retreat.

Now was seen the wisdom of Howard's orders for the concentration of the troops. As the different troops reported, he despatched them to the front and presently took the field with some three hundred soldiers. Joseph still remained in the valley of the Salmon. On June 27th, his scouts reported the approach of Howard. Waiting until Howard had almost reached the valley, Joseph moved down the Salmon River a few miles, crossed it and took up a strong position in the mountains on the other side. He had chosen his position with as much generalship as Washington displayed when he established his winter camp after Trenton and Princeton in the hills about Morristown. He threatened everything.

General Howard thus comments on the strategy of the great Nez Percé: "The leadership of Chief Joseph was indeed remarkable. No general could have chosen a safer position, or one that would be more likely to puzzle and obstruct a pursuing foe. If we present a weak force he can turn upon it. If we make direct pursuit he can go southward toward Boise, for at least thirty miles, and then turn our left. He can go straight to his rear, and cross the Snake at Pittsburg Landing. He can go on down the Salmon, and cross at several places and then turn either to the left, for his old haunts in the Wallowa Valley, or to the right and pass our flank threatening our line of supply, while he has, at the same time, a wonderful natural barrier between him and us in the Salmon, a river that delights itself in its furious flow."

The only way Howard could dislodge him was to cross the Salmon River and attack him in the fastnesses of the hills. Should he do that Joseph either could wait his attack with splendid prospects of success, or he could execute a counter-stroke by recrossing the Salmon to the north and falling upon Howard's communications. It was impossible for Howard to keep his army in idleness staring at Joseph across the river. He decided to follow him. Howard was not deceived as to the possibilities of the situation, for he despatched Major Whipple with two troops of cavalry to move toward Cottonwood Creek where Looking Glass and his men had encamped.

Looking Glass was very much disaffected, especially since the news of the victory in White Bird Cañon, and Howard hoped to prevent him from joining Joseph. Whipple had orders to force Looking Glass on the reservation. Incidentally, Whipple was to hold Joseph in check in case he attempted to cut Howard's communications.

Things did not happen as they were planned. Howard crossed the Salmon River; Joseph made off to the north, crossing the river with all his women, children and horses; Whipple fell in with Looking Glass and succeeded in capturing eight hundred ponies, but the chief and his people escaped. Joseph descended from the mountains and marched rapidly across Camas Prairie, while Howard was still entangled in the mountain country, and fell upon Whipple's force which was hastily intrenched at Cottonwood Ranch. A scouting-party under Lieutenant Rains, comprising a sergeant and nine men, was surrounded and killed to a man on the 3rd of July. On the 4th another party of civilians proceeding to the succor of Whipple was surrounded, its commander and others desperately wounded and the whole party placed in grave peril from which they were only extricated by a gallant cavalry charge by a troop sent from the position to rescue them. Whipple was closely invested. Howard learned of these disasters and again acted promptly. He retraced his steps across the Salmon, up White Bird Cañon and followed Joseph post-haste to the Cottonwood Ranch.

Joseph, well served by his scouts, was aware of Howard's movements. He raised the siege and retreated to the south fork of the Clearwater where it is joined by

Cottonwood Creek. There he effected a junction with Looking Glass which raised his numbers to some two hundred and fifty fighting men, with about four hundred and fifty women and children.

His campaign so far had been a brilliant success. The untried Nez Percé had beaten the enemy in detail. In the face of a more numerous and entirely unencumbered body of fighters, he had succeeded in concentrating his own men, — all this while accompanied by over two thousand ponies, large herds of cattle, and his women and children.

Joseph remained quiet waiting Howard's next move. So soon as he got his little army in hand Howard, with some four hundred men, mostly cavalry, with a small body of artillery, and some mounted infantry, advanced to attack him. Although greatly outnumbered Joseph did not retreat. He had chosen his position on the bank of the Clearwater, a mountain stream with steep banks rising to level plateaus cut by deep ravines. On the banks of the river he had thrown up some rude fortifications. When Howard's army appeared, Joseph did not wait, but instantly attacked him. Though his force was small he made skilful attempts to outflank the American soldiers and nearly succeeded. Indeed, only the timely arrival of reinforcements prevented the capture of Howard's supply-train.

The night of July 11th left both contestants on the field, each confident that the morrow would give him the victory. There were a number of wounded among the soldiers, and their condition was the more aggravated because the Indians had seized the only spring whence the troops could get water while the Indians held the river. The fighting during the day had been fierce and in several instances hand-to-hand. The Indians had charged directly upon the troops again and again as before led by Joseph in person. He seemed to bear a charmed life for, although horses were killed under him, he escaped without a wound.

The Indian fire was terribly accurate and very fatal, the proportion of wounded to killed being about two to one. "A large number of the casualties occurred in the short time before each man had protected himself by earth thrown up with his trowel bayonet. At one point of the line, one man, raising his head too high, was shot through the brain; another soldier, lying on his back and trying to get the last few drops of warm water from his canteen, was robbed of the water by a bullet taking off the canteen's neck while it was at his lips. An officer, holding up his arm, was shot through the wrist; another, jumping to his feet for an instant, fell with a bullet through the breast." *

The next day the battle was renewed. Howard, by making good use of his artillery, succeeded in driving the Indians back to their intrenchments. Employing his preponderance of force he concentrated a column under Maj. Marcus P. Miller, which he launched against the Indian left. The cavalry charged most gallantly, and in spite of a desperate resistance crossed the ravine and turned the Indian intrenchments, taking them in reverse. Joseph's position was now untenable. By a dashing countercharge he checked Miller, and by a vigorous resistance he held off Howard so that he finally brought off his force in good order. Extricating himself with great skill he retreated up the river, crossing it at Kamiah Ford where he halted ready for further battle.

* Quotation from Col. C. E. S. Wood's brilliant article in the *Century* for 1884, by permission of the publishers.—C. T. B.

In these two days of hard fighting the troops lost thirteen killed and twenty-seven wounded. The Nez Percés lost twenty-three killed and forty-six wounded. Forty were captured. Although defeated Joseph had not lost credit. He had inflicted serious loss upon the enemy. He had fought a two days' battle against a force outnumbering his own in the ratio of eight to five, and when defeated had withdrawn in good order. He had reëstablished himself in another formidable position.

General Howard's summary of the campaign thus far is both just and generous: "The Indians had been well led and well fought. They had defeated two companies in a pitched battle. They had eluded pursuit, and crossed the Salmon. They had turned back and crossed our communications, had kept our cavalry on the defensive, and defeated a company of volunteers. They had been finally forced to concentrate, it is true, and had been brought to battle. But, in battle with regular troops, they had held out for nearly two days before they were beaten, and after that were still able to keep together, cross a river too deep to be forded, and then check our pursuing cavalry and make off to other parts beyond Idaho. The result would necessitate a long and tedious chase.

"Still, on our side, the Indians had been stopped in their murders, had been resolutely met everywhere, and driven into position, and beaten; and, by subsequent pursuit, the vast country was freed from their terrible presence."

The indefatigable Howard marched up the Clearwater in pursuit, and finding that Joseph's position at Kamiah could not successfully be attacked in front he proceeded past him to Dunnell's Ford, intending to cross there and turn by the right flank and fall upon Joseph's rear. Joseph divined this, and desiring to reorganize his troops and prepare for a desperate venture he resorted to stratagem for delay. He sent word to Howard that he would like to talk with him. Howard thereupon halted at Dunnell's Ford where Joseph sent one of his warriors to talk with him, playing for time!

Meanwhile, the Nez Percés made every preparation to carry out the momentous decision to which their chief had come. Since Idaho had become too hot for him, Joseph determined to lead his people across the mountains to the hunting-ground in Montana and thence to that haven of malcontent Indians, British Columbia. Once across the British line they would be safe. This involved a retreat of from fifteen hundred to two thousand miles with a certainty of pursuit. It meant hard marching and harder fighting. It was a desperate resolution, but perhaps the only one save surrender — which he did not consider for a moment — to which the great Nez Percé could come.

"Joseph's last appeal was to call a council in the dale, and passionately condemn the proposed retreat from Idaho. 'What are we fighting for?' he asked. 'Is it for our lives? No. It is for this land where the bones of our fathers are buried. I do not want to take my women among strangers. I do not want to die in a strange land. Some of you tried to say once that I was afraid of the whites. Stay here with me now and you shall have plenty of fighting. We will put our women behind us in these mountains and die on our own land fighting for them. I would rather do that than run I know not where.'" *

He did not decide upon this course without great reluctance. He knew that he was leaving, and probably forever, the land which had been the home of his fathers.

* From Colonel Wood's *Century* article.— C. T. B.

Would he ever come back to it? Would he ever reach the desired haven across the far-off boundary line?

Howard was soon convinced that Joseph had no intention of coming in, so he crossed the Clearwater and struck for his rear in accordance with his plan. If he could drive Joseph back toward the Salmon he could get him eventually by surrounding him in the limited country at his disposal for marching and fighting. His advance was delayed at Weippe on July 17th by a body of Indians whom Joseph had thrown forward for that purpose. This and the time lost in the negotiations gave Joseph the start he wanted. When Howard with the loss of one man killed and one wounded had dispersed the Indians at Weippe and dashed down the river he discovered that Joseph was gone. With his flocks and his herds, his women and his children, his old and his young, he had struck the famous Lo-lo Trail and was hurrying northward and eastward with all the speed he could command.

There is no worse trail in North America than the Lo-lo. At times it straggled over huge boulders and jagged ravines; again through forests primeval, every foot so encumbered with prostrate trees as to be well-nigh impassable.

The following description of the trail and a typical march of the troops over it is from the pen of Captain Farrow:

"The ascent of the heights beyond Kamiah was tedious in the extreme. It was raining hard, and the muddy, slippery trail was almost impassable, filled with rugged rocks and fallen timber. The descent to the Lo-lo Fork was made by slipping, crawling and scrambling over rocks and through thick underbrush. At the 'We-ipe' was an opening in the forest with water and grass. Here was a camp made for the weary, footsore animals and exhausted men, after a sixteen mile march of the greatest severity.

"The trail ahead being obstructed by fallen trees of all sizes and descriptions, uprooted by the winds and matted together in every possible troublesome way, a company of forty 'pioneers,' with axes, was organized and sent ahead to open the trail, wherever possible. It is true that the Indians had gone over this trail ahead of the troops; but they had jammed their ponies through, over and under the rocks, around, over and under logs and fallen trees and through the densest undergrowth, and left blood to mark their path, with abandoned animals with broken legs or stretched dead on the trail.

"It is remarkable that the average daily march of sixteen miles was made over the Lo-lo Trail, when we realize the necessity of climbing ridge after ridge, in the wildest wilderness, the only possible passageway filled with timber, small and large, crossed and crisscrossed. The following, from the record of August 2nd, will serve to show the nature of these daily marches:

"The command left camp at seven A.M. Artillery at head of column. The trail led through woods of the same general character; a 'slow trail,' owing to mountainous country and fallen timber. The summit of the hills was covered with rough granite boulders, making the path quite difficult. Our men travel it well, and are in good order. We march sixteen miles and encamp on a slope of the mountain. Poor grazing; the only feed consists of wild dwarf lupine and wire-grass. Several mules were exhausted, and some packs of bacon were abandoned by the way. Dead and broken-down Indian ponies very numerous along the trail. Camp made about four P.M."

The Indian, unlike the Arab, has no affection for his horse. An Indian can get more out of a horse than any other man on earth, because he doesn't hesitate to kill him in the process. Joseph had enough horses to remount his tribe several times. The ponies were often ridden until they dropped. The cavalry in pursuit had no remounts. The infantry had to go afoot. That Howard was able to keep so close behind the Indians is marvelous. That the infantry could keep up is even more remarkable. For seventy-five days the average *per diem* of the soldiers, including all stops and haltages, was eighteen miles. On one occasion the cavalry marched one hundred and forty-five miles in four days. On another the entire command, cavalry, infantry, and wagons, seventy-five miles in three days.

The Indians marched greater distances. They were forced to make wide detours while the pursuers followed direct lines. Yet Joseph managed always to keep two or three days ahead of Howard.

The telegraph had been busy and the troops in the northern detachments were being made ready to intercept the Nez Percés. Captain C. C. Rawn commanded Fort Missoula. With fifty regulars and one hundred citizen volunteers he hastily fortified Lo-lo Pass through the Cœur d'Alenes. When Joseph got there he demanded free passage to march down the Bitter Root Valley. He pledged himself to commit no depredations if the permission were granted. Rawn refused except on condition of Indian disarmament. On the failure of negotiations Joseph, on July 28th, made a tremendous demonstration in front of the works with a thin skirmish-line, while he led the rest of his people through cañons hitherto impassable, over unheard mountain trails, past the flank of Rawn's command and into the valley.

Learning this too late to prevent it Rawn hastily moved back on his rear-guard which was already slightly engaged. The citizens, realizing that Joseph had no intention of molesting them, deserted Rawn and there was nothing left for him but to return to Missoula.

Joseph kept his word although there was no obligation upon him to do so, since he had not been granted free passage but had forced it. The inhabitants of the Bitter Root Valley did a lucrative business with the Indians, who were thus enabled to acquire much-needed supplies, including guns and ammunition!

From Helena, Montana, Gen. John Gibbon started for Missoula with a portion of his regiment, the Seventh Infantry. By hard marching he reached the fort August 3rd. With one hundred and forty-six men, seventeen officers, and thirty-four citizen volunteers, he started down the valley. He loaded his troops in wagons and made splendid time in spite of bad roads and mountain-ranges. Joseph, ignorant of the approach of Gibbon, knowing that he was a long distance ahead of Howard, moved leisurely and had no scouts out.

On the 8th of August, Gibbon's advance discovered the Indians. At ten o'clock at night Gibbon, leaving his wagons and his one piece of artillery with a small guard, started for the camp. He reached the vicinity about two o'clock in the morning. Without betraying his presence he led his men to high ground one hundred and fifty yards from the camp. Joseph had pitched his tepees in a meadow on the south side of the Big Hole River. The banks of the river were covered with a thick growth of willows and underbrush. The meadow was rolling and the farther side rose in hills covered with trees. The tree clad hills bordered the river on the north side. From Gibbon's position the smoldering fires disclosed the

Indian camp. The tepees were pitched in a V-shape with the apex westward. Below were several hundred ponies grazing and on the hills on the other side were large herds.

As day broke the soldiers advanced. Captains Comba and Sanno deployed their men and, dropping down the bluffs, waded silently through the river flowing breast-high. Captains Logan and Rawn swung to the right to attack the Indians on the left flank. Lieutenant Bradley, supported by Captain Williams, moved to the left to cut off the herd. The advance was made in perfect silence until one of the herd guards detected Bradley's movement. He fired a shot and gave the alarm. Gibbon's orders had been that so soon as the first shot was fired the men were to charge.

Dashing across the river and forcing their way through the undergrowth they fell on the camp like a storm. The surprise was complete. The Indians had barely time to seize their weapons and fly. In twenty minutes after the signal was given the camp was in Gibbon's hands.

"The soldiers poured into the camp, firing into the tepees, and, in the gray light, shooting indiscriminately everything that moved. Naked warriors, with only their rifles and cartridge-belts, ran into the willows and to the prairie knolls overlooking the camp and instantly from these positions of vantage opened a telling fire. Women and children, roused from sleep, ran away screaming with terror, or surrounded by enemies, begged by signs for mercy. (It is needless to say that no women or children were intentionally killed.) Some few women armed themselves in desperation, but most of them fled or hid under the overhanging banks of the creek or in the bushes." *

* From Colonel Wood's *Century* article.—C. T. B.

Maj.-Gen. O. O. Howard, U. S. A. (Retired)

In every other Indian battle which I have considered such a surprise meant a crushing defeat for the Indians and the destruction of the camp. Not so in this instance. Joseph, White Bird, and Looking Glass at once rallied their men. The Indians fled to the thickets on the banks of the river and the wooded knolls and bluffs surrounding the camp. Some of them took shelter in the river itself. Logan's men, having crossed the river, found the Indians on their backs. The battle was sharp and furious. The casualties on both sides were fearful. Again and again the Indians made charges on the soldiers in the village, and the fighting was hand-to-hand. Instead of a victory Gibbon found that he was fighting for life. The Indian riflemen — and these Indians could shoot straighter than any on the continent — were decimating his men.

Forming his command in two lines back-to-back, Gibbon charged through the undergrowth in both directions. The Indians retreated a short distance and finally checked the charges and began to swarm into the meadow. Gibbon had to retire or be cut to pieces. He recrossed the river and took position on a wooded knoll well adapted for defense. The Nez Percés attacked him furiously, and under cover of their own fire broke camp and sent the women, children, and horses to the southward.

The fighting raged all day. Joseph tried every device to dislodge the soldiers. He set fire to the grass and would have burned them out had not a fortunate change of wind turned the fire away at that critical moment. At eleven o'clock at night Joseph withdrew. Gibbon had lost three officers killed or mortally wounded, Captain Logan and Lieutenants Bradley and English. Four officers wounded, including himself, Captain Williams with two wounds, and Lieutenants Coolidge and Woodruff with three each. Twenty-one soldiers were dead and six civilians. There were thirty-one soldiers and four civilians wounded, making a total loss out of one hundred and ninety of sixty-nine.

During the day the wagon-train was attacked by a detachment. The howitzer which was being brought up to the battle-field was captured, one of the detachment killed, three others wounded. The howitzer was dismantled and twenty-five hundred rounds of ammunition seized. Gibbon had sent messages to Howard of his predicament and on the 12th, the day after the fighting, Howard arrived with an advance-party of fifty of his best mounted men. Taking with him a number of volunteers from Gibbon's command Howard pushed on after Joseph while Gibbon, with his wounded, returned to Fort Missoula.

The account of this battle given to General Howard in General Gibbon's own words, in the latter's camp, is most interesting: *

"When the Nez Percés had avoided Rawn with his small force, in the Lo-lo, they ascended the Bitter Root. At first they traveled slowly enough, delaying to trade with inhabitants. Wasn't it a shame in those Bitter Root people to traffic with the horrid murderers, giving them fresh horses, and all sorts of provisions, as readily as if they had been the best friends in the world? I am glad to say that one man had courage enough to shut his store in their faces. I set out with a little short of one hundred and fifty rifles, on the 4th (August, 1879), from Missoula, using wagons, to make all the distance possible. I don't think we could have got through to this

* Quoted from General Howard's book, "Chief Joseph, His Pursuit and Capture."
—C. T. B.

place, if I hadn't been most lucky in running across Mr. Blodget, a frontiersman, who had piloted wagons over this country before. The packs were on hand, if we had failed with the wagon-train. Wasn't it a rough road, though ? It took us a long time to get over the divides, but in the bottoms we made grand time.

"We ran across a number of the Indians' camps, and they made some twelve or fifteen miles a day; so that, by doubling on them, I knew I would, in time, catch up. But we were delayed beyond measure at the Rocky Mountains. Our men had to draw the wagons up with ropes. It took us hours to get to the top. Well, we accomplished it, and worked our way down this slope, into Big Hole; rested a while; then leaving a small detachment, three or four miles back, with the howitzer, where you saw the camp, with the remainder I came on, slowly and silently, under cover of the night. We heard the sound of Indian ponies on the next spur, over there, to my left. Pushing along quietly between them and the bottom, we at last discovered the Indian lodges.

"Here I halted my command, for it was altogether too dark to move to the attack. We could catch sounds from the tepees; occasionally a dog would bark, or a child cry; but, evidently, our presence was not discovered.

"On the edge of the bottom, I deployed my companies into line, putting the citizens on the left, for quite a number of them had volunteered to come on and help us. You notice the big sloughs there beside the creek! The willows are thicker in spots. The command now moved forward rapidly; but the Indians discovered the attack as soon as we had started, and several of them put themselves across this creek, into that bend, and, using the bank as cover, opened fire. Some of our men swept past these, and through the tepees, driving the Indians before them.*

"At first we had passed the low ground, and had taken the camp, and appeared to have carried everything; but I soon found that the Indians had not given up. Some were in the willows, working as skirmishers; some rallied up yonder on the hill, and started across the bottom to retake their herd, while others got behind the trees and rocks, and were picking off our men, one by one, and you know, we couldn't well spare any. Some of my officers were wounded already, and myself among the number.

"At last I ordered the move back to this side, and we took this wooded point. Here we were a good deal exposed to the sharp-shooters, and several officers were wounded, but we drove them back, defeated every attempt to assault our camp, and inflicted great loss upon the Indians. Of course they yelled, crept up close at times, fired, and set the grass on fire, but all that time we were digging those trenches, and barricading, giving to the hostiles as good as they sent.

"Next day, until night, parties of them were lurking about, between me and my train. The attempt to fetch up the howitzer brought on a severe skirmish, and the howitzer was lost; but that night (evening of the 10th) the last of them gave us a sharp volley, about eleven o'clock, and cleared out. And here you find us, some killed, many wounded, but in no way discouraged."

Eighty-nine dead Indians were left on the field, a number of them being women and children. Among them

* "He pointed to where women, during the battle, with their little ones in their arms, had waded into the deep water to avoid the firing; and told me how it touched his heart when two or three extended their babies toward him, and looked as pleasant and wistful as they could for his protection; this was while the balls were whistling through the willows near by."— General Howard.

was Looking Glass. The honors of the fight were with Joseph. That he was not annihilated after the surprise was wonderful. Joseph crossed the Bitter Root Mountains into Idaho again and made his way westward over Camas Meadows. He succeeded in getting two hundred and fifty fresh horses here with which to remount his people. On the 20th of August, Howard, believing himself to be only one day behind Joseph, halted to give some rest to his exhausted men. He had sent a detachment under Lieutenant Bacon to seize Thacher's Pass, the entrance into the Yellowstone Park, for which he believed the Indians were heading. Bacon, traveling on inside lines, reached the pass in plenty of time; but seeing no Indians, after waiting a couple of days concluded to rejoin the main body and marched away, leaving the pass open.

Joseph had no mind to enter it without crossing swords with Howard again. He knew of the absence of Bacon's detachment. Forming forty of his men in a column of fours he boldly advanced toward the camp, trusting that they would be mistaken for Bacon's detachment. The sentry, completely deceived by the soldierlike appearance of the approaching column in the darkness, allowed them to draw near before he challenged and gave the alarm. The Indians immediately deployed and dashed for the herd into which daring Indian scouts had already penetrated. Fortunately for Howard the cavalry-horses had been picketed for the night and only the pack-mules were stampeded. They were driven off under cover of a terrific fire upon the camp from the mounted Indians.

Howard immediately ordered his cavalry in pursuit of Joseph. The Indians retreated rapidly until the pursuing troops fell into a cunningly contrived ambush.

The Indians attacked them in the center and on both flanks amid some rocky lava-beds to the northward of the road. So sudden was the attack that the cavalry retreated post-haste. Norwood's company was not able to get off with the others and was surrounded. Fortunately they were caught in a strong defensive position. The men dismounted and made a gallant fight of it until Howard came to their relief with the main body. Some of the mules were recaptured, but were not retained, and the command, as the result of this brilliant midnight dash, found itself without a pack-train. As Joseph phrased it, he was tired of having General Howard on his heels and he wanted "to put him afoot." He nearly succeeded in his purpose.

Howard was forced to halt until he could supply the mules that he had lost and get supplies from Virginia City for his men who were by this time in a state of destitution. Joseph marched through Yellowstone Park over trails hitherto considered impassable. He surprised a party of tourists there, killed or wounded the men and captured the women. The women were well treated and finally released unharmed. Joseph feared they might fall into the hands of the young braves. So by his direction White Bird led them secretly to their ponies, mounted them and assisted in their escape. He dismissed them with these words, "Go. That is the way. Do not stop to water your horses. Hurry! Hurry!"

Howard was soon on the trail again. Where Joseph had gone he could go, what the Nez Percés had surmounted the soldiers could overcome. He was close on Joseph's track when the Nez Percés entered Wyoming. Joseph delayed him by burning Baronet's Bridge over the Clarke Fork of the Yellowstone and entered Montana.

Captain Farrow thus describes the march through the Yellowstone country:

"August 23rd, the command was nearing the head-waters of the Snake River and camped in a beautiful glade between the Snake and a small tributary. Here preparations were made for an early and forced march to 'Thatcher's Pass,' the entrance to the Yellowstone country, hoping to force the Indians, only a few miles ahead, to battle before they could enter the pass. Lieutenant Bacon and his party, on arrival two days previously at Henry Lake, which was in plain sight of Thatcher's Pass, not seeing any Indians, had turned back and took up a stern chase to overtake the command. The exhausted troops went into camp at Henry Lake for four days, and supplies and some fresh stock were rushed from Virginia City, seventy miles away. Then, on the morning of August 27th, the command, by a brisk movement, passed around Henry Lake, on through the mountain gorge to fields of danger and suffering still unknown.

"Here began the march through the rough western gateway into the National Park. For the first three days a most pleasant change was afforded by the beautiful mountain streams, lengthy openings, grassy bottoms, and numerous 'buttes,' beautifully dressed with trees. Then came the magnificent geyser landscape, with its vast seas of barren sulphur-crust.

"Here a party of tourists had been surprised and taken by the Indians. In this party were the wife of Mr. Cowan and her sister and brother. These were spared by Joseph and under protection were sent to the pursuing column. Two of the men in the party attempted to escape from the Indians. One was killed, but Mr. Cowan and a Mr. Oldham, left unconscious, recovered and found their way into camp.

"A picket-post was established on a woody height, a little south of the camp. From this point, a barren sulphur plain stretched to the south, filled with beautiful mounds and water-spouts, many of them throwing immense jets of water high into the air. These strange phenomena were witnessed and investigated by the officers and men with much delight. One of the most curious results of the intense chemical actions in progress were numerous muddy fermentations of various colors, from clayey white, through various shades of red, purple and brown, to black. There was no end of surprises in this wonderful country.

"Following the Indians' crooked trail, the command ascended a steep and difficult mountain, bristled with forests of small trees. Numerous forest fires had swept over these trees and had killed and hardened them. After a laborious zigzag climb, the top of this mountain was reached and camp made just beyond Mary Lake, a beautiful sheet of water on the very mountain-top.

"Joseph crossed the Yellowstone and went up the river toward the Yellowstone Lake and then proceeded along a tributary creek in the direction of Stinking Water River; and then, turning squarely to the left (because the prairie ahead of him was on fire and burning), made his way through a dense and tangled forest. General Howard took a course on the Chord of the Arc traveled by the Indians and thus saved nearly one hundred miles. He abandoned his wagons and with a pack-train proceeded over fearful steeps, through Devil's Cañon, across deep and rough ravines, to Baronet's Bridge on the Yellowstone. At this point the hostile Indians were abreast of the troops on the other side of the Yellowstone.

"The Indians had burnt a portion of Baronet's Bridge, a light structure across the Yellowstone torrent. This bridge was repaired in a few hours by the troops, bringing into requisition all the lumber which constituted Mr. Baronet's small house, which stood a few hundred yards away, on Joseph's side of the river. This was a shaky structure, fifty feet above the torrent, with slight intermediary support, as patched up by the improvised bridgemen. The command crossed in safety, and proceeded down the river twenty miles to Mammoth Falls, finding abundant evidence of murder and rapine all along the way.

"At Mammoth Falls, it was learned that Lieutenant Gilbert, with two companies of cavalry, had been there a few hours before; but the proximity of the hostile Indians and want of knowledge of the whereabouts of General Howard's command, caused him to make a remarkable detour, finally striking General Howard's trail one hundred miles in his rear. He made a stern chase after General Howard until his horses were exhausted, and then, in weariness, turned back to Fort Ellis."

The Seventh Cavalry was in the field. Six companies of it under the command of Colonel Sturgis endeavored to head off Joseph. Sturgis threw himself across Joseph's route so that the Nez Percés were between him and Howard. Joseph, however, outwitted Sturgis. Feinting flight along the Stinking Water River when Sturgis rushed after him in hot pursuit, Joseph by a forced march through a dense forest, which concealed his movements, avoided him and crossed the Yellowstone, escaping from between the two.

Sturgis soon found that he had been tricked and turning pursued the Nez Percé with all the speed of his fresh horses. He came up with him on the 13th of September at Cañon Creek and at once attacked him with three hundred and fifty men. The troops advanced most gallantly. The Indians occupied the ridges on either side of the cañon, from which they were driven by a series of magnificent charges. Every step of the retreat, however, was marked by hard fighting for delay, and when night fell Joseph again succeeded in making his escape. The soldiers lost three killed and eleven wounded. Twenty-one Nez Percés were killed and, most serious loss, Sturgis captured nine hundred ponies. But Sturgis had shot his bolt. His men and horses were in a state of complete exhaustion. He could pursue no farther.

Away off to the eastward at Fort Keogh was General Miles with detachments of the Fifth Infantry and the Second and Seventh Cavalry. Messengers were sped to him from Howard and Sturgis, detailing the escape of the Nez Percés and suggesting that he march to intercept them. In order to give him time to catch Joseph, Howard and Sturgis deliberately delayed their pursuit, knowing from experience that the great Nez Percé would keep just so far ahead of them.

Joseph moved forward leisurely with the remnant of his tribe. On the 23rd of September he crossed the Missouri at Cow Island, the head of low-water navigation and a large freight depot. Twelve men and a sergeant in a small fort guarded the place. Joseph destroyed a wagon-train, and after replenishing his stores, burned the rest of the freight at the station. The fort was stoutly defended, although three of the garrison were killed in an attack upon it. Joseph wasted no time over it and at once moved northward. On this march, Major Ilges, with a troop of the Seventh Cavalry, came down from Fort Benton by steamer and came in touch with him. Joseph easily repulsed his small force and after a slight loss Ilges wisely retired.

Joseph finally halted on Snake Creek on the north slope of the Bear Paw Mountains within a short distance of the boundary line. It would have been quite easy for him to cross the line and thus make good his escape. Yet his men and horses were tired beyond measure. He had many wounded. Hunting was good. He determined to rest there.

By this time Howard and Sturgis had been left far in the rear. Joseph knew that he had nothing to apprehend from them. He was ignorant of Miles' expedition. He made his great mistake by not having scouts scouring the country in all directions, in which case he might have given the pursuing soldiers the slip and crossed the boundary line.

Miles had with him two troops of the Second Cavalry, three of the Seventh, four companies of the Fifth Infantry mounted on captured Indian ponies, a Gatling and a twelve pound Napoleon cannon and a wagon-train, with two unmounted companies of the Fifth Infantry as a guard. He moved with great rapidity from Fort Keogh to the junction of the Mussel Shell and the Missouri. He believed that the Indians were south of the latter river, but learned that they had crossed at Cow Island some eighty miles to the westward a short time before. Fortunately he had detained the last steamer of the season. By means of this his troops were ferried across the river on the 25th of September. He marched north and then westward along the north slope of the Little Rockies, heading toward the Bear Paw Mountains where he had learned Joseph had halted. At 2:30 A.M., on the

3rd of October, he broke camp and started for the mouth of Snake Creek. A few hours later his scouts apprised him of the location of Joseph's camp which was some six or eight miles farther on.

The weather was extremely stormy and inclement. "My God!" exclaimed Captain Hale as they stopped to get in shape for the last dash, "have I got to go out and be killed in such cold weather!" The men were in excellent spirits. The march was taken up at a trot which soon became a gallop. In high glee they raced along. Early in the morning they came in sight of the Indian camp. It was spread along a crescent-shaped ravine from which a number of lateral ravines opened, and the whole position was dominated by high bluffs. Miles deployed his troops on the run. A battalion of the Second Cavalry was ordered to swing to the left and cut off the herds which were grazing on a high plateau behind the camp. The Seventh Cavalry supported by the Fifth Infantry was to make a direct attack upon the camp.

The surprise was not complete. The troops came into view in time for the Indians to prepare for them. The inequalities of the ground caused the Second Cavalry to incline to the left farther than was intended. They were not seriously engaged, but succeeded in getting possession of the greater part of the horses. The three troops of the Seventh Cavalry became separated in the advance. Captain Hale leading the battalion with K Troop struck the enemy first. The slaughter among his men was frightful. Captains Godfrey and Moylan found further progress checked by a high bluff lined with fire which they could not scale. The two captains promptly moved their troops to the rear and then marched them by the right flank to join K Troop. Godfrey, keeping between his men and the Indians, had his horse shot under him. The animal fell so suddenly that he pitched the officer on the ground where he lay stunned. Trumpeter Herwood left the line and interposed between Godfrey and the advancing Indians until the prostrate soldier could scramble to his feet. Moylan was severely wounded. By this time the two troops had joined Hale, and the whole party, save the officer, dismounted and advanced. They got within twenty yards of the Indians. Hale was shot and instantly killed — yes, on that cold morning! Godfrey was shot from his horse. Lieutenant Biddle was killed. In that fierce battle there was but one officer of the battalion, Lieutenant Eckestrom, unwounded. The battalion lost fifty-three killed and wounded out of one hundred and fifteen. K Troop's loss was over sixty per cent.

But the men held on and drove the Indians back to the ravines behind the camp. By this time the Fifth Infantry had got into action and also the Second Cavalry and the battle was general. The troops made several charges, but could not rush the camp. By contracting their lines, however, they drove the Indians closer and closer together. The position was splendidly defensible, and Miles, after making several attempts to dislodge the Nez Percés, in which Carter's company of the Fifth Infantry lost over thirty-five per cent, concluded that he would have to starve them out. White Bird and a number of others, estimated from twenty to fifty, succeeded in making their escape. They crossed into British Columbia and joined Sitting Bull.

Miles' position was precarious. Sitting Bull with two thousand Indians was only a day's march to the north of him. If he could be persuaded to join Joseph the situation would be terrible. Sitting Bull, however, had had enough of Miles and refused. The artillery was brought up and the Indian camp was shelled with fearful effect. Miles sent word to Howard that he had Joseph corralled at last and that gallant officer dashed off with a few men and joined Miles on the 3rd of October. The weather was very cold and snowy and both sides suffered severely.

Joseph afterward stated that he could have escaped if he had abandoned his women, children, and wounded. Unwilling to do this there was nothing left him but surrender. He gave up the unequal game on the 4th of October. Surely he had fought a good fight! In the battle Miles had lost twenty-four killed and fifty wounded, or over twenty per cent of his force. Joseph had lost seventeen killed. He surrendered eighty-seven warriors, of whom forty were wounded, one hundred and eighty-four squaws, and one hundred and forty-seven children. This was his pathetic message to General Howard:

Tell General Howard that I know his heart. What he told me before — I have it in my heart. I am tired of fighting. Our chiefs are killed. Looking Glass is dead. *Too-hul-hul-suit* is dead. The old men are all dead. It is the young men now, who say "yes" or "no" [that is, vote in council]. He who led the young men [Joseph's brother Ollicut] is dead. It is cold, and we have no blankets. The little children are freezing to death. My people — some of them — have run away to the hills, and have no blankets, no food. No one knows where they are — perhaps freezing to death. I want to have time to look for my children, and to see how many of them I can find; maybe I shall find them among the dead. Hear me, my chiefs, my heart is sick and sad. From where the sun *now* stands, I will fight no more forever.

Colonel Wood thus describes the scene and pictures the great chieftain:

"It was nearly sunset when Joseph came to deliver himself up. He rode from his camp in the little hollow. His hands were clasped over the pommel of his saddle and his rifle lay across his knees; his head was bowed

Chief Joseph Surrenders to Gen. Miles

" From where the sun now stands I fight no more with the white
man "

down. Pressing around him walked five of his warriors; their faces were upturned and earnest as they murmured to him; but he looked neither to the right nor to the left, yet seemed to listen intently. So the little group came slowly up the hill to where General Howard, with an aide-de-camp, and General Miles waited to receive the surrender. As he neared them, Joseph sat erect in the saddle, then gracefully and with dignity swung himself down from his horse, and with an impulsive gesture threw his arm to its full length and offered his rifle to General Howard. The latter motioned him toward General Miles, who received the token of submission.

"Those present shook hands with Joseph, whose worn and anxious face lighted with a sad smile as silently he took each offered hand. Then, turning away, he walked to the tent provided for him.

"His scalp-lock was tied with otter fur. The rest of his hair hung in a thick plait on each side of his head. He wore buckskin leggings and a gray woolen shawl, through which were the marks of four or five bullets received in this last conflict. His head and wrist were also scratched with bullets."

Perhaps one of the truest tests of greatness is ability to bear worthily defeat. By any standard Joseph acquitted himself well in this his most trying hour.

Joseph, whose force never amounted to three hundred fighting men, had engaged at different times some two thousand soldiers. Of these one hundred and twenty-six had been killed and one hundred and forty wounded. During the long retreat and the hard fighting Joseph had lost one hundred and fifty-one killed and eighty-eight wounded. He had fought eleven engagements, five being pitched battles, of which he had won three, drawn one and lost one. Some of the troops in pursuit of him had marched sixteen hundred miles. His own march had been at least two thousand miles. This constitutes a military exploit of the first magnitude and justly entitled the great Indian to take rank among the great Captains.

Joseph claimed, and there is no doubt as to the facts, that General Miles agreed that the remnant of the Nez Percés should be returned to Idaho. How did the United States keep that promise? It repudiated it entirely! Joseph and his band were sent down to Fort Leavenworth. I saw them often during the winter. In the spring they were given the unhealthiest reservation in the Indian Territory. These were mountain Indians, not used to the hot malarious climate of low lands and low latitudes. They died like sheep. Joseph protested in vain. To the everlasting credit of General Miles he also used his powerful influence in order to have the tardy Government keep faith with its poor captives. It was not until 1885 that the Indians were sent back to their beloved mountain home.

The other day a gray-headed old chief, nodding by the fire, dreaming perhaps of days of daring and deeds of valor, by which, savage though he was, he had written his name on the pages of history, slipped quietly to the ground and fell into his eternal sleep. Peaceful ending for the Indian Xenophon, the Red Napoleon of the West!

In reviewing this remarkable campaign, General Howard said: *

"I was sent to conduct a war without regard to department and division lines. This was done with all the energy, ability and help at my command, and the campaign was brought to a successful issue. As soon as the Indians reached General Terry's department, Gibbon

* Op. cit., p. 271, et seq.— C. T. B.

was despatched to strike his blow; then Sturgis, in close alliance, and, finally, Miles, in the last terrible battle. These troops participated in the struggle with exposure, battle, and loss, as we have seen. They enjoyed the appreciation and thanks of their seniors in command, and of their countrymen. But when, with the fullness of an honest and generous recognition of the work, gallantry, losses, and success of all coöperating forces, I turn my attention to the troops that fought the first battle, and then pursued the swift-footed fugitives with unparalleled vigor and perseverance, amid the severest privations, far more than a thousand miles, would it be wonderful if I magnified their doings, and gave them, were it possible, even an overplus of praise for the part they bore in this campaign?

"At the obstructing barricades in Montana, which were dangerous to pass, Looking Glass appeared as the diplomat. He succeeded by his ability in deceiving the commander of the defenses, and brought past the hindering works Joseph's whole people in complete safety. He was killed and buried under the river-bank at Gibbon's battle-field in Montana.

"After Gibbon's battle, Joseph showed his influence over the Indians by rallying them on a height, just beyond the reach of the long-range rifles. He gathered the warriors, recovered lost ground, and recaptured his numerous herd of ponies, which had already been cut off by Gibbon's men, buried the most of his dead, and made good his retreat before the force with me was near enough to harm him. Few military commanders, with good troops, could better have recovered after so fearful a surprise.

"At the Camas Meadows, not far from Henry Lake, Joseph's night march, his surprise of my camp and capture of over a hundred animals, and, after a slight battle, making a successful escape, showed an ability to plan and execute equal to that of many a partisan leader whose deeds have entered into classic story.

"Again, his quick penetration into my plan of delaying my march between the Mussel shell and the Missouri, so as to make all speed, cross the broad river at Cow Island, defeat the guard, and then destroy an immense freight-wagon-train, replenish his supplies, and make off beyond danger from the direct pursuit, is not often equaled in warfare.

"And even at the last, the natural resources of his mind did not fail him. Broken in pieces by Miles' furious and unexpected assault; burdened with his women, children, and plunder; suffering from the loss of his still numerous though badly crippled herd of ponies, yet he was able to intrench, and hold out for several days against twice his numbers, and succeeded in pushing out beyond the white man's pickets a part of his remnant to join his allies in Canada.

" From the beginning of the Indian pursuit across the Lo-lo Trail, until the embarkation on the Missouri River for the homeward journey, including all halts and stoppages, from July 27th to October 10th, my command marched one thousand three hundred and twenty-one miles in seventy-five days. Joseph, the Indian, taking with him his men, women, and children, traversed even greater distances, for he had to make many a loop in his skein, many a deviation into a tangled thicket, to avoid or deceive his enemy.

"So that whichever side of the picture we examine, we find there evidence of wonderful energy and prolonged endurance. It will be, indeed, fortunate for mankind, if these same qualities which we cannot help commending, can hereafter be turned into a common channel, and used for the promotion of the arts of peace. What glorious results would have been effected, could these non-treaties have received the same direction that the worthy missionaries were, in early days, able to give to the remainder of their tribe, and have shown the same ability and persistence in peace that they did during this fearful Indian War."

CHAPTER TWO

Chief Joseph's Own Story

With an Introduction by the Rt. Rev. W. H. Hare, D.D.,
Bishop of South Dakota *

I WISH that I had words at command in which to express adequately the interest with which I have read the extraordinary narrative which follows, and which I have the privilege of introducing to the readers of this *Review*. I feel, however, that this apologia is so boldly marked by the charming naïveté and tender pathos which characterizes the red-man, that it needs no introduction, much less any authentication; while in its smothered fire, in its deep sense of eternal righteousness and of present evil, and in its hopeful longings for the coming of a better time, this Indian chief's appeal reminds us of one of the old Hebrew prophets of the days of the Captivity.

I have no special knowledge of the history of the Nez Percés, the Indians whose tale of sorrow Chief Joseph so pathetically tells — my Indian missions lying in a part at the West quite distant from their old home —

---

* This and the following chapter are taken from *The North American Review* for 1879, by the gracious permission of Messrs. Harper and Brothers, the present publishers of the magazine and the owners of the copyright.— C. T. B.

and am not competent to judge their case upon its merits. The chief's narrative is, of course, *ex parte*, and many of his statements would no doubt be ardently disputed. General Howard, for instance, can hardly receive justice at his hands, so well known is he for his friendship to the Indian and for his distinguished success in pacifying some of the most desperate.

It should be remembered, too, in justice to the army, that it is rarely called upon to interfere in Indian affairs until the relations between the Indians and the whites have reached a desperate condition, and when the situation of affairs has become so involved and feeling on both sides runs so high that perhaps only more than human forbearance would attempt to solve the difficulty by disentangling the knot and not by cutting it.

Nevertheless, the chief's narrative is marked by so much candor, and he is so careful to qualify his statements, when qualification seems necessary, that every reader will give him credit for speaking his honest, even should they be thought by some to be mistaken, convictions. The chief, in his treatment of his defense, reminds one of those lawyers of whom we have heard that their splendid success was gained, not by disputation, but simply by their lucid and straightforward statement of their case. That he is something of a strategist as well as an advocate appears from this description of an event which occurred shortly after the breaking out of hostilities: "We crossed over Salmon River, hoping General Howard would follow. We were not disappointed. He did follow us, and we got between him and his supplies, and cut him off for three days." Occasionally the reader comes upon touches of those sentiments and feelings which at once establish a sense of kinship between all who possess them. Witness his description of his desperate attempt to rejoin his wife and children when a sudden dash of General Miles' soldiers had cut the Indian camp in two. . . . "I thought of my wife and children, who were now surrounded by soldiers, and I resolved to go to them. With a prayer in my mouth to the Great Spirit Chief who rules above, I dashed unarmed through the line of soldiers. . . . My clothes were cut to pieces, my horse was wounded, but I was not hurt." And, again, when he speaks of his father's death: "I saw he was dying. I took his hand in mine. He said: 'My son, my body is returning to my mother earth, and my spirit is going very soon to see the Great Spirit Chief. . . . A few more years and the white men will be all around you. They have their eyes on this land. My son, never forget my dying words. This country holds your father's body — never sell the bones of your father and mother.' I pressed my father's hand, and told him I would protect his grave with my life. My father smiled, and passed away to the spirit-land. I buried him in that beautiful valley of Winding Waters. I love that land more than all the rest of the world. A man who would not love his father's grave is worse than a wild animal."

His appeals to the natural rights of man are surprisingly fine, and, however some may despise them as the utterance of an Indian, they are just those which, in our Declaration of Independence, have been most admired. "We are all sprung from a woman," he says, "although we are unlike in many things. You are as you were made, and, as you are made, you can remain. We are just as we were made by the Great Spirit, and you cannot change us; then, why should children of one mother quarrel? Why should one try to cheat another? I do not believe that the Great Spirit Chief gave one kind of

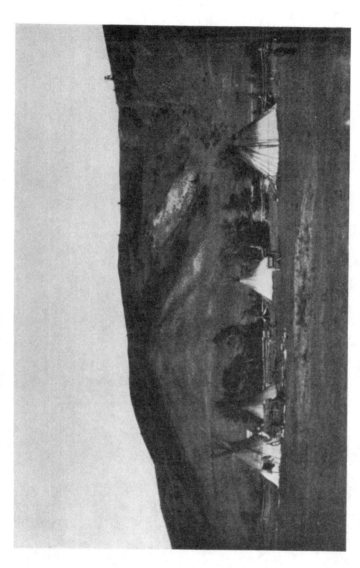

Last Home of Chief Joseph, where he Dropped Dead at the Camp Fire, September, 1904—Nespelum, Colville Reservation of Moses Indians, Washington State

From the collection of J. W. Redington

men the right to tell another kind of men what they must do."

But I will not detain the readers of the *Review* from the pleasure of perusing for themselves Chief Joseph's statement longer than is necessary to express the hope that those who have time for no more will at least read its closing paragraph, and to remark that the narrative brings clearly out these facts which ought to be regarded as well-recognized principles in dealing with the redman:

1. The folly of any mode of treatment of the Indian which is not based upon a cordial and operative acknowledgment of his rights as our *fellow-man*.

2. The danger of riding roughshod over a people who are capable of high enthusiasm, who know and value their national rights, and are brave enough to defend them.

3. The liability to want of harmony between different departments and different officials of our complex Government, from which it results that, while many promises are made to the Indians, few of them are kept. It is a home-thrust when Chief Joseph says: "The white people have too many chiefs. They do not understand each other. . . . I cannot understand how the Government sends a man out to fight us, as it did General Miles, and then break his word. Such a Government has something wrong about it."

4. The unwisdom, in most cases, in dealing with Indians, of what may be termed *Military short-cuts*, instead of patient discussion, explanations, persuasion, and reasonable concessions.

5. The absence in an Indian tribe of any truly representative body competent to make a treaty which shall be binding upon all the bands. The failure to recognize

this fact has been the source of endless difficulties. Chief Joseph, in this case, did not consider a treaty binding 'which his band had not agreed to, no matter how many other bands had signed it; and so it has been in many other cases.

6. Indian chiefs, however able and influential, are really without power, and for this reason, as well as others, the Indians, when by the march of events they are brought into intimate relations with the whites, should at the earliest practicable moment be given the support and protection of our Government and of our law; not *local* law, however, which is apt to be the result of *special* legislation adopted solely in the interest of the stronger race.   WILLIAM H. HARE.

My friends, I have been asked to show you my heart. I am glad to have a chance to do so. I want the white people to understand my people. Some of you think an Indian is like a wild animal. This is a great mistake. I will tell you all about our people, and then you can judge whether an Indian is a man or not. I believe much trouble and blood would be saved if we opened our hearts more. I will tell you in my way how the Indian sees things. The white man has more words to tell you how they look at him, but it does not require many words to speak the truth. What I have to say will come from my heart, and I will speak with a straight tongue. Ah-cum-kin-i-ma-me-hut (the Great Spirit) is looking at me, and will hear me.

My name is In-mut-too-yah-lat-lat (Thunder-travel-ing-over-the-mountains). I am chief of the Wal-lam-wat-kin band of Chute-pa-lu, or Nez Percés (nose-pierced Indians). I was born in eastern Oregon, thirty-eight winters ago. My father was chief before me. When

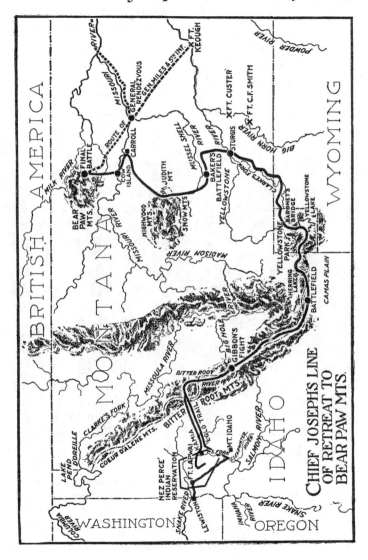

a young man he was called Joseph by Mr. Spaulding, a missionary. He died a few years ago. There was no stain on his hands of the blood of a white man. He left a good name on the earth. He advised me well for my people.

Our fathers gave us many laws, which they had learned from their fathers. These laws were good. They told us to treat all men as they treated us; that we should never be the first to break a bargain; that it was a disgrace to tell a lie; that we should speak only the truth; that it was a shame for one man to take from another his wife, or his property, without paying for it. We were taught to believe that the Great Spirit sees and hears everything, and that He never forgets; that hereafter He will give every man a spirit-home according to his deserts; if he has been a good man, he will have a good home; if he has been a bad man, he will have a bad home. This I believe, and all my people believe the same.

We did not know there were other people besides the Indian until about one hundred winters ago, when some men with white faces came to our country. They brought many things with them to trade for furs and skins. They brought tobacco, which was new to us. They brought guns with flintstones on them, which frightened our women and children. Our people could not talk with these white-faced men, but they used signs which all people understood. These men were Frenchmen, and they called our people "Nez Percés," because they wore rings in their noses for ornaments. Although very few of our people wear them now, we are still called by the same name. These French trappers said a great many things to our fathers, which have been planted in our hearts. Some were good for us, but some were bad. Our people were divided in opinion about these men. Some thought they taught more bad than good. An

Indian respects a brave man, but he despises a coward. He loves a straight tongue, but he hates a forked tongue. The French trappers told us some truths and some lies.

The first white men of your people who came to our country were named Lewis and Clarke. They also brought many things that our people had never seen. They talked straight, and our people gave them a great feast, as a proof that their hearts were friendly. These men were very kind. They made presents to our chiefs and our people made presents to them. We had a great many horses, of which we gave them what they needed, and they gave us guns and tobacco in return. All the Nez Percés made friends with Lewis and Clarke, and agreed to let them pass through their country, and never to make war on white men. This promise the Nez Percés have never broken. No white man can accuse them of bad faith, and speak with a straight tongue. It has always been the pride of the Nez Percés that they were the friends of the white men. When my father was a young man there came to our country a white man (Rev. Mr. Spaulding) who talked spirit law. He won the affections of our people because he spoke good things to them. At first he did not say anything about white men wanting to settle on our lands. Nothing was said about that until about twenty winters ago when a number of white people came into our country and built houses and made farms. At first our people made no complaint. They thought there was room enough for all to live in peace, and they were learning many things from the white men that seemed to be good. But we soon found that the white men were growing rich very fast, and were greedy to possess everything the Indian had. My father was the first to see through the schemes of the white men, and he warned his tribe to be careful about trading with them. He had a suspicion of men who seemed so anxious to make money. I was a boy then, but I remember well my father's caution. He had sharper eyes than the rest of our people.

Next there came a white officer (Governor Stevens) who invited all the Nez Percés to a treaty council. After the council was opened he made known his heart. He said there were a great many white people in the country, and many more would come; that he wanted the land marked out so that the Indians and white men could be separated. If they were to live in peace it was necessary, he said, that the Indians should have a country set apart for them, and in that country they must stay. My father, who represented his band, refused to have anything to do with the council, because he wished to be a free man. He claimed that no man owned any part of the earth, and a man could not sell what was not his own.

Mr. Spaulding took hold of my father's arm and said, "Come and sign the treaty." My father pushed him away and said: "Why do you ask me to sign away my country? It is your business to talk to us about spirit matters, and not to talk to us about parting with our land." Governor Stevens urged my father to sign his treaty, but he refused. "I will not sign your paper," he said, "you go where you please, so do I: you are not a child, I am no child; I can think for myself. No man can think for me. I have no other home than this. I will not give it up to any man. My people would have no home. Take away your paper. I will not touch it with my hand."

My father left the council. Some of the chiefs of the other bands of the Nez Percés signed the treaty, and then Governor Stevens gave them presents of blankets. My father cautioned his people to take no presents, for "after awhile," he said, "they will claim that you accepted pay for your country." Since that time four bands of the Nez Percés have received annuities from the United States. My father was invited to many councils, and they tried hard to make him sign the treaty, but he was firm as the rock, and would not sign away his home. His refusal caused a difference among the Nez Percés.

Eight years later (1863) was the next treaty council. A chief called Lawyer, because he was a great talker, took the lead in this council, and sold nearly all of the Nez Percés country. My father was not there. He said to me: "When you go into council with the white man, always remember your country. Do not give it away. The white man will cheat you out of your home. I have taken no pay from the United States. I have never sold our land." In this treaty Lawyer acted without authority from our band. He had no right to sell the Wallowa (*winding water*) country. That had always belonged to my father's own people, and the other bands had never disputed our right to it. No other Indians ever claimed Wallowa.

In order to have all people understand how much land we owned, my father planted poles around it and said:

"Inside is the home of my people — the white man may take the land outside. Inside this boundary all our people were born. It circles around the graves of our fathers, and we will never give up these graves to any man."

The United States claimed they had bought all the Nez Percés country outside the Lapwai Reservation, from Lawyer and other chiefs, but we continued to live on this land in peace until eight years ago, when white men began to come inside the bounds my father had set. We warned them against this great wrong, but they would not leave our land, and some bad blood was raised. The white man represented that we were going upon the war-path. They reported many things that were false.

The United States Government again asked for a treaty council. My father had become blind and feeble. He could no longer speak for his people. It was then I took my father's place as chief. In this council I made my first speech to white men. I said to the agent who held the council:

"I did not want to come to this council, but I came hoping that we could save blood. The white man has no right to come here and take our country. We have never accepted presents from the Government. Neither Lawyer nor any other chief had authority to sell this land. It has always belonged to my people. It came unclouded to them from our fathers, and we will defend this land as long as a drop of Indian blood warms the hearts of our men."

The agent said he had orders, from the Great White Chief at Washington, for us to go upon the Lapwai Reservation, and that if we obeyed he would help us in many ways. "You *must* move to the agency," he said. I answered him: "I will not. I do not need your help; we have plenty, and we are contented and happy if the white man will let us alone. The reservation is too small for so many people with all their stock. You can keep your presents; we can go to your towns and pay for all we need; we have plenty of horses and cattle to sell, and we won't have any help from you; we are free now; we can go where we please. Our fathers were born here. Here they lived, here they died, here are their graves. We will never leave them." The agent went away, and we had peace for awhile.

Soon after this my father sent for me. I saw he was dying. I took his hand in mine. He said: "My son, my body is returning to my mother earth, and my spirit is going very soon to see the Great Spirit Chief. When I am gone, think of your country. You are the chief of these people. They look to you to guide them. Always remember that your father never sold his country. You must stop your ears whenever you are asked to sign a treaty selling your home. A few years more, and white men will be all around you. They have their eyes on this land. My son, never forget my dying words. This country holds your father's body. Never sell the bones of your father and your mother." I pressed my father's hand and told him that I would protect his grave with my life. My father smiled and passed away to the spirit-land.

I buried him in that beautiful valley of winding waters. I love that land more than all the rest of the world. A man who would not love his father's grave is worse than a wild animal.

For a short time we lived quietly. But this could not last. White men had found gold in the mountains around the land of the winding water. They stole a great many horses from us, and we could not get them back because we were Indians. The white men told lies for each other. They drove off a great many of our cattle. Some white men branded our young cattle so they could claim them. We had no friend who would plead our cause before the law councils. It seemed to me that some of the white men in Wallowa were doing these things on purpose to get up a war. They knew that we were not strong enough to fight them. I labored hard to avoid trouble and bloodshed. We gave up some of our country to the white men, thinking that then we could have peace. We were mistaken. The white man would not let us alone. We could have avenged our wrongs many times, but we did not. Whenever the Government has asked us to help them against other Indians, we have never refused. When the white men were few and we were strong we could have killed them off, but the Nez Percés wished to live at peace.

If we have not done so, we have not been to blame. I believe that the old treaty has never been correctly reported. If we ever owned the land we own it still, for we never sold it. In the treaty councils the commissioners have claimed that our country had been sold to the Government. Suppose a white man should come to me and say, "Joseph, I like your horses, and I want to buy them." I say to him, "No, my horses suit me, I will not sell them." Then he goes to my neighbor, and says to him: "Joseph has some good horses. I want to buy them, but he refuses to sell." My neighbor answers, "Pay me the money, and I will sell you Joseph's horses." The white man returns to me and says, "Joseph, I have bought your horses, and you must let me have them." If we sold our lands to the Government, this is the way they were bought.

On account of the treaty made by the other bands of Nez Percés, the white men claimed my lands. We were troubled greatly by white men crowding over the line. Some of these were good men, and we lived on peaceful terms with them, but they were not all good.

Nearly every year the agent came over from Lapwai and ordered us on to the reservation. We always replied that we were satisfied to live in Wallowa. We were careful to refuse the presents or annuities which he offered.

Through all the years since the white man came to Wallowa we have been threatened and taunted by them and the treaty Nez Percés. They have given us no rest. We have had a few good friends among white men, and they have always advised my people to bear these taunts without fighting. Our young men were quick-tempered, and I have had great trouble in keeping them from doing rash things. I have carried a heavy load on my back ever since I was a boy. I learned then that we were but few, while the white men were many, and that we could not hold our own with them. We were like deer. They were like grizzly bears. We had a small country. Their country was large. We were contented to let things remain as the Great Spirit Chief made them. They were not; and would change the rivers and mountains if they did not suit them.

Year after year we have been threatened, but no war was made upon my people until General Howard came to our country two years ago and told us that he was the white war-chief of all that country. He said: "I have a great many soldiers at my back. I am going to bring them up here, and then I will talk to you again. I will not let white men laugh at me the next time I come. The country belongs to the Government, and I intend to make you go upon the reservation."

I remonstrated with him against bringing more soldiers to the Nez Percés country. He had one house full of troops all the time at Fort Lapwai.

The next spring the agent at Umatilla Agency sent an Indian runner to tell me to meet General Howard at Walla Walla. I could not go myself, but I sent my brother and five other head men to meet him, and they had a long talk.

General Howard said: "You have talked straight, and

it is all right. You can stay at Wallowa." He insisted that my brother and his company should go with him to Fort Lapwai. When the party arrived there General Howard sent out runners and called all the Indians to a grand council. I was in that council. I said to General Howard, "We are ready to listen." He answered that he would not talk then, but would hold a council next day, when he would talk plainly. I said to General Howard: "I am ready to talk to-day. I have been in a great many councils, but I am no wiser. We are all sprung from a woman, although we are unlike in many things. We cannot be made over again. You are as you were made, and as you were made you can remain. We are just as we were made by the Great Spirit, and you cannot change us; then why should children of one mother and one father quarrel? — why should one try to cheat the other? I do not believe that the Great Spirit Chief gave one kind of men the right to tell another kind of men what they must do."

General Howard replied: "You deny my authority, do you? You want to dictate to me, do you?"

Then one of my chiefs — Too-hool-hool-suit — rose in the council and said to General Howard: "The Great Spirit Chief made the world as it is, and as He wanted it, and He made a part of it for us to live upon. I do not see where you get authority to say that we shall not live where He placed us."

General Howard lost his temper and said: "Shut up! I don't want to hear any more of such talk. The law says you shall go upon the reservation to live, and I want you to do so, but you persist in disobeying the law" (meaning the treaty). "If you do not move, I will take the matter into my own hand, and make you suffer for your disobedience."

Too-hool-hool-suit answered: "Who are you, that you ask us to talk, and then tell me I shan't talk ? Are you the Great Spirit ? Did you make the world ? Did you make the sun ? Did you make the rivers to run for us to drink ? Did you make the grass to grow ? Did you make all these things that you talk to us as though we were boys ? If you did, then you have the right to talk as you do."

General Howard replied: "You are an impudent fellow, and I will put you in the guard-house," and then ordered a soldier to arrest him.

Too-hool-hool-suit made no resistance. He asked General Howard: "Is this your order ? I don't care. I have expressed my heart to you. I have nothing to take back. I have spoken for my country. You can arrest me, but you cannot change me or make me take back what I have said."

The soldiers came forward and seized my friend and took him to the guard-house. My men whispered among themselves whether they would let this thing be done. I counseled them to submit. I knew if we resisted that all the white men present, including General Howard, would be killed in a moment, and we would be blamed. If I had said nothing, General Howard would never have given an unjust order against my men. I saw the danger and while they dragged Too-hool-hool-suit to prison, I arose and said: "*I am going to talk now.* I don't care whether you arrest me or not." I turned to my people and said: "The arrest of Too-hool-hool-suit was wrong, but we will not resent the insult. We were invited to this council to express our hearts, and we have done so." Too-hool-hool-suit was prisoner for five days before he was released.

The council broke up that day. On the next morning

General Howard came to my lodge, and invited me to go with him and White Bird and Looking Glass, to look for land for my people. As we rode along we came to some good land that was already occupied by Indians and white people. General Howard, pointing to this land, said: "If you will come on to the reservation, I will give you these lands and move these people off."

I replied: "No. It would be wrong to disturb these people. I have no right to take their homes. I have never taken what did not belong to me. I will not now."

We rode all day upon the reservation, and found no good land unoccupied. I have been informed by men who do not lie that General Howard sent a letter that night telling the soldiers at Walla Walla to go to Wallowa Valley, and drive us out upon our return home.

In the council next day General Howard informed us in a haughty spirit that he would give my people *thirty days* to go back home, collect all their stock, and move on to the reservation, saying, "If you are not here in that time, I shall consider that you want to fight, and will send my soldiers to drive you on."

I said: "War can be avoided and it ought to be avoided. I want no war. My people have always been the friends of the white man. Why are you in such a hurry? I cannot get ready to move in thirty days. Our stock is scattered, and Snake River is very high. Let us wait until fall, then the river will be low. We want time to hunt our stock and gather our supplies for the winter."

General Howard replied, "If you let the time run over one day, the soldiers will be there to drive you on to the reservation, and all your cattle and horses outside of the reservation at that time will fall into the hands of the white men."

I knew I had never sold my country, and that I had

Colonel W. R. Parnell,
U. S. A., retired

First Lieutenant Robert H.
Fletcher, U. S. A., retired

Brigadier-General David
Perry, U. S. A., retired

Major J. G. Trimble, U. S. A.,
retired

Distinguished Officers of the Nez Percé War

no land in Lapwai; but I did not want bloodshed. I did not want my people killed. I did not want anybody killed. Some of my people had been murdered by white men, and the white murderers were never punished for it. I told General Howard about this, and again said I wanted no war. I wanted the people who live upon the lands I was to occupy at Lapwai to have time to gather their harvest.

I said in my heart that, rather than have war I would give up my country. I would rather give up my father's grave. I would give up everything rather than have the blood of white men upon the hands of my people.

General Howard refused to allow me more than thirty days to move my people and their stock. I am sure that he began to prepare for war at once.

When I returned to Wallowa I found my people very much excited upon discovering that the soldiers were already in the Wallowa Valley. We held a council, and decided to move immediately to avoid bloodshed.

Too-hool-hool-suit, who felt outraged by his imprisonment, talked for war, and made many of my young men willing to fight rather than be driven like dogs from the land where they were born. He declared that blood alone would wash out the disgrace General Howard had put upon him. It required a strong heart to stand up against such talk, but I urged my people to be quiet, and not to begin a war.

We gathered all the stock we could find, and made an attempt to move. We left many of our horses and cattle in Wallowa, and we lost several hundred in crossing the river. All my people succeeded in getting across in safety. Many of the Nez Percés came together in Rocky Cañon to hold a grand council. I went with all my people. This council lasted ten days. There was a great deal of war talk and a great deal of excitement. There was one young brave present whose father had been killed by a white man five years before. This man's blood was bad against white men and he left the council calling for revenge. .

Again I counseled peace, and I thought the danger was past. We had not complied with General Howard's order because we could not, but we intended to do so as soon as possible. I was leaving the council to kill beef for my family, when news came that the young man whose father had been killed had gone out with several hot-blooded young braves and killed four white men. He rode up to the council and shouted: "Why do you sit here like women? The war has begun already." I was deeply grieved. All the lodges were moved except my brother's and my own. I saw clearly that the war was upon us when I learned that my young men had been secretly buying ammunition. I heard then that Too-hool-hool-suit, who had been imprisoned by General Howard, had succeeded in organizing a war party. I knew that their acts would involve all my people. I saw that the war could not then be prevented. The time had passed. I counseled peace from the beginning. I knew that we were too weak to fight the United States. We had many grievances, but I knew that war would bring more. We had good white friends, who advised us against taking the war-path. My friend and brother, Mr. Chapman, who has been with us since the surrender, told us just how the war would end. Mr. Chapman took sides against us and helped General Howard. I do not blame him for doing so. He tried hard to prevent bloodshed. We hoped the white settlers would not join the soldiers. Before the war commenced we had discussed this matter all over, and many of my people were in favor of warning them that if they took no part against us they should not be molested in the event of war being begun by General Howard. This plan was voted down in the war-council.

There were bad men among my people who had quarreled with white men, and they talked of their wrongs until they roused all the bad hearts in the council. Still I could not believe that they would begin the war. I know that my young men did a great wrong, but I ask, Who was first to blame? They had been insulted a thousand times; their fathers and brothers had been killed; their mothers and wives had been disgraced; they had been driven to madness by the whiskey sold to them by the white men; they had been told by General Howard that all their horses and cattle which they had been unable to drive out of Wallowa were to fall into the hands of white men; and, added to all this, they were homeless and desperate.

I would have given my own life if I could have undone the killing of white men by my people. I blame my young men and I blame the white men. I blame General Howard for not giving my people time to get their stock away from Wallowa. I do not acknowledge that he had the right to order me to leave Wallowa at any time. I deny that either my father or myself ever sold that land. It is still our land. It may never again be our home, but my father sleeps there, and I love it as I love my mother. I left there, hoping to avoid bloodshed.

If General Howard had given me plenty of time to gather up my stock, and treated Too-hool-hool-suit as a man should be treated, there *would have been no war.* My friends among white men have blamed me for the war. I am not to blame. When my young men began the killing, my heart was hurt. Although I did not justify them, I remembered all the insults I had endured, and my blood was on fire. Still I would have taken my people to the buffalo country without fighting, if possible.

I could see no other way to avoid a war. We moved over to White Bird Creek, sixteen miles away, and there encamped, intending to collect our stock before leaving; but the soldiers attacked us and the first battle was fought. We numbered in that battle sixty men, and the soldiers a hundred. The fight lasted but a few minutes, when the soldiers retreated before us for twelve miles. They lost thirty-three killed, and had seven wounded. When an Indian fights, he only shoots to kill; but soldiers shoot at random. None of the soldiers were scalped. We do not believe in scalping, nor in killing wounded men. Soldiers do not kill many Indians unless they are wounded and left upon the battle-field. Then they kill Indians.

Seven days after the first battle General Howard arrived in the Nez Percés country, bringing seven hundred more soldiers. It was now war in earnest. We crossed over Salmon River, hoping General Howard would follow. We were not disappointed. He did follow us, and we got between him and his supplies, and cut him off for three days. He sent out two companies to open the way. We attacked them, killing one officer, two guides, and ten men.

We withdrew, hoping the soldiers would follow, but they had got fighting enough for that day. They intrenched themselves, and next day we attacked again. The battle lasted all day, and was renewed next morning. We killed four and wounded seven or eight.

About this time General Howard found out that we were in his rear. Five days later he attacked us with three hundred and fifty soldiers and settlers. We had two hundred and fifty warriors. The fight lasted twenty-seven hours. We lost four killed and several wounded. General Howard's loss was twenty-nine men killed and sixty wounded.

The following day the soldiers charged upon us, and we retreated with our families and stock a few miles, leaving eighty lodges to fall into General Howard's hands.

Finding that we were outnumbered, we retreated to Bitter Root Valley. Here another body of soldiers came upon us and demanded our surrender. We refused. They said, "You cannot get by us." We answered, "We are going by you without fighting if you will let us, but we are going by you anyhow." We then made a treaty with these soldiers. We agreed not to molest any one and they agreed that we might pass through the Bitter Root country in peace. We bought provisions and traded stock with white men there.

We understood that there was to be no war. We intended to go peaceably to the buffalo country, and leave the question of returning to our country to be settled afterward.

With this understanding we traveled on for four days, and, thinking that the trouble was all over, we stopped and prepared tent-poles to take with us. We started again, and at the end of two days we saw three white men passing our camp. Thinking that peace had been made, we did not molest them. We could have killed, or taken them prisoners, but we did not suspect them of being spies, which they were.

That night the soldiers surrounded our camp. About daybreak one of my men went out to look after his horses. The soldiers saw him and shot him down like a coyote. I have since learned that these soldiers were not those we had left behind. They had come upon us from another direction. The new white war-chief's name was Gibbon. He charged upon us while some of my people were still asleep. We had a hard fight. Some of my men crept around and attacked the soldiers from the rear. In this battle we lost nearly all our lodges, but we finally drove General Gibbon back.

Finding that he was not able to capture us, he sent to his camp a few miles away for his big guns (cannons), but my men had captured them and all the ammunition. We damaged the big guns all we could, and carried away the powder and lead. In the fight with General Gibbon we lost fifty women and children and thirty fighting men. We remained long enough to bury our dead. The Nez Percés never make war on women and children; we could have killed a great many women and children while the war lasted, but we would feel ashamed to do so cowardly an act.

We never scalp our enemies, but when General Howard came up and joined General Gibbon, their Indian scouts dug up our dead and scalped them. I have been told that General Howard did not order this great shame to be done.

We retreated as rapidly as we could toward the buffalo country. After six days General Howard came close to us, and we went out and attacked him, and captured nearly all his horses and mules (about two hundred and fifty head). We then marched on to the Yellowstone Basin.

On the way we captured one white man and two white women. We released them at the end of three days. They were treated kindly. The women were not insulted. Can the white soldiers tell me of one time when Indian women were taken prisoners, and held three days and then released without being insulted? Were the Nez

Percés women who fell into the hands of General Howard's soldiers treated with as much respect? I deny that a Nez Percé was ever guilty of such a crime.

A few days later we captured two more white men. One of them stole a horse and escaped. We gave the other a poor horse and told him that he was free.

Nine days' march brought us to the mouth of Clarke's Fork of the Yellowstone. We did not know what had become of General Howard, but we supposed that he had sent for more horses and mules. He did not come up, but another new war-chief (General Sturgis) attacked us. We held him in check while we moved all our women and children and stock out of danger, leaving a few men to cover our retreat.

Several days passed, and we heard nothing of General Howard, or Gibbon, or Sturgis. We had repulsed each in turn, and began to feel secure, when another army, under General Miles, struck us. This was the fourth army, each of which outnumbered our fighting force, that we had encountered within sixty days.

We had no knowledge of General Miles' army until a short time before he made a charge upon us, cutting our camp in two, and capturing nearly all of our horses. About seventy men, myself among them, were cut off. My little daughter, twelve years of age, was with me. I gave her a rope, and told her to catch a horse and join the others who were cut off from the camp. I have not seen her since, but I have learned that she is alive and well.

I thought of my wife and children, who were now surrounded by soldiers, and I resolved to go to them or die. With a prayer in my mouth to the Great Spirit Chief who rules above, I dashed unarmed through the line of soldiers. It seemed to me that there were guns on every side, before and behind me. My clothes were cut to pieces and my horse was wounded, but I was not hurt. As I reached the door of my lodge, my wife handed me my rifle, saying: "Here's your gun. Fight!"

The soldiers kept up a continuous fire. Six of my men were killed in one spot near me. Ten or twelve soldiers charged into our camp and got possession of two lodges, killing three Nez Percés and losing three of their men, who fell inside our lines. I called my men to drive them back. We fought at close range, not more than twenty steps apart, and drove the soldiers back upon their main line, leaving their dead in our hands. We secured their arms and ammunition. We lost, the first day and night, eighteen men and three women. General Miles lost twenty-six killed and forty wounded. The following day General Miles sent a messenger into my camp under protection of a white flag. I sent my friend Yellow Bull to meet him.

Yellow Bull understood the messenger to say that General Miles wished me to consider the situation; that he did not want to kill my people unnecessarily. Yellow Bull understood this to be a demand for me to surrender and save blood. Upon reporting this message to me, Yellow Bull said he wondered whether General Miles was in earnest. I sent him back with my answer, that I had not made up my mind, but would think about it and send word soon. A little later he sent some Cheyenne scouts with another message. I went out to meet them. They said they believed that General Miles was sincere and really wanted peace. I walked on to General Miles' tent. He met me and we shook hands. He said, "Come, let us sit down by the fire and talk this matter over." I remained with him all night; next morning, Yellow Bull came over to see if I was alive, and why I did not return.

General Miles would not let me leave the tent to see my friend alone.

Yellow Bull said to me: "They have got you in their power, and I am afraid they will never let you go again. I have an officer in our camp, and I will hold him until they let you go free."

I said: "I do not know what they mean to do with me, but if they kill me you must not kill the officer. It will do no good to avenge my death by killing him."

Yellow Bull returned to my camp. I did not make any agreement that day with General Miles. The battle was renewed while I was with him. I was very anxious about my people. I knew that we were near Sitting Bull's camp in King George's land, and I thought maybe the Nez Percés who had escaped would return with assistance. No great damage was done to either party during the night.

On the following morning I returned to my camp by agreement, meeting the officer who had been held a prisoner in my camp at the flag of truce. My people were divided about surrendering. We could have escaped from Bear Paw Mountain if we had left our wounded, old women, and children behind. We were unwilling to do this. We had never heard of a wounded Indian recovering while in the hands of white men.

On the evening of the fourth day, General Howard came in with a small escort, together with my friend Chapman. We could now talk understandingly. General Miles said to me in plain words, "If you will come out and give up your arms, I will spare your lives and send you back to the reservation." I do not know what passed between General Miles and General Howard.

I could not bear to see my wounded men and women suffer any longer; we had lost enough already. General

Miles had promised that we might return to our country with what stock we had left. I thought we could start again. I believed General Miles, *or I never would have surrendered.* I have heard that he has been censured for making the promise to return us to Lapwai. He could not have made any other terms with me at that time. I would have held him in check until my friends came to my assistance, and then neither of the generals nor their soldiers would have ever left Bear Paw Mountain alive.

On the fifth day I went to General Miles and gave up my gun, and said, "From where the sun now stands I will fight no more." My people needed rest — we wanted peace.

I was told we could go with General Miles to Tongue River and stay there until spring, when we would be sent back to our country. Finally it was decided that we were to be taken to Tongue River. We had nothing to say about it. After our arrival at Tongue River, General Miles received orders to take us to Bismarck. The reason given was, that subsistence would be cheaper there.

General Miles was opposed to this order. He said: "You must not blame me. I have endeavored to keep my word, but the chief who is over me has given the order, and I must obey it or resign. That would do you no good. Some other officer would carry out the order."

I believe General Miles would have kept his word if he could have done so. I do not blame him for what we have suffered since the surrender. I do not know who is to blame. We gave up all our horses — over eleven hundred — and all our saddles — over one hundred — and we have not heard from them since. Somebody has got our horses.

General Miles turned my people over to another soldier, and we were taken to Bismarck. Captain Johnson, who now had charge of us, received an order to take us to Fort Leavenworth. At Leavenworth we were placed in on a low river bottom, with no water except river water to drink and cook with. We had always lived in a healthy country, where the mountains were high and the water was cold and clear. Many of our people sickened and died, and we buried them in this strange land.* I cannot tell how much my heart suffered for my people while at Leavenworth. The Great Spirit Chief who rules above seemed to be looking some other way, and did not see what was being done to my people.

During the hot days (July, 1878) we received notice that we were to be moved farther away from our own country. We were not asked if we were willing to go. We were ordered to get into the railroad-cars. Three of my people died on the way to Baxter Springs. It was worse to die there than to die fighting in the mountains.

We were moved from Baxter Springs (Kansas) to the Indian Territory and set down without our lodges. We had but little medicine and we were nearly all sick. Seventy of my people have died since we moved there.

We have had a great many visitors who have talked many ways. Some of the chiefs (General Fish and Colonel Stickney) from Washington came to see us, and selected land for us to live upon. We have not moved to that land, for it is not a good place to live.

The Commissioner Chief (E. A. Hayt) came to see us. I told him, as I told every one, that I expected General Miles' word would be carried out. He said it "could not be done; that white men now lived in my country and all the land was taken up; that, if I returned to Wallowa, I could not live in peace; that law-papers were out against my young men who began the war, and that

* I can corroborate this.   I saw them there often.—C. T. B.

the Government could not protect my people." This talk fell like a heavy stone upon my heart. I saw that I could not gain anything by talking to him. Other law chiefs (Congressional Committee) came to see us and said they would help me to get a healthy country. I did not know whom to believe. The white people have too many chiefs. They do not understand each other. They do not talk alike.

The Commissioner Chief (**Mr.** Hayt) invited me to go with him and hunt for a better home than we have now. I like the land we found (west of the Osage Reservation) better than any place I have seen in that country; but it is not a healthy land. There are no mountains and rivers. The water is warm. It is not a good country for stock. I do not believe my people can live there. I am afraid they will all die. The Indians who occupy that country are dying off. I promised Chief Hayt to go there, and do the best I could until the Government got ready to make good General Miles' word. I was not satisfied, but I could not help myself.

Then the Inspector Chief (General McNiel) came to my camp and we had a long talk. He said I ought to have a home in the mountain country north, and that he would write a letter to the Great Chief in Washington. Again the hope of seeing the mountains of Idaho and Oregon grew up in my heart.

At last I was granted permission to come to Washington and bring my friend Yellow Bull and our interpreter with me. I am glad we came. I have shaken hands with a great many friends, but there are some things I want to know which no one seems able to explain. I cannot understand how the Government sends a man out to fight us, as it did General Miles, and then breaks his word. Such a Government has something

wrong about it. I cannot understand why so many
chiefs are allowed to talk so many different ways, and
promise so many different things. I have seen the Great
Father Chief (the President); the next Great Chief
(Secretary of the Interior); the Commissioner Chief
(Hayt); the Law Chief (General Butler), and many other
law chiefs (Congressmen), and they all say they are my
friends, and that I shall have justice, but while their
mouths all talk right I do not understand why nothing is
done for my people. I have heard talk and talk, but
nothing is done. Good words do not last long until they
amount to something. Words do not pay for my dead
people. They do not pay for my country, now overrun
by white men. They do not protect my father's grave.
They do not pay for my horses and cattle. Good words
will not give me back my children. Good words will not
make good the promise of your War Chief, General
Miles. Good words will not give my people good health
and stop them from dying. Good words will not get my
people a home where they can live in peace and take
care of themselves. I am tired of talk that comes to
nothing. It makes my heart sick when I remember all
the good words and all the broken promises. There has
been too much talking by men who had no right to talk.
Too many misrepresentations have been made, too many
misunderstandings have come up between the white
men about the Indians. If the white man wants to live in
peace with the Indian he can live in peace. There need
be no trouble. Treat all men alike. Give them all the
same law. Give them all an even chance to live and
grow. All men were made by the same Great Spirit Chief.
They are all brothers. The earth is the mother of all
people, and all people should have equal rights upon it.
You might as well expect the rivers to run backward as

that any man who was born a free man should be contented penned up and denied liberty to go where he pleases. If you tie a horse to a stake, do you expect he will grow fat? If you pen an Indian up on a small spot of earth, and compel him to stay there, he will not be contented nor will he grow and prosper. I have asked some of the great white chiefs where they get their authority to say to the Indian that he shall stay in one place, while he sees white men going where they please. They cannot tell me.

I only ask of the Government to be treated as all other men are treated. If I cannot go to my own home, let me have a home in some country where my people will not die so fast. I would like to go to Bitter Root Valley. There my people would be healthy; where they are now they are dying. Three have died since I left my camp to come to Washington.

When I think of our condition my heart is heavy. I see men of my race treated as outlaws and driven from country to country, or shot down like animals.

I know that my race must change. We cannot hold our own with the white men as we are. We only ask an even chance to live as other men live. We ask to be recognized as men. We ask that the same law shall work alike on all men. If the Indian breaks the law, punish him by the law. If the white man breaks the law, punish him also.

Let me be a free man — free to travel, free to stop, free to work, free to trade, where I choose, free to choose my own teachers, free to follow the religion of my fathers, free to think and talk and act for myself — and I will obey every law, or submit to the penalty.

Whenever the white man treats the Indian as they treat each other, then we shall have no more wars. We shall be all alike — brothers of one father and one mother, with one sky above us and one country around us, and one government for all. Then the Great Spirit Chief who rules above will smile upon this land, and send rain to wash out the bloody spots made by brothers' hands upon the face of the earth. For this time the Indian race are waiting and praying. I hope that no more groans of wounded men and women will ever go to the ear of the Great Spirit Chief above, and that all people may be one people.

In-mut-too-yah-lat-lat has spoken for his people.

YOUNG JOSEPH.

CHAPTER THREE

General Howard's Comment on Joseph's Narrative

By Maj.-Gen. O. O. Howard, United States Army (Retired)

ON reading in the *North American Review* for April the article entitled "An Indian's View of Indian Affairs," I was so pleased with Joseph's statement — necessarily *ex parte* though it was, and naturally inspired by resentment toward me as a supposed enemy — that at first I had no purpose of making a rejoinder. But when I saw in the *Army and Navy Journal* long passages quoted from Joseph's tale, which appeared to reflect unfavorably upon my official conduct, to lay upon me the blame of the atrocious murders committed by the Indians, and to convict me of glaring faults where I had deemed myself worthy only of commendation, I addressed to the editor of that journal a communication (which has been published) correcting misstatements, and briefly setting forth the facts of the case.

If I had had the power and management entirely in my hands, I believe I could have healed that old sore, and established peace and amity with Joseph's Indians. It could only have been done, first, by a retrocession of Wallowa (already belonging to Oregon) to the United

States, and then setting that country apart forever for the Indians without the retention of any Government authority whatever; and, second, by the removal therefrom of every white settler, making to each a proper remuneration for his land and improvements. But this power I did not have, and the Indian management did not belong to my department.

Now permit me to present a few simple facts which will show whether, in manner or matter, I have failed to meet the requirements of the situation. . . . Governor Stevens and Joel Palmer, in 1855, made a treaty with the Nez Percés, including all the different bands. Joseph's bands were parties to the treaty, and Joseph's father signed it. This ceded and relinquished to the United States all land that the Nez Percés claimed outside of the limits then fixed and agreed upon.

This treaty, be it remembered, included Wallowa and Imnaha Valleys. In 1863 the United States, by their commissioners, made another treaty with the Nez Percés — fifty-one chiefs participating. This treaty reduced the limits so as to constitute the reservation in Lapwai, as it now is, and ceded all the land outside to the United States. Wallowa and Imnaha were left out.

Joseph's band, and a few other bands, now known as the Salmon River or White Bird's band, lived east of the reservation, and the Palouse or Hush-hush-cute's band, west of the same. These, with a few more, on and off the reserve, constitute what are called "non-treaties." The vast majority who made the treaty have kept good faith and are called "treaty Indians." James Lawyer, the present head-chief, is an excellent man; dresses as a white man, and has a good house and farm. Now, notice the difference; Joseph says: "Governor Stevens urged my father to sign the treaty (1855), but he refused";

and then he goes on to give us a graphic account of this refusal and its consequences. He "cautioned his people to take no presents." He "was invited to many councils, and they tried hard to make him sign the treaty, but he was firm as a rock and would not sign away his home," etc. Now, all this is very fine; yet his father did sign the treaty. His name is the third on the list, and there are eleven white witnesses, besides the makers of the instrument.

Governor Grover says in his message: "The reservation named became the common property of the whole tribe." Joseph and his band acknowledged these conclusions also, by accepting the benefit of the treaty of 1855.

Such is the record of history, in precise contradiction to Young Joseph's traditional statement. But he states truly the *claim* (based on the treaty of 1863), of the United States to Wallowa, and Joseph's constant demurrer thereto. The underlying cause of all the troubles, finally resulting in the war, is Joseph's assumption that, as sub-chief, he is not bound by this treaty, inasmuch as he has ever refused to sign it.

Again, the account of Joseph concerning his father's death, and his home, is beautiful and quite affecting. I dislike to mar the effect of it, yet it is a known fact that when the United States agents sought to make some definite arrangement, proposing to give this land to the tribe as *a home*, the offer was refused. The Governor of Oregon writes in 1873: "This small band wish the possession of this large section of Oregon simply to gratify a wild, roaming disposition, and *not for a home*." And even up to the last peace council the objection was not that "you take from us our *home*" (for they intended to live part of the year with the remainder of the tribe), but "you take away our liberty; fix bounds to our habitation, and give law to us. The land is ours, and not yours."

Joseph's pictures of frontier troubles between whites and Indians are graphic and true. The killing of a member of his tribe by a white man he refers to. This came near causing an outbreak. The troops intervened between the settlers and the Indians, and the latter quieted down. But the slow process of the civil law, and the prejudice against Indians in all frontier courts, almost invariably prevent the punishment of crimes against Indians. I did what I could to further the ends of justice, in bringing the guilty to trial; but my efforts in this case resulted in nothing. The Indian has a complaint against us (army and agents), because we can and do punish *him*, but do not and cannot punish *white men* who steal the Indian's property and take life.

"But no war was made on my people until General Howard came to our country two years ago," etc. This has all the summary brevity of Shakspere's history, but is not more accurate. The facts are, that I had been in command of the department since the fall of 1874, and had many dealings with Joseph and his people.

The "non-treaties" became suspiciously restless during the Modoc troubles. This was quieted by my worthy predecessor, by sending a considerable force among them just after the Modoc War.

General Davis, speaking of a large gathering of Indians that boded difficulty at the Wee-ipe, says: "The troops did not interfere with the council (twelve hundred Indians), but their presence there for about ten days had the effect to disperse it. General dissatisfaction, however, seemed to prevail among the 'non-treaty Nez Percés.' This was particularly the case with Joseph's band, the claimants of Wallowa Valley."

Again, the *same year* (1874), these Indians were so restless and threatening that Maj. John Green, First Cavalry, was sent to Wallowa Valley with two companies, and remained till the Indians left for their winter quarters.

The next year (1875), I say in my report: "The troubles at Lapwai and Wallowa Valley have not thus far resulted in bloodshed; but it has been prevented by great carefulness and provision on the part of the Government agents."

The year following (1876), my report goes into the trouble again at length, mentioning the grave fact that "an Indian was killed by a white man in a dispute concerning some stock," and winds up with these words: "And renew my recommendation of a commission to hear and settle the whole matter, before war is even thought of." The commission was at last ordered, but not until after blood had been shed — not till after the Indians had stood up in battle array against armed citizens in Wallowa; and a conflict was averted only by the intervention of regular troops. The commission came, held its memorable sessions at Lapwai in November of 1876, and labored hard and long to get the consent of the disaffected "non-treaty Indians" to some measures of adjustment.

Here are a few of the facts developed by this commission: "The Dreamers, among other pernicious doctrines, teach that the earth being created by God complete, should not be disturbed by man; and that any cultivation of the soil or other improvements to interfere with its natural productions; any voluntary submission to the control of the Government; any improvement in the way of schools, churches, etc., are crimes from which they shrink. This fanaticism is kept alive by the superstition of these Dreamers, who industriously teach that if they continue steadfast in their present belief a leader will be raised up (in the East), who will restore all the dead Indians to life, who will unite with them in expelling the whites from their country, when they will again enter upon and repossess the lands of their ancestors.

"Influenced by such belief, Joseph and his band firmly declined to enter into any negotiations, or make any arrangements that looked to a final settlement of the question pending between him and the Government . . . yet, in view of the fact that these Indians do not claim simply this (rights of occupancy), but set up an absolute title to the lands, an absolute and independent sovereignty, and refuse even to be limited in their claim and control, necessity, humanity, and good sense constrain the Government to set metes and bounds and give regulations to these non-treaty Indians. . . . And if the principle usually applied by the Government, of holding that the Indians with whom they have treaties are bound by majorities, is here applied, Joseph should be required to live within the limits of the present reservation."

The commission, though firm and strong in the expression of its opinion, was very patient with and kind to the Indians. I was a member of this commission, and earnestly desired peace. I took Joseph's brother by himself and showed him how much it would be for the Indians' advantage to come to some settlement and spent a long time in giving him and his brother, in the kindest manner, the benefit of my counsel. They appeared at one time almost on the point of yielding, but bad advice intervened to renew the Dreamer sophistry. The commission promised that they should annually visit Wallowa, and so recommended. But here are a few closing words: "If these Indians overrun land belonging to the whites and commit depredations on their property, disturb the peace by threats or otherwise, or commit other overt acts of hostility, we recommend the employment of sufficient force to bring them into subjection, and to place them upon the Nez Percés Reservation. The Indian agent at Lapwai should be fully instructed to carry into execution these suggestions, relying at all times upon the department commander for aid when necessary."

Now, there was nothing like precipitancy in all this; so that the wonderfully abrupt advent of General Howard, with a fear of the laughter of the white man in his heart, and a threat of violence on his tongue, is all fiction.

Doubtless Joseph was told that the commission had

recommended "that Wallowa should be held by military occupation," to *prevent* and not to make war, and that I should have the work to do.

This commissioner's report was approved at Washington. The Indian Agent, Mr. Monteith, did all that lay in his power to carry out the recommendations at first without military aid.

The Indians called me to an interview first at Walla Walla, afterward at Lapwai. At Walla Walla the talk with Joseph's brother Ollicut was exceedingly pleasant. I write of it, "The old medicine-man looks happy, and Ollicut believes we shall have no trouble. . . .

"I made the appointment for Lapwai in twelve days, but I went to Lewiston immediately to meet the officers of Fort Lapwai, and Indian Agent Monteith, to read to them carefully the full instructions from the Honorable Secretary of War, General Sherman, and the commanding general of the military division, in relation especially to the agency the military was to have in placing the Indians upon the reservation."

I made a visit to Wallula and then returned by stage to meet the non-treaties at Lapwai the 3rd of May (1877). This is the council to which Joseph invited me, and not I him, as he alleges.

Before giving points in this interview in answer to Joseph's statements, I must state that Mr. Monteith, Indian Agent, had been instructed by his chief at Washington, to bring the "non-treaty Nez Percés" upon their reservation. He had made his official demand upon me. I had been positively ordered to give the essential aid. There was now nothing left to parley about, yet to please the Indians I had promised to meet them again, and I did.

These picturesque people came in sight, after keeping

Ollicut, Chief Joseph's Brother. Killed in One of the
Last Battles of the Nez Percé War

From the collection of J. W. Redington

us waiting long enough for effect. They drew near the hollow square of the post and in sight of us, the small company to be interviewed. They struck up their song. They were not armed except with a few "tomahawk-pipes" that could be smoked with the peaceful tobacco or penetrate the skull-bone of an enemy, at the will of the holder"; yet, somehow, this wild song produces a strange effect. Our ladies, thinking it a war-song, ask with some show of trepidation, "Do you think Joseph means to fight?" The Indians sweep around the fence and make the entire circuit, still keeping up the song as they ride, the buildings breaking the refrain into irregular bubblings of sound till the ceremony was completed.

After all had finally gathered at the tent, and Father Cataldo had opened by a prayer in the Nez Percés language, I turned to Joseph and said through Mr. Whitman (the interpreter): "I heard from your brother Ollicut, twelve days ago at Walla Walla, that you wished to see me. I am now here to listen to what you have to say."

Joseph then told me of other Indians coming and said, "You must not be in a hurry to go till all get in, to have a talk."

I replied: "Mr. Monteith, the Indian Agent, and I have our instructions from Washington. They send us to your people. If you decide at once to comply with the wishes of the Government, you can have the first pick of vacant land. We will wait for White Bird if you desire it. Instructions to him are the same as to you. He can have his turn." And an old Dreamer intimating that they wished a long talk, the answer is: "Mr. Monteith and I wished to hear what you have to say, whatever time it may take; but you may as well know at the outset that, in any event, the Indians must obey the orders of the Government of the United States."

Mr. Monteith then read his instructions from the Indian Bureau to the Indians and had them carefully interpreted to them, and also explained how he had already informed them of the orders to come on the reservation through Reuben (then head-chief at Lapwai) and that they had scorned his message. "Now, you *must* come, and there is no getting out of it. Your Indians, and White Bird's, can pick up your horses and cattle and come on the reservation. . . . General Howard will stay till matters are settled."

Ollicut replied at length, objecting to considering matters settled.

I rejoined: "Joseph, the agent, Mr. Monteith, and myself are under the same Government. What it commands us to do, that we must do. The Indians are to come on the reservation first; *then* they may have privileges, as the agent has shown, to hunt and to fish in the Imnaha Valley. If the Indians hesitate to come to the reservation, the Government directs that soldiers be used to bring them hither. Joseph and Ollicut know that we are friends to them, and that if they comply there will be no trouble."

Everybody at this council was in good humor, except two old Dreamers who tried to make a disturbance. I told them pointedly to give good advice. My manner I will not judge of. It is my usual manner, proceeding from the kindest of feelings, and from an endeavor to behave as a gentleman to the weakest or most ignorant human being. The Indians, excepting the two I have named, made no angry remarks. We shook hands and separated, to wait as Joseph had requested.

Joseph has turned this right about in the article

published in the *Review* where it is stated that he said, "I am ready to talk to-day," and that General Howard would not. His account runs two days' interviews into one. Joseph never made that interesting speech ending with "I do not believe that the Great Spirit Chief gave one kind of men the right to tell another kind of men what they must do." And I did never reply, "You want to dictate to me, do you?" We always treated each other with the most marked courtesy.

On May 4th Joseph made a brief speech: "This is White Bird; I spoke to you of him; this is the first time he has seen you and you him. I want him and his Indians to understand what has been said to us."

White Bird was a demure-looking Indian, about five feet eight inches in height. His face assumed the condition of impassability while in council; he kept his ceremonial hat on, and placed a large eagle's wing in front of his eyes and nose.

The sub-chief and Dreamer, Too-hool-hool-suit, was broad-shouldered, deep-chested, five feet ten in height, had a deep guttural voice, and betrayed in every word a strong and settled hatred of all Caucasians. This man the Indians now put forward to speak for them — not that they had already decided to indorse his sentiments, but because he always counseled war; they evidently desired to see what effect his public utterance would produce upon us.

Now, instead of the mild and respectful speech attributed to this surly Indian by Joseph, a speech that was followed by my causeless loss of temper, Mr. Monteith and I heard him patiently, for quite a length of time, asserting his independence and uttering rebellious speeches against the Washington authority. We replied firmly and kindly as before, explaining everything and showing the imperative nature of our instructions.

The White Bird Indians were very tired that day, and Joseph again asked for delay. The record reads: "Let the Indians take time; let them wait till Monday morning, and meanwhile talk among themselves. So, with pleasant faces and cordial handshaking, the second interview broke up."

How different this is from Joseph's account of the affair, in which he condenses the whole narrative into the arrest of Too-hool-hool-suit upon his first appearance, and without provocation.

Now (Monday, May 7th), we came together again. The "non-treaties" had received large accessions. The display (previous to seating themselves) gave them great boldness. Our garrison was but a handful, and the manner of the Indians was now defiant. Mr. Monteith began in the kindest manner to show the Indians that their religion would not be interfered with, nor their ceremonies, unless the peace was disturbed by excessive drumming.

Then Too-hool-hool-suit began in the most offensive style. We listened to the oft-repeated Dreamer nonsense with no impatience, till finally he accused us of speaking untruthfully about the chieftainship of the earth.

I thought the time had come to check his tirade. I was not in the least angry, if I recall my mood with accuracy; I did not lose my temper, but I did assume a severity of tone sufficient to show that I understood the drift of the council, and that we were not to be intimidated. My first words were: "I do not want to interfere with your religion, but you must talk about practicable things. Twenty times over I hear that the earth is your mother, and about the chieftainship of the earth; I want to hear it no more, but to come to business at once."

He then talked against the treaty Indians, and said they had no law, or their law was born of to-day; then against us white people for attempting to divide the earth, and defiantly asking, "What do you mean?"

Mr. Monteith explained: "The law is, you must come to the reservation. The law is made in Washington; we don't make it." Then, again, the Dreamer goes over the same ground and becomes fiercer and fiercer. The crowd of Indians are becoming excited, and I saw that I must act, and that very promptly. The record is: "The rough old fellow, in his most provoking tone, says something in a short sentence, looking fiercely at me. The interpreter quickly says: 'He demands what person pretends to divide the land and put me on it?' In the most decided voice I said: 'I am the man; I stand here for the President, and there is no spirit, good or bad, that will hinder me. My orders are plain and will be executed. I hoped that the Indians had good sense enough to make me their friend and not their enemy.'"

From various unmistakable signs (I am no novice with Indians) I saw that immediate trouble was at hand. Joseph, White Bird, and Looking Glass indorsed and encouraged this malcontent. I must somehow put a wedge between them; so I turned to this Dreamer and said, "Then you do not propose to comply with the orders of the Government?"

After considerable more growling and impudence of manner, he answered with additional fierceness, "The Indians may do what they like, but I am not going on the reservation." After telling the Indians that this bad advice would be their ruin, I asked the chiefs to go with me to look at their land. "The old man shall not go. I will leave him with Colonel Perry." He says, "Do you want to scare me with reference to my body?" I said, "I will leave your body with Colonel Perry." I then arose and led him out of the council, and gave him in charge of Colonel Perry.

The whole tone of the Indians now changed, and they readily agreed to go with me to look at their new homes. They may have thought of killing me then and there; but a bold, quick, unexpected action will often save you in extreme peril. Joseph's manner was never defiant. He rode with me to look at what Mr. Monteith had intended for him. A few Indians and some white sojourners would have to remove to other lands, to put Joseph's people together. We lunched together at Mr. Colwell's and then returned to the fort. White Bird and Looking Glass appeared to be happy and contented. They pleaded for the release of Too-hool-hool-suit; but I told them to wait until I had shown them their land which Mr. Monteith would designate. The next day we rode to Kamiah (sixty-five miles), and the next went to the lands intended. White Bird picked his near Looking Glass's farms, and then we returned to Kamiah, and the next day following to Lapwai.

Too-hool-hool-suit was released on the pledge of Looking Glass and White Bird, and on his earnest promise to behave better and give good advice.

Now we must have our final interview, May 14th. Joseph concluded to go, too, near Kamiah with the rest. The promises were put in writing. No objection was made to thirty days, except by Hush-hush-cute. I gave him thirty-five days because he had not had so early notice of removal.

I withheld the protection papers from Hush-hush-cute because of something he said, which indicated that he was attempting to conceal his intentions. So I left his papers with the agent. There was general joy among the treaty Indians, non-treaty Indians, and whites, at the peaceful outcome of the councils, and I returned to Portland.

This idea that General Howard caused the war is an after-thought.

That story that Joseph asked me for more time is not true. That I sent orders to the soldiers to drive them out on their return to Wallowa is, of course, untrue; that would have disconcerted everything; on the contrary, the officers and soldiers were simply to occupy Wallowa in the interest of peace, and not use constraint unless forced to do so.

The statements with reference to our losses and those of the Indians are all wrong, and Joseph does not tell how his own Indians, White Bird and his followers, who treacherously escaped, after the terms of the surrender had been agreed upon between us at General Miles' battle-field, being permitted by himself, did in fact utterly break and make void the said terms of surrender.

These Indians were to return to Idaho, not because of any promise, but because of General McDowell's orders, requiring all the Nez Percé prisoners to be kept in my department. This order was changed by General Sherman, or at Washington.

CHAPTER FOUR

The Battle of White Bird Cañon

By Maj. and Brev. Col. W. R. Parnell, United States
Army (Retired)

THE Wallowa Valley is fifteen or twenty miles east of the Grande Ronde Valley in eastern Oregon, and had long been a bone of contention between the whites and a band of non-treaty Nez Percé Indians under Chief Joseph. The whites claimed the right of settlement under the United States Land Acts, and while no determined effort on their part was made to take up homestead, preëmption or other claims, yet they kept it as a grazing ground for their cattle, while the Indians denied them the right to such privileges, claiming to themselves the entire control of the valley and surrounding hills for hunting and fishing. They were confirmed in this right by the Government, I believe, in 1855; but by subsequent authority from Washington the land was thrown open for settlement and still later on again withdrawn.

These conflicting rulings the Indian did not clearly understand, and he evidently did not propose to be trifled with like a child with a toy, to be taken away from and given again in pleasure. Quarrels were continually arising between the red-men and the white; an occasional steer would be missing from the white man's herd, and ponies would, in turn, be missing from that of the Indian. Fort Walla Walla was the nearest military station to this disputed territory and the cavalry troops were constantly moving to and from the Grande Ronde and Wallowa Valleys, settling differences and preserving the peace, from the date of regarrisoning it in 1873 until hostilities commenced in 1877.

During the summer months two troops of cavalry were kept in camp in the Wallowa Valley, returning to Walla Walla for the winter. Even the severity of winter did not appear to cool the hot blood, or bad blood, of either the white man or the Indian, for on New Year's Day 1876 — the year of the Centennial — two troops of the First Cavalry under my command had to forego their New Year calls, egg-nog and other attractions, and start out on an expedition across the Blue Mountains to Grande Ronde Valley, to quell an anticipated outbreak of the Indians for some grievance against the whites. The temperature was twelve degrees below zero with from two to four feet of snow on the ground.

On reaching the valley we found, however, that there was no evidence of any trouble whatever on the part of the Indians. The report was a ruse of some white men in Grande Ronde Valley to get cavalry into the valley, hoping, thereby, to dispose of their hay, grain and provisions at prices at inverse ratio to the mercury in the thermometer. Imagine their chagrin when they found that the Government contractor had made all necessary arrangements in the premises before we reached the valley!

It would seem an anomaly to the military mind to read the regular annual Presidential Message to Congress that "the country was at peace," etc., when war within our own borders was never ceasing; that for acrimony and deviltry on the part of the Indians, and of hardships, suffering and privations on the part of the troops engaged in it, was absolutely unknown in a war of any other character.

A few years ago not a month passed that war did not exist in one section or another within the boundaries of the United States; if not in Washington, Oregon, Nevada, or California, we had it in Montana and the Dakotas, or down in Arizona, New Mexico or Texas. So far as the cavalry arm of the service was concerned, cessation from hostilities did not exist. The cavalry was continually on the alert, the ever watchful eyes of the army were either in the saddle, or virtually "standing to horse." And they are doing the same thing in the Philippines to-day!

General Howard, commanding the Department of the Columbia, was instructed from Washington to proceed to Fort Lapwai, Idaho, and hold council with Chief Joseph and his tribe regarding the disputed territory. He was directed to formulate a plan by which the non-treaty Indians should come on the Nez Percé Indian Reservation at Lapwai or Kamai.

There were stationed at Fort Lapwai in May, 1877, Troop F, First United States Cavalry, and a small command of the Twenty-first United States Infantry, the post being under the command of Col. David Perry, Captain First Cavalry. General Howard ordered Troop H, First Cavalry, from Walla Walla to Lewiston, Idaho, a small town at the junction of the Snake and Clearwater Rivers. This troop was to remain in camp on the west bank of the Snake so as to be ready to move up the Snake River on either side, or to move rapidly into the Wallowa Valley and reinforce Troops

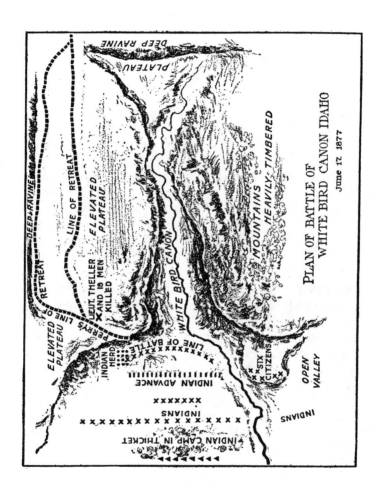

PLAN OF BATTLE OF
WHITE BIRD CANON IDAHO
June 17, 1877

E and L, First Cavalry, should occasion require it, as it was well known that the Indians were ugly and strongly opposed to going on a reservation, or surrendering their alleged rights to the Wallowa.

The Nez Percé Reservation covers an immense tract of perhaps the most fertile soil in Idaho, abundantly supplied with water and timber land. The agency is beautifully situated on the Clearwater, about three miles from the military post of Fort Lapwai. It has a sub-agency at Kamai, sixty miles higher up on the Clearwater. It is there that the celebrated Lo-lo Trail across the Bitter Root Mountains in Montana commences.

It was with much difficulty that the Indians could be induced to come in and hold council, several preliminary "talks" had occurred with one or another of the sub-chiefs. On the 15th of May, the grand council was held in a large tent pitched on the parade-ground at Fort Lapwai. The attitude of the Indians indicated anything but friendly feelings; they wore a sullen, dogged and defiant demeanor; treachery on their part was anticipated at least, and although the stipulations were that each party should appear unarmed, it was afterward discovered that many Indians present at the council, beside many on the outside, were armed with revolvers, rifles and knives hid away under their blankets. To provide against such an emergency, the General gave orders to have all the troops remain in quarters and "under arms." The Indians were represented by Chief Joseph, Ollicut, his younger brother, White Bird, Looking Glass, Hush-hush-cute, chief of the Palouse Indians, who were strong allies, through intermarriage, of the Nez Percés; and a goodly sprinkle of sub-chiefs, warriors and squaws.

The council lasted from about ten o'clock in the

morning until late in the afternoon. Many times during the day hot and defiant words fell from the lips of the Indians, more particularly from those of White Bird, who was the worst devil of the lot. I use the phrase advisedly, knowing from past experience the horrible cruelties practised by Indians on helpless and unprotected white women and children on our frontier.

Toward the close of the council the excitement grew intense. Every moment General Howard and the officers present anticipated an attack by the Indians whose every motion indicated that they were armed, though no weapons were shown. So arrogant and defiant were they that few white men could have restrained themselves; indeed, at one time, General Howard was on the point of committing one of them to the guard-house in irons, but his cooler and better judgment and proverbial desire for peace restrained him, and the storm subsided for the time being.

The most trivial spark of indiscretion on the part of any officer present would have caused the massacre of the entire party. Let the so-called Indian philanthropist of the East, the admirers of the Fenimore Cooper type of the noble red-man, cavil as they may about army officers and the regular army, generally, on that question. There never have been any better friends of the Indian than the officers and enlisted men of our little regular army. When they go out on a campaign, they go in obedience of orders. They go for business strictly, and not for a picnic. They go to protect the lives and property of our sturdy pioneers on our frontier against the most bloodthirsty and relentless foe of our race, and then, when success and victory crown their efforts, they in turn feed, clothe and protect the people they have subdued.

Chief Joseph and Looking Glass favored the proposition of going on the reservation. White Bird and Ollicut opposed it, but the decision of the council was that Chief Joseph's band of non-treaty Indians, which included all of the smaller bands, was to go on the reservation. Thirty days were allowed for this purpose. The 14th of June was to see the entire band on the Nez Percé Reservation among their own people. To this the Indians agreed.

During the conference Chief Joseph's brother, Ollicut, sometimes called Young Joseph, exhibited a map of the disputed territory of the Wallowa which was, to say the least, unique. It was a novel specimen of draughtsmanship, if I remember correctly. It was on a peculiar piece of paper or parchment of a muddy yellow tinge, about sixteen or eighteen inches square, the ink being of a pale green color; the geography was delineated by natural history; for instance, the Wallowa Lake was represented by a single ink line showing the boundary line, and a crude drawing of a fish in the center; the mountains were represented by the figures of deer; the Wallowa River by a zigzag line, with trees here and there along its length. The wagon-road was probably the most peculiar and interesting part of it, a double column of very small circles running the entire length of the valley was the impression we received at first glance, the circles not larger than a pin's head; but upon closer inspection the circles were found to be incomplete; they were minute representations of horse-shoes, indicating the impress of the shoe upon the soft earth.

A tragedy that occurred a short time before, in which an Indian was killed by a white man, occasioned by a dispute about the removal of a rail fence to allow horses to pass through, was shown on the map as near the vicinity as guesswork could make it, by figures representing a white man and two or three Indians struggling for the possession of a gun. The figures of men and animals were a good deal after the Egyptian types, straight lines and angles.

An effort was made by General Howard and Lieutenant Fletcher of the Twenty-first Infantry to make an exact copy of the map, but under no consideration would the Indians allow them to retain it long enough for that purpose.

General Howard returned to Portland next day to await the termination of the allotted month, and the Indians returned to their camp on the Salmon River. As the 14th of June drew near, speculation was rife as to the probabilities of the Indians abiding by the decision of the council, or otherwise. Nothing had been heard from them, nor had any of them as yet "come in."

The morning of the 14th of June arrived and with it brought General Howard from Department Headquarters. The day wore along, clear, warm and peaceful; troops were to return to their stations if all went well. But all did not go well, for about six o'clock P.M. a messenger arrived from Mount Idaho with a letter to the General stating that Joseph's band was giving the settlers much trouble and annoyance, causing fears of an outbreak. Early next morning four cavalrymen and the interpreter from the agency started for Mount Idaho to learn particulars.

Much uneasiness was manifest throughout the little garrison. We knew that the Indians should now be within the boundary of the reservation, and they were not. We were satisfied in our own minds that they did not intend to obey the mandate of the council and from their demeanor, during the deliberations of that body,

we could see no other prospect than war. The Nez
Percés were a brave and warlike type of the Indian,
tall, strong and well formed, armed with weapons
equal, if not superior, to our own, for theirs were Winchesters, sixteen shooters; ours were the Springfield,
single-shot, breech-loading carbines. They had a large
herd of good, strong ponies, giving them almost un-
limited relays for their remounts, either for pursuit or
retreat. We, therefore, made our preparations for business on the return of the messengers.

Scarcely three hours had elapsed ere the party came
galloping into camp very much excited. They had been
fired upon and driven back by a squad of Indians concealed in the timber, who were watching the road to
Mount Idaho, about ten miles from Fort Lapwai. Our
dream of a peaceful settlement of the question was now
at an end. Hostilities had commenced, and another protracted and bloody Indian war was confronting us.

The Indians had failed to comply with the terms
agreed upon in the council. The young bloods had defied
the counsel and advice of the older and wiser heads of
their tribe, and demanded approval from their people
for the cold-blooded murder of innocent and unsus-
pecting white settlers along the Salmon River.

On the 14th of June, the day they should have been
on the reservation, under treaty stipulations, three of
their young men went to a store and post-office some
six miles above Slate Creek on the Salmon River, kept
by a Mr. Elfers, whom they shot and killed while he was
plowing. His unfortunate wife witnessed the murder of
her husband and then fled from the house and sought
shelter in the thick underbrush along the creek.

The Indians thoroughly ransacked the house, procured one or two rifles and shot-guns, a quantity of

ammunition and a large supply of provisions. A party, fleeing from Cottonwood to Mount Idaho, eighteen miles distant, was also attacked; one man was killed, one wounded and one woman badly wounded. A settler at the mouth of White Bird Creek on the Salmon River was also killed, his wife made prisoner and his house burned. These were the acts which demanded recognition and approval at the hands of the tribe, or at least the condonation of them. We learned afterward that a grand council was held by the leading men of the tribe, and after a long debate it was determined to give their support to the murderers and defy the United States authorities. In other words, they determined to get to war rather than surrender the offenders against law, or go on the reservation.

Troops F and H, First Cavalry, therefore left Fort Lapwai for Mount Idaho at eight o'clock on the evening of June 15th. The command mustered about eighty men. Capt. and Brev. Col. David Perry was in command. After marching until about one o'clock A.M., on the 16th, skirmishers and flankers were thrown out. We were in the mountains; heavy timber, deep ravines, and a wild, broken country confronted us. The night was dark and at any moment we might be saluted with a volley from the usually unerring rifles of the Indians, but the men were vigilant and careful and we reached Cottonwood Ranch unmolested. We knew that Indian scouts were watching our every move, as we proceeded on our march, but they carefully avoided being seen by us by taking to the high ridges or hiding in the thick underbrush in the ravines and cañons along the line of march.

We halted at Cottonwood long enough to cook coffee and unsaddle our animals for a roll and an hour's grazing and then proceeded across Camas Prairie to Mount

Idaho, which we reached in the afternoon. We found the citizens armed and very much excited. In the course of the evening a delegation from the small town waited on Colonel Perry, urging him to move down to the Salmon River where the Indians were camped, and attack and punish them for the murders committed by them. Perry called the officers of the command together and after a prolonged conversation with the citizens, who professed to know the situation and strength of the Indians, claiming an easy victory, it was decided to make the attempt. The citizens were deceived in their supposed knowledge of Indian affairs as events subsequently proved.

We fed our men and horses and started at ten o'clock P.M. for the Salmon River, distant about twenty miles. We were now two days and on our second night without rest or sleep, but fully awake and alive to the possibilities of the serious business before us. Half a dozen citizens accompanied us to act as guides and assist in the prospective fight and defeat of the Indians; their leader being George Shearer, an ex-Confederate Major, a brave man and a genial good fellow.

We plodded along in the dark until about one o'clock in the morning when we reached the head of White Bird Cañon, where we made a halt until dawn. Colonel Perry ordered perfect quiet and under the circumstances no light of any kind was to be made, yet one man of his own troop lighted a match to light his pipe; two hours later that man paid the penalty of his disobedience with his life. Almost immediately the cry of a coyote was heard in the hills above us, a long, howling cry, winding up, however, in a very peculiar way not characteristic of the coyote. Little heed was paid to it at the time, yet it was a fatal cry to the command. It was made by an

Scouts of Nez Percé Warriors

Indian picket on the watch for the soldiers who they knew were already on the march. Probably he had seen the light. The signal was carried by others to the camp, so that they were thoroughly prepared for our coming.

As dawn approached we continued our march down the ravine into White Bird Cañon. A trail led us down a narrow defile, now and again crossing a dry creek bed with here and there a heavy growth of willows and underbrush. At one time we would be skirting along the steep hillside, at another following the creek bed. High bluffs and mountains lined each side of the cañon while the trail led over rolling country, up and down little knolls but still descending.

About three o'clock that fatal morning, as we passed in single file along the side of the hill, a sad and pitiable sight presented itself to us. We discovered an unfortunate woman, whose husband had been killed by the Indians, concealed in the gulch below us with a little four year old girl in her arms. The child's head was broken, yet bearing it with fortitude the poor mother and child, shivering with cold, were thanking God for their deliverance. They had been hiding in the brush from the Indians since the 14th and it was now the morning of the 17th of June. I have never seen a sight that called for sympathy, compassion, and action like it. It was a terrible illustration of Indian deviltry and Indian warfare. The contents of the haversacks were freely given to the unfortunates and we passed into the woods before us.

In a short time we found the cañon widening out as we descended, the bluffs on either side appeared to grow higher and higher; bearing around to the east as we entered a valley four or five hundred yards wide. We had advanced about a hundred yards when I noticed Perry's Troop moving into line at a trot. It was now fairly daylight, the Indians were seen advancing and firing commenced at once. Troop H moved up and formed line on the right of Perry. The citizens were on the extreme left and in good position in a rocky knoll which virtually commanded all approaches from the left. The ground to the right of the line was a steady rise at an angle of about twenty degrees for a distance of perhaps two hundred yards, then quite a steep ascent for some distance to the plateau above. The ground to the left of Troop H, occupied by F, gradually swayed downward and then upward to the position held by the citizens.

It was bad judgment and certainly not tactical to put the entire command on the line, leaving no reserves whatever in either troop, and, to increase the danger of such a fatal error, the men were in the saddle in an exposed position, while the Indians were on foot, taking cover in the grass and behind rocks. Very soon the men dismounted of their own account. Some were shot off their horses, and as the firing became hotter many loose horses were soon galloping away in the rear of the line.

About half an hour had elapsed and several men had either been killed or wounded when Perry's men began moving by the right flank to the higher ground on our right. An attack had been made on the position held by the citizens, two of whom were wounded and the rest driven from their stand. This left it an easy matter for the Indians to pass around Perry's left under cover of the knoll and get a position on his right. In the meantime, the Indians had driven a large herd of loose ponies through our line, and scattered in among the ponies were some sixty or seventy warriors who immediately attacked us in the rear, demoralizing the troop, many of whom were recruits, but a short time out from Eastern rendez-

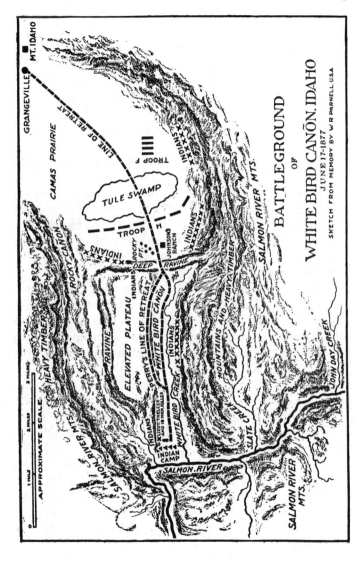

BATTLEGROUND
OF
WHITE BIRD CAÑON, IDAHO
JUNE 17-1877
SKETCH FROM MEMORY BY W R PARNELL U.S.A

vous, so that it became utterly impossible to control them.

As Perry passed in to the right I supposed he would halt the line when in position on the right of Troop H, but not so. He kept on gaining ground to the right and rear until I saw him finally ascend the steep rise to the bluffs above and disappear from sight. He afterward explained this officially by the statement "that the men were beyond control."

I now found my position one of extreme danger. The other two officers of the command had followed the movement of Perry's troop to the elevated plateau on our right. Lieutenant Theller and eighteen men were killed by an overwhelming body of Indians before they could reach Perry's men. The quantity of empty shells found where their bodies lay indicated that they fought to the bitter end.

With what men I could collect together I now commenced falling back, fighting, by the way we came; that is, up the White Bird Cañon. I saw that it would be suicidal to attempt to reach the bluffs on our right, so we slowly retreated up the ravine, holding the Indians in check from knoll to knoll. I saw that halt must be made pretty soon to tighten up our saddle-girths, so, posting a few men in a little rise in front to hold the Indians, I dismounted and readjusted my saddle, directing the men to do the same. We then took position on the right knoll and from knoll to knoll we fell back, waiting at every halt until the Indians came near enough to receive the contents of our carbines. They were swarming in front of us and on the hillsides on both flanks, but the few brave fellows with me obeyed every command with alacrity. I think there were thirteen or fourteen men altogether.

The Indians dared not approach too closely, yet at one time they were near enough for my last pistol cartridge to hit one of them in the thigh. We had several miles of this kind of work up through the cañon, but the men were now cool and determined and fully alive to the perilous situation we were in. When we reached the head of the cañon, we were rejoiced to find Perry's men, who had been falling back in a line nearly parallel with us, on the mesa above. He had eighteen or twenty men with him. I had not seen him since he reached the bluffs two hours before, and neither of us knew anything about the whereabouts or fate of the other. Our meeting no doubt saved the massacre of either or both parties, for we had yet about eighteen miles to fight our way back ere we could hope for succor.

Immediately in our rear was a deep ravine to be crossed. Perry requested me to hold the ridge we were on while he crossed and he would then cover my passage from a commanding position on the other side. I watched his crossing so as to be ready to move when he had his men in position, but again they failed him. They had not yet recovered from their unfortunate stampeded condition. I crossed the ravine at a gallop and halted on the other side to welcome the Indians, who appeared to swarm on every hill. They halted abruptly on receiving a salute from our carbines.

We then moved quietly down to an abandoned ranch, a mile to the rear, where Perry had his men dismounted in what appeared to be a good position in the rock. I dismounted our men, tied our horses to a rail fence and took position in the rocks; the house and barn were to our left a short distance, and a small creek between us and the house. Presently, shots came flying over our heads from the front and right flank. The Indians had taken stand in a clump of rocks in our front and flank on higher ground, and therefore commanded our position. At the same time I noticed some of them coming down on our left, under cover of a fence that ran from the house up the hill perpendicular to our front. I mentioned this to Perry. Our ammunition was getting very short, as we had but forty rounds per man when we started.

After a brief consultation under a hot fire we determined to abandon our positions and continue a retreating fight back to Mount Idaho. When we first reached the ranch, Perry suggested that we should hold the position until dark and then fall back, as it was then seven o'clock, and it would soon be dark. I could not understand his remark and looked at him in astonishment. I said:

"Do you know that it is seven o'clock in the morning — not evening — that we have been fighting nearly four hours and have but a few rounds per man left?"

I thought he was what is commonly called confused. He requested me to hold the position while he mounted his men, and he would then hold it until I had my men in the saddle.

He moved down and mounted. I then ordered my small detachment down, waiting until every man was away. I followed and to my consternation found the command gone and my horse with it. I hallooed out to the command now more than a hundred yards distant, but, evidently, nobody heard me as they continued to move on.

The Indians were now gaining on me and shots kept whizzing past me from every direction in rear. I looked around for a hiding-place, but nothing presented itself that would secure me from observation. I fully made up my mind that I would not be taken prisoner, and determined to use my hunting-knife or a small derringer pistol I always carried in my vest-pocket. These thoughts and final determination flashed through my mind in a few seconds, as I kept moving on trying to overhaul the command.

Finally, some of my own men missed me, and looking back, saw me and reported to Colonel Perry. The troops were halted, my horse caught and led back to me. A few minutes after Perry halted the men and requested me to reorganize the command. I did so quickly for there was little to organize, and requesting Perry to support me at a distance not greater than one hundred yards, I stated that I would take charge of the skirmish-line. The line was deployed at unusually great intervals, so as to cover as much front as possible and then, after a few words of caution and instruction, we waited the coming of the Indians, who at a distance had been closely watching us.

We did not have a long time to wait, for they came upon us with a yell. Not a shot was fired until the red devils rode up to within seventy-five or a hundred yards of us when I gave the order to "commence firing." Several redskins and half a dozen horses went down from our fire. We then moved "to the rear" at a walk, and again halted, the Indians waiting for us, but once more our fire sent some to grass and we quietly fell back eighty or ninety yards more. Thus we continued retreating for several miles. Chief White Bird with about seventy warriors made several attempts to drive us off to the right into Rocky Cañon, which, had they succeeded in doing, would have sounded our death knell, but Perry moved his men so as to prevent it and gave them a few well-directed volleys which drove them back.

In passing over a marsh my attention was called to a man struggling through the swampy ground and long grass about half-way between us and the Indians. We could just see his head above the grass. A few minutes more and the Indians would have his scalp. I advanced the line firing, driving the Indians back, and rescued a man of H Troop whose horse had been shot. The poor fellow was almost played out, he was taken up behind another man and we continued our retreat.

When we got to within a few miles of Mount Idaho, a party of citizens came out to our assistance. While we fully appreciated their action, it was too late for them to be of any service as the Indians disappeared as they came into view. Men and horses were now completely exhausted. We had been on the move ever since Friday without rest or sleep, and under too much excitement to hope for sleep now that we had reached comparative safety.

Late in the fall of 1877 I was shown a copy of the *New York Herald* containing an account of the Nez Percé Indian War from "White Bird" fight to its termination in Montana in November, and this is what is stated of the White Bird affair:

The hostiles commenced operations by murdering all the white settlers they could find, of whom there were many; burning their houses, driving off their stock, and taking all the valuables they wanted. . . . The terrible massacre of thirty-three of these soldiers, under command of Captain Perry, on June 17th, first attracts our attention. . . . Captain Perry attacked the Indians in White Bird Cañon, situated on a creek of the same name at a point about three miles from where the stream empties into the Salmon River. This cañon is very deep and extensive, and the trail leading down to it is very steep, and in places extremely narrow, necessitating for part of the way a march by "file." It is seven miles from the point of descent to the creek, the first three miles being almost perpendicular. The canon gradually widens as you approach the creek, sloping down to the water's edge. The width of the cañon contiguous to the stream is about five miles. It here presents the appearance of a rolling prairie, being dotted here and there with wave-like swells.

The correspondent is somewhat in error about the width of the cañon, as in no place is it anywhere near half that distance. There are also some slight discrepancies in his account of the order given and the conduct of the engagement. I have no knowledge of the source of his information. We had no correspondent with us, nor was there one with any of the troops who subsequently passed through the cañon. Further, he says:

Captain Perry led his command down the narrow trail at daylight in the morning of June 17th after marching all night, with men and horses hungry and weary. The Indians permitted him to advance to within seventy-five yards without resistance, or even showing themselves to the troops. When the redskins were visible, the command was given, "Left front into line; forward, charge!"

The correspondent then goes on to explain the action, in which are many errors, so that I am satisfied the author could not have been one familiar with military affairs. He, however, says truly that Captain Perry did attempt to rally his men, but he could not get one-twentieth of them together, scattered as they were, especially as he could not find either of his trumpeters. One was killed and the other was demoralized and had got out of range of the Indian rifles as soon as the retreat commenced. He says again:

However, with the few men under his immediate eye, he occupied a semicircle of knolls, with himself and a few citizens inside the curve thus defended, until an opportunity occurred to retreat still farther in a similar manner, and his party reached the top of the cañon, where all who had horses ran as if for their lives.

Captain Perry did not retreat up the cañon, he did just what I have stated: *i. e.*, he ascended to the plateau above the cañon near where the fight commenced and retreated along that until our parties united at the head of the cañon, mine out of it, and his on the right above us. Neither did all those who had horses run as if for their lives. That some did, I know.

He, the so-called correspondent, speaks in generous and flattering terms of my humble, but happily successful attempts to hold the Indians in check with the few gallant fellows who fought up the cañon. He says:

> There is no doubt but the Indians would have pursued and massacred every one of the command had it not been for the bravery and determined pluck of Lieutenant Parnell of the First Cavalry. This officer, gathering a few men around him, occupied knolls here and there after gaining the high ground, and so vigorous and effective was the fire poured into the victorious Indians that they — the Indians — did not deem it prudent to come within range, but instead circled to the right and left when Lieutenant Parnell would so change his position as to again check them.

It might seem a pity to spoil a good story, especially where one is so particularly interested as the *Herald* correspondent indicates, but he is in error when he says that "they — the Indians — did not deem it prudent to come within range." The jubilant devils did come within range, and pretty close range, too, on more occasions than one, but the men were now steady and gave them a withering fire every time.

White Bird Cañon was a terrible defeat to the troops engaged in it. It put the Indians in "high feather." It largely increased their warriors from among those on the reservation as well as from the small tribes along the Palouse, Snake, and Spokane Rivers, resulting, as it did, in the massacre of the brave young Lieutenant Rains,

First Cavalry, and his party of ten men at Cottonwood; the battle of Clearwater, July 11th and 12th, when we had abundance of hard fighting with more than four hundred troops engaged, in contrast to the numerical strength of our little squad at White Bird.

CHAPTER FIVE

The Battle of White Bird Cañon, Continued

By Brig.-Gen. David Perry, United States Army (Retired)

WHEN the first alarming news came into Fort Lapwai, where General Howard, the Department Commander, then was, viz: the morning of the 15th, I got my little command ready to move, and the quartermaster was despatched to Lewiston, distant twelve miles, to procure pack animals while I waited for some confirmation of the disturbing rumor. This reached us late in the afternoon in the shape of a letter from one L. P. Brown of Mount Idaho, stating that the Indians were murdering settlers on Salmon River ranches.

The quartermaster not having returned at retreat, I proposed to General Howard that I move at once to the relief of Mount Idaho, carrying three days' rations in my saddle-bags. The General sanctioned my doing so and at eight o'clock P.M., on June 15th, I left Fort Lapwai with my command, consisting of my own Troop F, First Cavalry, Lieutenant Theller attached, Lieutenant Parnell and forty-one men. My troop was fifty strong. Five packs with five days' rations in addition to the three days' cooked rations carried in saddle-bags accompanied us. We reached Cottonwood, forty miles distant, at nine A.M. on the 16th.

I lost much time waiting for the pack-mules to come up, as the road was very muddy in places. Rested the command here three hours. From the high ground we saw three large smokes, which proved to be the remains of straw stacks set on fire by the Indians, probably as signals of our coming. From Cottonwood to Mount Idaho the road passes over a rolling prairie for a distance of eighteen miles. We reached Grangeville about two and one-half miles short of Mount Idaho at six P.M.

Within three miles of Grangeville we met a party of armed citizens who informed me that the Indians had crossed the prairie at about eleven A.M., that day, traveling in the direction of White Bird crossing of the Salmon River. They also insisted that unless they were pursued and attacked early the following morning they would have everything over the river and be comparatively safe from immediate pursuit, with the buffalo trail *via* the Little Salmon open to them, thus escaping without punishment. While realizing that men and animals should have a night's rest, I also understood that if I allowed these Indians to escape across the river with all their plunder, and in the face of the representations made to me, without any effort on my part to prevent it, I should not only be justly open to censure, but bring discredit upon the army. So I told them I would give a definite decision after reaching Grangeville.

Upon my arrival there I laid the matter before my officers and, after considering all the circumstances, it was decided that to make the attempt to overtake the Indians before they could effect a crossing of the Salmon River was not only the best, but the *only* thing to do. It was also suggested that the Indians would most likely begin crossing at once and I would thus strike them while divided. I informed the citizens of the decision, and that I would be ready to start as soon as the horses had been fed and the men had cooked their coffee. At the same time I requested them to provide a guide and bring as many volunteers as they could muster, which they estimated at twenty-five to thirty, but only eight came back.

About nine o'clock that night I started for White Bird crossing of Salmon River. We reached the summit of the dividing ridge between the prairie and the river at midnight and halted there waiting for daylight. At dawn I started again, following the road which I saw led down a narrow gorge, but upon commenting upon this, I was assured by the guide that it opened out into a comparatively smooth valley. This proved to be a mistake or misstatement as it was very rough and broken all the way. I detailed Lieutenant Theller and eight men from my troop as an advance-guard, with instructions that if he saw any Indians to deploy, halt, and send me word. I also directed the command to load.

About four miles, as nearly as I can judge, from the summit where we had halted lay a point where two high ridges ran diagonally across the low ground we were traversing. This was flanked on the left by two round knolls of considerable height, and on the right by a high ridge running parallel with our road. Between this last ridge, however, and the two referred to lay a long, deep valley of considerable width, and beyond the knolls on my left ran White Bird Creek, the banks of which were covered with thick brush. On the more distant of these ridges Lieutenant Theller halted, deployed his advance-guard and at the same time sent me word that "the Indians were in sight."

I immediately formed my troop into line at a trot, but when I reached the advance position I saw the Indians coming out of the brush, and realized that to charge would only drive them back into the brush and under cover while my command would be in the open, exposed to their fire. I took in the situation at a glance; that the ridge I was on was the most defensible position in that vicinity. I accordingly dismounted my troop and deployed on the ridge, sending my horses into the valley between the two ridges before described. At the same time I directed the eight civilians to occupy the round knoll on my left and ordered Trimble "to take care of my right."

Having made these dispositions, being under fire at the time, I told Theller to take command of the line and then proceeded to consider the situation. I found the citizens well posted on the knoll on my left which not only protected my line, but the led horses in the valley between the two ridges before described. I then started for the right of the line to observe the conditions there, and, if possible, borrow a trumpet, as I discovered in making the deployment that mine had been lost. The necessity for one in action needs no explanation. When about three-fourths of the way to Trimble's position, I became aware of something wrong, and saw that the citizens had been driven off the knoll and were in full retreat and that the Indians were occupying their places, thus enabling them to enfilade my line and control the first ridge. The line on the left was already giving away under the galling fire.

Being too far away to charge and retake the hill, my only alternative was to fall back to the second ridge. Galloping down to the line and, having no trumpet, I directed the word to fall back to be passed along the line. Seeing the order in process of execution, I then went to Trimble for a trumpet. I found he was in the same plight as myself; namely, without a trumpet, and had only time to note that he occupied a high point on the right of the ridge and that some of his men were dismounted, when a commotion among my led horses showed that the left of my line had broken, and the men were in a mad scramble for their horses. I only had time to tell Trimble that if we could not hold this position, we must find one more easily defended, when I rushed to the left to head off those men who had gotten their horses, and endeavor to establish a new line.

The men on the left, seeing the citizens in full retreat and the Indians occupying their places and the right falling back in obedience to orders, were seized with a panic which was uncontrollable, and then the whole right of the line, seeing the mad rush for horses on the left, also gave way and the panic became general. I have never seen anything to equal it except when the Eighth Corps were jumped out of their beds by Gordon's men, October 19, 1864, at Cedar Creek.

To stem the onrush was simply impossible. I did everything in human power to halt and reform my line, but no sooner would one squad halt and face about than the other, just placed in position, would be gone. The panic soon extended to H Troop which disintegrated and melted away. It was on this second or rear ridge that I made my most desperate efforts to reform my line, but in vain. From that time on there was no organized fighting, but the battle was confined to halting first one squad and then another, facing them about and holding the position until flanked out. In this way we retreated up the low ground to the right of the road.

When nearing one of the trails leading up the bluff

on the side opposite the road, I saw to my rear a number of men occupying a point that looked as though it might be successfully defended, at least for a time, provided I could reach it before the men again retreated. My horse failed to respond to any further urging, and feeling that everything depended upon my reaching that point quickly, I jumped off and asked one of my men to carry me on his horse, which he did. When I dismounted, I called to Trimble, who was some way to the rear, to halt a squad of men near by and place them on a point indicated by me. This he did, at the same time telling me that one of the citizens told him that there was a better place to defend higher up. I then turned to a sergeant of H Troop, who had a little squad of men on another point, and told him to hold it until I could place some men on the trail to command it and our position. Having done this, I found that the other men were already going to the rear. Being dismounted, I could exercise no control over them.

I then, with the few men left, made my way up the bluff, keeping under cover as much as possible and avoiding the trail until near the summit, part of the men halting to fire while a portion kept on to repeat this maneuver in turn. The Indians were all the time pressing us hard, but were a little more wary, as our ascending position gave us a little better command of the lower positions. As we came into the trail near the summit, I caught a loose horse which I rode the rest of the day.

When we reached the summit the Indians were already coming up the trail, and also making their way around on the ridge that I have heretofore mentioned as being on my extreme right, and running parallel with the road. I saw Trimble some distance away, too far to make myself heard, but motioned him toward the road which we went down, and up which I believed Parnell and Theller to be working their way, but evidently was misunderstood. I then turned to the right (late left) with the few men I had, and made my way to the head of the cañon just as Parnell emerged with about a dozen men. Our united squads made about twenty-eight.

We had only time to acknowledge each other's presence when the Indians were upon us and we were obliged to continue our retreat, fighting and in the same disorder, our men being still too panicky to be depended upon, until we reached Johnson's Ranch, two or three miles from the summit. Here was a rocky knoll that I thought might be defended, so I halted and dismounted the men. But discovering the Indians crawling down to kill our horses, I gave the order to mount, and as we had an open prairie to cross we were at last able to keep the Indians off. Parnell with the H Troop men deployed on the firing-line while I kept mine closed up and ready to reinforce him should it be necessary.

Once a large party of Indians charged us but, finding they could not stampede our small party that we now had well in hand, they gave up the pursuit. Soon we reached a fence around which the road ran. They also made an attempt to cut us off from the road by reaching the fence ahead of us. This, however, I observed in time to frustrate by charging them with my small squad. From here we continued on to Grangeville, where I waited for General Howard with reinforcements.

Parnell received a " Brevet " and a " Medal of Honor " for his most gallant conduct on this day, both of which he fully deserved.—C. T. B.

Memorandum by Capt. E. S. Farrow

(late United States Army), to Accompany Colonel
Perry's Account

With daylight, Perry's command began the descent
of the rugged cañon following a horse-trail, by a long
and tortuous descent, to the rolling country at the bottom of the cañon.

A few individuals were seen stirring at the Indian
camp, well down in the cañon. Ollicut's quick eye soon
caught sight of Colonel Perry's command and soon, with
Joseph and White Bird, with the aid of an immense
field-glass, a part of their careful preparation for war,
every movement of the troops and those of the friendly
scouts, Jonah and Reuben, watching on the distant and
commanding hill nearer the Salmon River, were carefully noted.

Joseph then gave his orders for the first battle. The
women, children, and plunder were prepared to be taken
across the swift Salmon if necessary, while Mox-Mox
would look after the herd and supply fresh horses if
required. White Bird and his braves were to turn the
troops when they got to a certain ridge. Joseph and a
hundred warriors were near by, lying in wait behind the
rocks. Every Indian was ready to mount, and quietly
awaited the attack of the soldiers.

Lieutenant Theller and a detachment of eight men
were in the lead, followed by Colonel Perry and his company and a small party of volunteer citizens, with Captain Trimble's company about fifty yards farther to the
rear, all proceeding in column of fours. As the column
approached two small "Buttes," the Indians appeared

"in skirmish order," in an irregular line, White Bird executing a flank movement to the left, while absolute resistance was made to any further advance of the troops. The air was full of noise and smoke — many of the horses became wild and unmanageable, while many Indians were pressing up to higher ground to the right of the troops.

In a few moments the battle was lost, and only by the magnificent coolness of Colonel Perry and the quick coöperation of his good officers was it possible to commence a retreat. Several futile attempts were made by the panic-stricken troops to hold high ground among the rocks, along the line of retreat; but the Indians were too quick. Horses were galloping without riders, men were falling while the Indians passed along faster and faster, gaining the trails up the flanks of White Bird Cañon, which trails they knew well.

In many places, where the trail became steep and narrow, there were desperate struggles for life, as shown by the location of the bodies of the men who had fallen, one after another. Defeated, and losing their brave officer — Lieutenant Theller, the men made every effort to gain the top of the cañon ridge. Here Perry and Parnell succeeded in rallying the remnant left, and beat a rapid retreat to Mount Idaho, closely pursued and fought by the Indians to within four miles.

More than one-third of the command, including Lieutenant Theller, was killed and left on the field. Joseph, Ollicut, and White Bird, with their chosen warriors, pushed forward in this pursuit to within sight of Grangeville, and then withdrew and slowly rode back to White Bird Cañon to gather up the arms and ammunition and clothing of the destroyed command and to enjoy the first animating thrill of victory.

Note by Dr. Brady in justification of Colonel Perry

As is usually the case after a defeat, Colonel Perry was much censured by the press and general public for the disaster at White Bird Cañon. In this censure, unfortunately, some of his officers joined, at least by implication. At the close of the war Colonel Perry demanded a Court of Inquiry as to his conduct during the campaign, with particular reference to the disaster at White Bird Cañon and the skirmish at Cottonwood. In justice to Colonel Perry the opinion of the said court is herewith appended. This report was received with expressions of approval and satisfaction by both the department and division commanders, Generals Howard and McDowell, and effectually disposes of any charge reflecting in the least degree upon Colonel Perry. I am glad to include it here and thus do justice, even at this late day, to a brave officer.— C. T. B.

OPINION:

"That up to the time of the fight at White Bird Cañon (except that no evidence appears that a suitable quantity of ammunition had been provided in case of an emergency), every precaution that good judgment dictated was taken by Captain PERRY; that at White Bird Cañon the disposition of the troops was judicious and proper, with the exception of leaving his left to be protected by some citizens,— possibly unavoidable. That soon after the fight began, this point was abandoned by the citizens in a panic extending to nearly all the troops, who became so disorganized and dispersed as to be unmanageable.

"That Captain PERRY, after the panic took place, did all in his power to collect and organize the men for a defense, without success, owing partly to the troops not being well drilled in firing mounted; and the Court does not deem his conduct deserving of censure.

"In regard to the affair at Cottonwood, it does not appear probable that, had Captain PERRY attacked under the circumstances, any great advantage would have been gained, while, by so doing, he would have jeopardized the safety of his supplies of provisions, and more especially, ammunition for the main column of the field. His conduct there appears to have been in accordance with the dictates of good judgment and prudence, particularly as the enemy was flushed with success, and a part of his command at least had but recently suffered from a severe disaster.

"As regards the affair at the Clearwater, he appears to have done all required of him, and all that, under the circumstances, could have been reasonably expected of him,— the Commanding General being present.

"It further appears to the Court, from the written statements of some of the officers of the First Cavalry, submitted to the Court, a coloring by insinuations has been given, prejudicial to the conduct of Captain PERRY, unwarranted by the evidence."

The Reviewing Officer approves the proceedings, findings, and opinion of the Court, excepting this shade of difference: that it does not appear to him, from the evidence, that Captain PERRY is at all answerable for the limited quantity of ammunition on hand at the engagement of White Bird Cañon; neither is it clear that the citizens (volunteers) were misplaced upon his left. Their subsequent conduct could not have been foreseen.

CHAPTER SIX

The Affair at Cottonwood

By Brig.-Gen. David Perry, United States Army (Retired)

I WAS returning July 4th from Fort Lapwai to General Howard's command in charge of a pack-train loaded with ammunition. It had been expected that Captain Jackson's troop of cavalry would reach Lapwai in time to furnish a safe escort. Fearing that the ammunition might be needed, I decided not to wait longer and pushed ahead with a small detachment. No one believed the hostiles to be within striking distance, as the last reports located them in the Salmon River Mountains. Imagine then my surprise at meeting Whipple's command that afternoon several miles from Cottonwood deployed in two lines with his mountain guns between them.

Then it was that I learned of the appearance in that neighborhood of a large body of hostiles and the fate of Rains and detachment. It appears that Whipple's scouts reported seeing Indians in the hills back of Cottonwood where the command lay and in the direction of Lapwai. Orders were immediately given to "saddle up." As soon as they could get their horses, an advance-guard under Rains started off at a gallop. In their eagerness to get away they outstripped by several minutes the command, which was just in the act of mounting when firing was heard in the direction of the advance-guard. Proceeding at a gallop they reached the scene of the firing only to find that the entire detachment had been cut off.

The Indians evidently had seen them coming, or perhaps — which is more likely — had prepared for the whole command a trap which was sprung by the advance-guard and which undoubtedly prevented a greater disaster. They had so skilfully secreted a large party that Rains passed through without discovering them. He was thus caught between two lines of hostiles. He at once abandoned his horses and took position by a big boulder out in the open, but undoubtedly commanded on all sides by Indian guns where all were killed.

After meeting Whipple I assumed command by virtue of seniority and pushed on to Cottonwood, where the positions previously occupied were again taken up. It seems that Whipple knew of my coming, and thinking that the hostiles might know of my whereabouts and of the ammunition and take me in, determined to go to my relief. The hostiles were in communication with the reservation, it is believed, and it would have been an easy matter for a runner to have notified Joseph that I had left for the front, and of the size of the detachment with me, about twenty men.

The place was called Cottonwood Ranch House and Corrals, and was situated close to the open prairie on the road running from Lewiston to Mount Idaho. At this point the road extends through the foot-hills, and the ranch was admirably located for defense, being surrounded by high ground, I might say a succession of hills. I found instructions to wait here for further orders from General Howard.

All the morning of the 5th, the Indians showed themselves at different points, in fact, seemed to be all around us. About the middle of the day they made a determined attack upon our position, striking all exposed places at the same time, thereby exhibiting a much stronger force than we had supposed they possessed, estimated at not less than two hundred and fifty warriors. Our positions were so strong that they could make no impression on them, though in some instances they crawled up the hills through the grass to within fifty feet of my men before being discovered. How long the main attack lasted I am unable to recall, but desultory firing continued for some time after the principal force had withdrawn and disappeared from view.

During the afternoon and after the Indians had gone, my attention was directed to a dust on the prairie, apparently coming toward us and from the direction of Mount Idaho or Grangeville. At first we took it to be loose stock (ponies) and then mounted men, but whether whites or Indians was the question. Some said one and some another. Being mindful of the trap set for Whipple's command, as before narrated, I was inclined to believe it a ruse on the part of the Indians to draw us out. All doubt, however, was soon dispelled as the Indians attacked the party, which proved to be a company of "home guards" from Mount Idaho.

I at once rushed my front line down the hill and sent a mounted detachment to their rescue, which drove the Indians off and brought the party in. Their casualties I do not now recall. Shortly after this the whole hostile "outfit," families, loose stock, etc., debouched from the foot-hills some six or eight miles from my position and started across the prairie at a furious pace in the direction of the Clearwater, where General Howard afterward engaged them.

Captain Whipple estimated two hundred and fifty warriors while my command of about one hundred had a valuable train to guard, so that to pursue them was not deemed judicious. It was now apparent that their hovering around my camp and their attack was not, as some had supposed, an attempt to capture the train, but to keep us occupied while their families and stock gained the open prairie and prevent our sending out scouting parties, who, in all probability, would have discovered them.*

* Another evidence of the subtilty and strategic skill of these remarkable Indians.— C. T. B.

CHAPTER SEVEN

The Salmon River Expedition

By Maj. and Brev.-Col. W. R. Parnell, United States
Army (Retired)

ON the 24th of June, 1877, seven days after the
battle of White Bird Cañon, Troop H, First
Cavalry, left Mount Idaho by the roundabout way of Florence for the little settlement of Slate Creek on the Salmon River. Slate Creek
empties into Salmon about six miles above the mouth of
White Bird. The Indians were still in camp on the river-
bank and had possession of all trails between the two
points.

The march was through the mountains over an old,
abandoned trail, obstructed by rocks and fallen timber;
and, although it was mid-summer, snow and rain fell
almost incessantly during the trip, which was completed
at two o'clock on the morning of the 25th. A few men,
and many women and children were found at the place,
all badly scared, not knowing what moment the redskins
might attack them and murder the entire party. But the
expected arrival of the troop and that of a volunteer
company of citizens from Lewiston relieved all anxiety.

We remained at Slate Creek until July 1st and then
crossed the Salmon River to join General Howard's

column in pursuit of the hostiles. After the battle of White Bird General Howard ordered all the available troops in his own department to report to him immediately for field duty. In addition to these, troops from the departments of California and Arizona were hurried to the front.

The Second United States Infantry was promptly put *en route* by rail and boat from Atlanta, Georgia, to Lewiston, Idaho; and the Fifth and Seventh Infantry, together with the Second and Seventh Cavalry in Montana, were prepared to attack the Indians, should they attempt to cross the Bitter Root Mountains, which it was supposed they would do if they could, hoping possibly to form a junction with some of Sitting Bull's warriors in the Sioux country, or else escape across the line into Canada.

After crossing the river the troop joined General Howard's column at Brown's Ranch at the head of Sink Creek, and then commenced a climb of twelve miles up the steep and rugged sides of the Salmon River Mountains. It rained all day and all that night. Several pack-mules were lost — overboard! — in the steep climb; the animals would slip and flounder in the mud, under heavy loads, and in the struggle to get foothold in some particularly steep places several lost their balance and went rolling down the mountain side, nearly two thousand feet, with frightful velocity. Of course, there was not much pack and very little serviceable mule left when the bottom was reached.

The howitzer battery and the infantry and pack-train were obliged to camp about half-way up the mountain; the foot artillery and cavalry troop, who had the advance, reached the summit about half past seven in the evening. The pack-train being behind, the artillery as well as the General and staff had to go without bedding or rations until noon the next day. Troop H led their own mules with the command and shared their coffee, hard bread and bacon, as far as it would go, with their less fortunate comrades. Our Fort Walla Walla Post surgeon, George M. Sternberg, now Surgeon-General, was ill and exhausted when he reached the summit. I, therefore, made him turn in under my blankets and canvas for the night, while I joined the large majority under the trees and kept the fire going all night.

Next day the troop was out scouting. We started at eight o'clock in the morning with our clothing soaking wet from the night's unpleasant experience in the rain, but after a while the sun came out and our garments began to steam and smoke, so that we were completely dry by the time we returned to camp late in the afternoon. We had a sweat bath in the saddle.

On the 4th the command moved at an early hour, following the trail of the Indians down the Salmon River again, and camped on the river-bank about fifteen miles below White Bird. The Indians had recrossed the river at the point two days before, then moved over to Cottonwood and Craig's Mountain, and had there ambushed and killed Lieut. S. M. Rains, First Cavalry, and ten or twelve more of Troop L, who had been sent out as an advance-guard of the troop. This occurred on July 3rd, the day our part of the command was engaged in dragging their guns and pack-mules up the slippery sides of the Salmon River Mountains.

The Indians had scuttled their canoes; the General therefore concluded to build a raft to cross the command. Lieut. H. G. Otis, Fourth Artillery, was detailed for this duty. His idea was to take all the cavalry lariats (light three-fifths rope), tie them together, make one end fast to a tree and the other to the raft, and then let the current carry the raft near enough to the other side to be able to throw a line from it to the shore.

When it is understood that the raft was constructed of closely laid twelve inch hewn logs, thirty or forty feet long, pounded by a current of water running not less than seven miles an hour, in a river more than two hundred and fifty feet wide, there was not much show for a slender rope that was not strong enough to hold even a single log.

I was detailed to take charge of and swim all the animals across. While I was engaged in this particularly interesting yet dangerous duty with fifteen men, naked and mounted on bare-backed horses, I was recalled, for "the raft went down the river, hal-le-lu." * The loss of lariats, alas! required the services of the troop "Affidavit Corps" to square accounts with the Chief of Ordnance and Second Auditor's Office. The failure of the raft was predicted by officers who had years of experience in that kind of business, but the young and inexperienced "sub," who was on his first campaign, knew better. He had worked out mathematically — to his own satisfaction at least — the positive success of his theory!

That afternoon we retraced our steps, crossed the river at White Bird by boats, and camped at Grangeville on the night of the 8th. The next day E, F, H, and L Troops, First Cavalry, marched to the Clearwater to await the arrival of the infantry and artillery.

On the 11th we crossed the Clearwater, moving down its eastern bank on the high bluffs above the valley. When nearly opposite the confluence of the Cottonwood, the Indians were discovered in force. Their camp was

---

* This was the refrain to a song of the campaign composed by some of the officers to the air of "Turn Back Pharaoh's Army."— C. T. B.

Nez Percés at Salmon River

down by the water's edge, but their warriors were scattered along the slope from base to summit, and fairly well fortified. They numbered about four hundred rifles. It took but a moment to wheel into line, deploy, and open fire on them, and the battle of Clearwater commenced. Troop H was on the right of the line, and took care of that flank as well as guarded a little spring of water at the head of a ravine, the only water we had for the entire command.

While our pack-train was coming into camp eighty or ninety Indians emerged from the timber on our left and made a daring attack on its center, killing two packers and a few mules, but a quick move of the troop and men from the left of the line drove them off, and the train reached the camp in safety.

During the afternoon and night and nearly all the next day the fighting continued more or less severely. The Indians were daring in their attacks, sometimes charging our line almost to bayonet distance. When in turn our men would charge down on them driving them from their rifle-pits, and from behind trees and stumps until stopped by the main body.

About three o'clock in the afternoon of the 12th, Captain Jackson's fine Troop B, of the First Cavalry, was seen in the distance escorting a large pack-train with supplies. The artillery battalion moved out to assist him in case of attack, and after escorting him safely within our lines Captain Miller moved his battalion, together with Troops E and L, First Cavalry, down on the right flank of the Indians and drove them from their position, the infantry and howitzers making it exceedingly hot for their left and center. The Indians crossed the river and retreated quietly on the other side, and the battle of the Clearwater was ended.

Our loss was, I believe, twelve men killed and two officers and twenty-five men wounded. The Indian loss was unknown, as they carried their dead and wounded with them.

The cavalry under Captain Perry, the Senior Cavalry Officer present, was ordered to cross the river and pursue the leisurely retreating Indians, but the movement was so dilatory and irritating that General Howard became annoyed and countermanding the order directed the cavalry to aid the fort troops in crossing the river. An opportunity was lost on that occasion for effective cavalry work that was inexcusable. Five troops of cavalry, eager and hoping for such a chance to wipe out the White Bird and Craig's Mountain disasters, were chafing to be ordered into action and avenge the death of their fallen comrades.

The retreat of the Indians was invitingly deliberate. We should have charged them on that open ground across the river, for ten times their number could not have stopped the onslaught of our men feeling as they did. The survivors of White Bird Cañon were especially anxious to show their comrades of the regiment that the disaster of the 17th of June was not their fault; but not until a year later was such an opportunity afforded, when on the 8th of July, 1878, Captain Bernard, in command of seven troops of the regiment at Birch Creek, Oregon, gave them the post of honor in leading the charge on the Bannock and Pi-ute Indians.

It is certain that had we vigorously attacked the Indians at that time, the hostiles would never have crossed the Lo-lo Trail, to add many more valuable lives to the already long list of "killed in action." Every available soldier in the Department of the Columbia, California and Arizona was in the field, and we had so far failed to accomplish what two small troops — many of them recruits — had tried to do but failed at White Bird Cañon. It is true that the result of that fight increased the strength of the Indians to three times their number from the reservation and from roving bands along the Snake, Columbia, and Palouse Rivers, but the warlike and fighting element, and the master minds, the leaders, men of ability, shrewdness, and diplomacy, were exclusively confined to the non-treaty Indians under Chief Joseph, Ollicut, and White Bird, who were the commanders at White Bird Cañon as they were during the whole campaign.

At the "Clearwater" the opposing forces were about equal. If anything the troops had the advantage in numbers as well as position. And yet, strictly speaking, the Indians were not defeated. Their loss must have been insignificant and their retreat to Kamai was masterly, deliberate and unmolested, leaving us with victory barren of results. Their strategy and fighting qualities, whether opposed to two troops of cavalry or to General Howard's command along the Clearwater, or to General Miles' troops in Montana, where they were so largely outnumbered, commanded the attention and admiration of all.

On the 13th the command camped on the west bank of the Clearwater, the Indians being in full view on the other side at the Kamai Sub-Agency. On the 15th the cavalry left camp for Durwald's Ferry, about sixty miles down the river. General Howard accompanied the command, his purpose being to cross the ferry and make a detour through the heavy timber, secure a good position in the rear of the Indians, and cut off their retreat over the Lo-lo Trail. This would have been a good move, as the artillery and infantry could have attacked them in front while the cavalry opened on them in the rear; they would have been completely hemmed in and must have surrendered or been annihilated.

The shrewd and wily Indian was not, however, to be caught in such a trap. It was no surprise to many of us, therefore, after we had marched about six miles to be overtaken by a courier with a message "that Chief Joseph had sent in a flag of truce," desiring to see General Howard.

The troops were ordered to continue the march twenty miles, and then return to Kamai. General Howard returned at once, only to find that Chief Joseph had adopted this ruse to stop the move of the cavalry and give him time to get possession of the Lo-lo Trail and all approaches to it. The cavalry made their forty odd miles march and then returned to Kamai, men and horses weary and jaded.

On the 16th thirty-two Indians, fourteen of whom were men, surrendered. They were part of those who had left the reservation to join the hostiles. Early on the morning of the 17th the cavalry made a reconnaissance over the Lo-lo Trail. We had marched about eighteen miles — by file — over the narrow trail, which was obstructed by works and fallen timber, when our advance was fired on by the Indian rear-guard. One scout was killed and two wounded. On either side of the narrow pathway over the Bitter Root Mountains the trees were so close together that a dog would have found it difficult to get through, so that there was nothing for us to do but return. We had, however, accomplished our object; *i. e.*, to find out the whereabouts of the Indians.

While we were at a halt, the pawing of the horses removed some leaves and dirt, and exposed a quantity of fresh sawdust. Upon investigation we found considerable of it covered over in a similar manner. We then discovered that many of the trees had been sawed off here and there, near the trail, at a height of three or four feet from the ground, leaving the trees still standing on their stumps and easily supported by the adjacent trees. The marks of the saw were covered over with dirt and bark, and no doubt would have escaped observation had we not been stopped by the attack on our advance. We overtook them too soon for their purpose, their object evidently being to let us pass until our rear-guard had advanced beyond that point, whereupon some fifty or sixty warriors who were concealed in the timber were to drop the trees across the trail and block our retreat while they would attack us in front and rear from behind the fallen trees, for they had done the same thing some distance ahead. For craft and deviltry the Indian is unequaled.*

When we returned to Kamai a change of program had taken place. Reinforcements had reached Lewiston and Mount Idaho. The Second Infantry from Atlanta, and some of the Twelfth from California were in camp at Lewiston, and several companies of the Eighth Infantry were at Mount Idaho. Col. John Green with a battalion of the First Cavalry was somewhere in the Salmon River range, *en route* from Fort Boise. A concentration of troops was ordered at Lewiston, and from there to proceed over the Mullan Road, *via* Spokane Falls into Montana. Troop H, First Cavalry, and a detachment of infantry and artillery were to remain at Mount Idaho and report to Colonel Green on his

---

* This appears to be entirely a legitimate war measure which the soldiers might have practised without reprehension. Why, therefore, couple the ruse with a suggestion of "deviltry" only because it was originated by the Indian? — C. T. B.

arrival. On the 19th these plans were again changed, the removal of the troops from Kamai, except Throckmorton's Battery, induced some of the Indians to return, destroy the agency and seriously threaten Throckmorton. General Howard then decided to pursue the Indians over the Lo-lo Trail with the troops who fought at the Clearwater with the exception of two depleted troops, F and H, First Cavalry, which were ordered to report to Colonel Wheaton, Second Infantry, at Lewiston.

The Lo-lo Trail troops constituted the main column; Colonel Wheaton's command, the "left wing," was ordered to Spokane Falls, and Colonel Green's Cavalry, the "right wing," changed its line of march in the direction of Luuhi.

Our left wing marched to Spokane Falls, where it remained until August 21st and then returned to Lapwai. The hostiles had no idea of taking a back track over the Mullan Road. They were anxious to cross the line into Canada, and were making it exceedingly interesting for the combined forces of Generals Howard and Miles in Montana in their efforts to do so.

The close of the war in October ended one of the most memorable campaigns in the history of Indian warfare.

CHAPTER EIGHT

The Battle of the Clearwater

By Maj. J. G. Trimble, United States Army, (Retired)

ON quitting camp at Slate Creek, Oregon, I marched my troop, consisting of thirty enlisted men and three officers, to a crossing some miles below the settlement on Salmon River and put them across — horses swimming, men and packs by canoe. This movement was in obedience to an order from General Howard to join his immediate command in pursuit of the Indians *via* the Salmon River hills.

The hostiles had been confronting the General's command at the mouth of the White Bird Creek, they, the hostiles, being on the farther side of the river, and the command under General Howard being camped on our battle-field of White Bird Creek. After the General had collected boats, some of which I sent him from Slate Creek, and was prepared for a forward movement, the Indians began a retreat. The troops followed about the third day after the Indians had disappeared from the vicinity of the river. On the first day's march I joined the General's command, and we all proceeded up and over the high bluffs. After a toilsome march of about ten miles the heights were reached and camp was made.

The infantry did not arrive until after dark and the pack-train not until midnight, some animals being lost *en route.*

That night a terrific rain-storm fell upon us. As there were no tents except for the staff all were drenched at daylight. I was ordered to make a reconnaissance, being the only mounted force with the command. My orders were to ascertain which way the enemy's trail led, though that was evident from our camp as it was very broad and resembled the trace of a vast moving population. In fact, their movements showed quite a leisurely march or retreat. Their camps were made at short intervals and no sign of alarm or hurry was apparent.

The troops took up the pursuit on the second day after, and made camp in the highlands after a march of about twenty miles. The next day's march brought us to the bluff overlooking the Salmon River again. As the river described a bend hereabouts, the Indians and the troops traversing a chord of the semicircle, it was soon discovered that the former had again crossed the stream, and though their skill and appliances made that quite easy for them, our utter want of the same rendered it impossible for us to follow, so here we were balked. An effort was made to swim some mounted men over, but without success, as the stream was deep and rapid and nearly the whole command inexperienced in such transit. A raft was constructed, but after being loaded and manned, went over the rapids and was lost. Fortunately, no one was lost with it.

Well, after one night's sojourn by the river side, it was determined to retrace our way and the command started in retrograde. On reaching the head of the cañon we were met by a messenger escorted by two friendly Nez Percé Indians. Here the disagreeable tidings were conveyed to the General that the hostiles had crossed Camas Prairie in our rear, or between us and our base, *i. e.*, Fort Lapwai, and after defeating a force of two troops of cavalry at Cottonwood House were there devastating the ranches and threatening the settlements. They had also met and defeated a small party of citizen volunteers, captured quite a herd of horses, and, in fact, had the whole country terrorized.

After making one more camp the command was put in march for our original crossing of the river, and arriving there in the afternoon were ferried over during the next day. Then we marched up through White Bird Cañon over our first battle-field and then on to Grangeville, near Mount Idaho. It was rather a sad sight to some of us to see the incomplete manner in which our dead had been buried, although I suppose that the heavy rains had washed the earth from the newly-made graves. Some bodies were quite exposed. However, in due course of time all were disinterred and decently buried in the cemetery at Walla Walla, where a handsome monument was erected over them by their comrades of the regiment. The fund for this memorial, I am pleased to say, was originated and secured principally by the efforts of an enlisted man, my own First Sergeant, Michael McCarthy, who witnessed a number of the victims perish and who came near sharing their fate.

The General reached Grangeville at dark escorted by my troops and one company of infantry. The next morning a delegation of citizens called upon me and related all the occurrences happening in or about the prairie, at the same time asking for guards, protection, etc. Some urgent messengers also arrived from the Clearwater River, who told of the stress of a party of volunteers surrounded by the hostiles, whereupon preparations were made for a march in that direction. Meanwhile, three troops of cavalry came up, Perry's, Whipple's, and Winter's. This command had been posted at Cottonwood House, distant about twenty-five miles, and were there besieged by the Indians while the latter were crossing the prairie with their immense herds. So on the morrow we set out for the position of the hostiles on the Clearwater, not waiting for the infantry command under Colonel Miller, which had been delayed in crossing the Salmon River.

On arriving within a few miles of the hostile camp, a halt was called and camp made, as it was deemed risky to attack the Indians without the infantry and Gatling guns. Here we learned that the volunteers, forty in number, who were surrounded, had abandoned their horses to the Indians and retreated on foot at dark.

The following day everything was prepared for a forward movement, the infantry and Gatling guns having joined the cavalry. Of course, our advance was well known to the Indians; it could not be otherwise. However, contrary to the custom of some hostiles, these, the Nez Percés, showed no disposition to flee, and our deliberate movements only gave them opportunity for greater defense, although I saw no evidence that even this advantage was improved by them. No doubt a peculiar state of feeling took possession of Joseph and his brother. Indeed, I am inclined to believe that he did not expect a serious effort would be made to drive them from his country, or even to coerce him *in extremis*, for the attack on and the dispersion of Looking Glass's band, which afterward joined his, should have been accepted as war without conditions on our part.

The command moved out on this, our last march, before engaging the hostiles in the following order, namely:

First, the cavalry, four troops, about one hundred and eighty men commanded by Brev.-Col. David Perry; being F Troop, Perry; L Troop, Whipple; H Troop, Trimble; E Troop, Winters, with Lieutenants Parnell, Shelton, Forse, and Knox attached. This command was armed with Springfield carbines and Colt's revolvers. After the cavalry marched the infantry, commanded by Capt. Evan Miles, four companies strong; namely: Burton's, Pollock's, Joslyn's, and Miles', with Lieutenants Wood, Eltonhead, Duncan, Bailey, and Farrow, about two hundred strong. After the infantry marched the artillery, acting as infantry, commanded by Brev.-Col. Marcus Miller, Fourth Artillery, four companies strong; Miller's, Bancroft's, Throckmorton's, and Rodney's, about two hundred men. Two Gatling guns drawn by horses followed with suitable cannoneers.

H Troop, First Cavalry, led the advance with six troopers in the extreme front. All were prepared for immediate contact with the enemy.

To proceed: the command had marched but about four miles when my advance reported the presence of two Indian herders driving stock over the bluffs down the Clearwater River. These men were plainly seen by me and, of course, immediately reported to the commanding officer. Quickly a number of men, or officers, left the main command, which was marching in column, and rode to the edge of the bluff, shortly after reporting that the Indians in the small valley below were in active movement. Their camp was clearly visible with lodges standing, so the Indians were now moving up the bluff to their defenses.

With the advance, and without any further orders or change of orders, I kept moving forward. The balance of the command moved by the flank to the bluff and presently became engaged with the enemy, but they were so hotly assailed by the Indians that they were forced back upon more easily defensible ground. Now, as I quietly proceeded, though with flankers thrown out, I became considerably separated from the main command, and meeting no opposition advanced up to the edge of the bluffs, which were then across my front as I approached obliquely from my original direction. I then halted and dismounted my troop, and seeing Indians crossing the river above me, at once divined their object, which was to get in our rear. However, being now out of employment, as soon as I heard the firing in the rear and saw the Indians crossing us, I sent my second subaltern, Knox, to report the condition of affairs and ask for orders.

In a few moments the lieutenant returned with orders from Colonel Mason, chief-of-staff, to withdraw my command to the vicinity of the main force. As I was doing this I encountered the whole pack-train, under the escort of Captain Rodney's company, halted on an open mesa, or plain. Rodney informed me that he had no orders and considered his company too small to defend the train, if attacked. I replied that if he wished to move the train back to the vicinity of the main command, I would deploy my troop on foot in his rear and thus afford support, as I suspected that the Indians would soon be all around us in accordance with their usual practice.

Upon our moving back the train was so attacked, but the hostiles were driven off with a loss of two men and two pack animals on our side. A small detached train of about six or seven animals loaded with the ammunition was also saved. All were moved to the high ground in the rear of the location where the principal fighting was going on, and Rodney's and my company forming a line in the rear, the whole position was thus defended.

The other troops of cavalry were, or had been, dismounted, the horses assembled on the plateau on which the train was halted, and the men became engaged beside the infantry in what was now a defensive fight. Assaults were made on the Indian position which was established in the woods on the edge of the bluff, but each one was repulsed by the hostiles, who finally only engaged the troops at long range, although there was some fierce fighting at times and a dozen or more men were killed with a proportion of wounded.

I cannot relate exactly what went on in front of the main command as I had our line to guard, though our firing was slight in comparison. Of course, there was the usual excitement of the battle-field, and many could, no doubt, describe things very graphically. Quite a number of the officers present were experiencing their first taste of real war, and very few of the men had been engaged with an enemy prior to this time. However, there were also quite a number who could contemplate the affair coolly and could not notice anything extraordinary either in the resistance of the Indians, the determination of the defense, or the strategy enacted.

The Nez Percés had on one or two occasions before this shown a very warlike spirit, a considerable generalship and undoubted bravery. The present position to which the troops fell back and on which they maintained themselves was in some respects good, as the ground was higher and sufficiently undulating to make temporary earthworks easy of erection. Furthermore, as the whole line was clear of the timber, any hostile seen emerging therefrom could easily be stopped. But the enemy had the advantage of the river, it being at their back though about a mile below by the trail. The lines were separated about eight hundred yards and extended about half the circle inclosed, though a defense was maintained around the whole. Yet the hostiles, after the assault on the pack-train, did not attempt anything except on the line next the timber where the first fighting took place.

But we were unfortunate in having no water until a small spring was discovered by one of my men, Private Fowler, who gallantly went forward under considerable fire and filled several canteens which were sorely needed by the wounded. So I may say, without disrespect to the commanding general, that the position taken up was without much regard seemingly to the necessities of a command curtailed in limits. The cavalry horses and pack animals to the number of about three hundred were collected and held in the center of the circumference, and suffered much from want of water. For thirty hours or more they were thus confined.

Well, the situation at dark was this: The troops were in the circle on the defensive, the Indians in similar manner, though upon a line or nearly so at the edge of the bluff and in the timber. A few were killed and wounded on both sides. I should think the area absolutely commanded by the hostiles was about twenty miles in every direction; that is, it would be unsafe for any one to venture out of our lines or immediate vicinity.

When night fell there was almost complete cessation of shooting, and the Indians could be distinctly heard in various forms of expression, sometimes in earnest talk, sometimes in harangue; the chief exhorting the hardy to greater bravery on the morrow and anon reproving the delinquent. Now and then the female voice could be detected in a plaintive wail of mourning, sometimes in low and tremulous unison, then breaking into a piercing cry. Those of us accustomed to Indians in all situations and to our own condition in like circumstances, could readily discern the different phases of their emotional expressions. The occasion was quite serious indeed. The clear sky, the stillness of the night, added to a feeling of weariness on our part, made the distant sounds strike the ear with an intensely mournful cadence.

At daylight both sides seemed alert and long shots were given and taken. About sunrise several of the hostiles essayed to discover if any reinforcements were on the way for us. They would shoot out from the timber and at top speed gain the trail. This fact required exposure, as each attempt was made a target for the long range rifle of our infantry. I saw one horse shot, but it was astonishing to see the swiftness of their ponies and the savage maneuvers performed by those expert horsemen.

I could not tell what designs were intended by our commander. The morning seemed to be taken up in strengthening our defenses, cooking, and the various duties of camp so far as these could be carried on in our situation. About the beginning of the afternoon a dust was descried in the direction whence we came, or toward the settlements. In due time a herd, or train, perhaps a column of troops, was made out in the distance. All eyes were strained and many memories recalled no doubt the traditional morning watch of "Sister Anne" in Bluebeard's tower, though where additional troops were to come from in that time I, for one, could not guess. However, a well-defined organization was soon espied. It was evidently relief of some kind. Colonel Miller's command was ordered out to meet it. These troops, four companies, marched out with very little molestation on the part of the hostiles. They interposed themselves, or rather Colonel Miller marched his command between the coming train and the position occupied by the enemy, a very pretty movement as we watched it from our greater elevation. Soon the pack-train, as it proved to be, guarded by Captain Jackson's troop, First Cavalry, was under due escort and rapidly approaching. This gallant officer had brought the train from Fort Lapwai, some eight miles distant, safely and courageously into our very invested lines, though how without a fight was certainly singular.

But now to relate the final act in the drama of "Clearwater." I wish the power of description were given me to recite this fine performance. Colonel Miller, who always takes a prominent position in matters of duty and gallantry on the field, determined that his command should not on this occasion simply "march up hill and down again." He, therefore, conceived a plan either to end the battle then and there, or to test the mettle of his troops to the utmost. After marching in escort, as it were, to the train and apparently returning with it, on reaching a point immediately in front of the Indian barricades, he quickly wheeled his battalions, and forming line moved forward at double time directly on the works. Soon both sides were engaged in deadly fusillade.

Simultaneously an advance and charge were ordered and taken up by all the troops on the line confronting the Indian position, firing by volley and in skirmish order. The yelling of the savages and the ever louder shouts of the soldiers soon changed the scenes and sounds from the setting heretofore pervading to wild exclamations and roars of impending strife.

The redskins were broken and driven fleeing before the same enemy whom they had only the day before forced back, but who, reinvigorated with the long drawn breath and serious reflection of the past day and night, had come to regard the matter in deadly earnest. The Indians fled down the high bluffs, crossed the river and joined their families. Soon they were seen slowly ascending the high hills beyond, though not in stampede. Our Gatling guns with my own troop in support moved quickly to a point on the brow and poured in a rapid, but as I suspect ineffective, fire upon the moving tribe and also upon the now deserted village.

The cavalry were soon mounted and moving down the trail in pursuit, but, owing to a rumor that a body of the hostiles were returning, after crossing the stream, they were ordered to dismount and take up a defensive position under the river-bank quite near the village, where a number of tepee frames were still standing.

As the main force of our command had to reform and prepare for an onward movement, the dead were to be collected, the wounded cared for, and the animals so long confined to be attended to, the time approached sunset before all was ready for the advance. Consequently, when the column had marched down the bluff and crossed the stream, it was decided to move no farther that night, and camp was made. During the evening a number of caches were discovered and much plunder was obtained.

The Indians here discarded all surplus baggage and household utensils, but, as subsequently transpired, carried off enough to serve their purposes for some months to come. The only living objects that were abandoned by them were about half a dozen crippled horses and one poor aged squaw.

Our dead were buried on the hill above and the wounded sent under escort of a troop of cavalry back to

Fort Lapwai the next day. The following morning our command broke camp in pursuit of Joseph. I will state some few details which may vary somewhat from other movements against Indians, and may perhaps also throw some light upon the methods and management of the Nez Percé campaign.

Our generals commanding had arrived at the conclusion that the Nez Percé Indians were no despicable foemen, and in this opinion the troops coincided to a man. At that time the newspapers contained no such encomiums as they displayed when recounting the wrongs suffered by the murderous Modocs, although sufficient information concerning this highly intelligent tribe was extant and their bravery in battle was well established. Before the campaign closed, however, much was written and spoken by our people in the "Far East" in eulogy of their prowess, the generalship of Joseph and the sad fate awaiting his followers, but not until the latter was assured.

If ever a tribe of aborigines was worthy of fostering and improving side by side with their more powerful brethren of the human race it was the Nez Percés. But no recollection of former service or common ties of humanity could stand before the white man's greed. This is human nature, I suppose, the possession of which attribute is in some cases extolled as a jewel of rich inheritance.

To resume, it was a lovely sight we beheld on arriving at the heights overlooking the Kamai Valley. The fields belonging to the still loyal bands of Nez Percés were green with grain not yet ripe, the hills beyond clad in spring attire, the beautiful river flowing between, and the Agency buildings shining white in the background. In fact, all nature appeared to bloom with loveliness, and to us, who had not viewed any ripening tillage since the year before, all this cultivation seemed most inviting, especially amid the scenes enacting around us and the warlike prospects ahead.

Joseph and his warriors, having nothing, passed through and among these possessions of their peaceful brothers. He crossed the river with his own means of transport and took his stand on the bluffs beyond. He also deployed a number of his men on the river-bank, either to dispute its passage or inflict some damage on the troops as they approached. This the cavalry did rather incautiously and receiving several volleys retired in some haste, if not confusion. After a slight skirmish the hostiles retired out of range.

I may say that here the second act or the second part of the campaign ended, as the troops remained here for some weeks, returned to Fort Lapwai leaving a guard — which was my troop — returned again, reinforced and refitted, made several scouts here and there, and finally followed the Indian on the Lo-lo Trail after an interval of about fifteen days from the date of their departure.

An incident or two connected with our scout on the Lo-lo Trail would rightfully belong to this paper to show the great assistance rendered by the loyal Nez Percés and also the brave spirit manifested by them on many occasions. From the time these Indians signed the treaty they never swerved from their allegiance to the Government, but tilled their land, attended the church and school, and were ever ready to give their services in all matters connected with frontier settlement and the discouragement of turbulent tribes.

Six of them accompanied us on this occasion and rode well ahead as advance, or flankers. As soon as the "hostiles" were met or discovered, they rushed forward to make a parley, but were greeted with a fusillade from the rifle and two were shot, one being killed. Then, in a further attempt, or perhaps retaliation, James Reuben, a very intelligent Indian, was wounded. He made a circuit to get into our lines and the timber being quite dense came near being killed before the soldiers recognized him.

Those of us who still survive that bloody affair will never forget the service rendered by these true Indians, nor the humanity and hospitality shown by their people in this our hour of adversity.

Captain E. S. Farrow, U. S. A.

Colonel J. W. Redington

Colonel C. E. S. Wood,
U. S. A., retired

Captain S. G. Fisher, chief of
Bannock Scouts during
Nez Percé campaign

Group of Officers who Fought in the Nez Percé War

CHAPTER NINE

The Assembling of the Soldiers and the Battle of Clearwater

By Capt. E. S. Farrow, late United States Army

I. The Gathering of the Troops

TROOPS were soon hastening to the scene of trouble from all directions. Captain Whipple, in Indian Valley, near the Wallowa, made forced marches with Company L, First Cavalry. The few troops at Fort Walla Walla and those near Wallula, and all available men from Forts Vancouver, Stevens, Canby, Townsend, Klamath, and Harney, were also in motion. The artillerymen about this time returning from Alaska were caught on the wing and turned toward Fort Lapwai. The call for troops was answered from California, Arizona, and even Georgia, whence came the Second Infantry.

The most fearful excitement prevailed at this time, and citizens and friendly Indians and their families flocked from all directions to Fort Lapwai for protection. All kinds of rumors as to Colonel Perry's destruction and indiscriminate massacres were flying in to the post from all sources and directions. Lewiston was made the base of supplies and the concentration of troops was actively pushed.

By June 21st, eight companies of troops (in the aggregate about two hundred and fifteen men) had arrived at Fort Lapwai, and a small organization of volunteers under Captain Paige had arrived with Captain Whipple. The friendly Indians generously supplied a sufficiency of Indian ponies. While preparations were being made for departure to the front, Capt. Evan Miles, with several companies of the Twenty-first Infantry, Capt. Marcus P. Miller, with several companies of the Fourth Artillery, and Captain Winters, with a company of the First Cavalry, by quick movements had arrived at Lewiston. Lieutenant Bomus improvised a mule pack-train and impressed into the service all the transportation that could be found available.

The moment of starting was solemn — the Indians were numerous and the air was full of rumors, and the daring messengers, who had skulked through from Colonel Perry to Lapwai, over roundabout and un-looked-for paths, largely magnified the dangers. The column consisted of cavalry, infantry, and artillery (on foot), flanked with two Gatling guns and an old mountain howitzer, formerly used as the morning and evening gun at Fort Lapwai, all followed by an unstable pack-train of noisy mules, every animal carrying its maximum load. Every foot of the march over Craig's Mountain was carefully skirmished, the column proceeding at ease, stretched out about a mile.

The column, under command of Captain Miller, went into camp on the 22nd of June, after the first day's march, at Junction Trail (Mount Idaho and Craig's Ferry Trail). The next morning reveille was sounded at four A.M., and a hard march was made to Norton's Ranch. The next day, June 24th, was Sunday, and was spent in concentrating the forces as far as possible, and ascertaining the then position of the victorious Indians.

On Monday a brisk movement was made forward, the infantry, bearing off to the right, went to "Johnson's Ranch," where Perry made his stand, when retreating, and enabled his stragglers to close in. General Howard, with the cavalry, deviated to Grangeville and there met the remnants of Perry's command and made provisions for additional supplies. Leaving the cavalry to rest until his return, the General made a hurried visit to Mount Idaho, nearly reassured the trembling, frightened congregation of people, and ministered to the many who had suffered outrages at the hands of the Indians.

Camp at "Johnson's Ranch" was broken early the next morning and the column was moved to the head of White Bird Cañon, with two objects in view — first, to bring Perry's dead, and to reconnoiter to locate Joseph and White Bird. These, with all their warriors, women, children and baggage, were well across the Salmon, and from high sharp-pointed hills were observing every movement of the troops. Joseph had at first intended to give General Howard battle before crossing the Salmon River; but changed his plans, great general that he was, and sought to draw the troops into the vicinity of the "Seven Devils," where they could be more easily cut off from supplies or flanked. Having buried the dead and made a satisfactory reconnaissance, the command gathered, over muddy trails, at the head of the cañon, and returned to Johnson's Ranch to camp for the night.

The troops were quickly gathered near the mouth of White Bird Cañon. From the high bluff lying between the forks of White Bird Creek could be seen the irregular mountain valley held by the Indians beyond the restless Salmon. Their sentries and outposts were shouting back and forth. While the troops were constructing rafts and preparing to cross, the Indians came from ravines and hilltops and opened fire. This was merely a ruse to engage the attention of the troops, while the main body of Indians were moving to recross

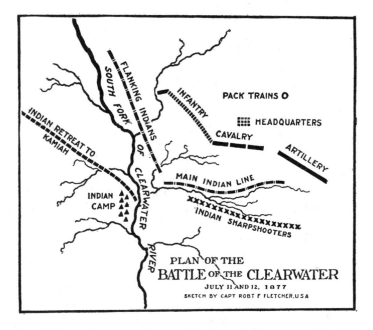

PACK TRAINS O

HEADQUARTERS

SOUTH FORK

FLANKING INDIANS

INFANTRY

CAVALRY

ARTILLERY

INDIAN RETREAT TO KAMIAH

OF CLEARWATER

MAIN INDIAN LINE

INDIAN CAMP

XXXXXXXXXXXXXXXXX
INDIAN SHARPSHOOTERS

RIVER

PLAN OF THE
BATTLE OF THE CLEARWATER
JULY 11 AND 12, 1877
SKETCH BY CAPT ROBT F FLETCHER,USA

the Salmon twenty-five miles lower down at Craig's Ferry.

Chief Looking Glass, in the rear, was now giving trouble. Captain Whipple was sent to the fork of the Clearwater to take him and his band to Mount Idaho. Looking Glass and his band escaped to join Joseph, and Captain Whipple's cavalry proceeded to Norton's

Ranch. On the morning of July 3rd, Captain Whipple sent two citizen scouts, Foster and Blewett, in the direction of Craig's Ferry in search of indications of the presence of any Indians. Blewett was killed; but Foster returned to camp and reported that he had seen Indians about twelve miles distant, proceeding from the direction of Craig's Ferry.

Captain Whipple then hastened to send Lieut. Sevier M. Rains, of his company, with ten picked men and the scout Foster to recover Blewett and ascertain the strength of the enemy. The command was soon in motion, and closely followed Lieutenant Rains. Firing was soon heard in the front. A rapid gait was assumed and after traveling two miles Indians were seen in force about half a mile distant; and on approaching nearer, it was found that Lieutenant Rains and *every man* of his detachment had been killed. This was a terrible disaster.

At the appearance of Captain Whipple's command the Indians took the back track and soon had the prairies to themselves and leisurely crossed the road between Grangeville and Cottonwood, where Colonel Perry and Captain Whipple had joined forces. At this time Joseph picked up Looking Glass, and his war parties made it very lively for the troops and volunteer detachments at Cottonwood and other points.

II. The Two Days of Hard Fighting

The 11th of July, the commencement of the Clearwater battle, was a memorable day. Early on this day the troops were moving carefully through rough forests and deep ravines, over ridges and through ravines, to the confluence of the two Clearwaters. About noon the

Indians were in close proximity in several deep ravines, near the mouth of Cottonwood Creek, and were watching the approach of the troops. As quickly as possible a howitzer and two Gatling guns, mounted by a detachment under Lieut. H. G. Otis, Fourth Artillery, were brought to bear on the masses of the Indians below.

The Indians lost no time in running their horses up the south fork of the Clearwater, on both sides, and quickly placing their stock beyond range. It was their intention to escape by a cañon on the left, leading to the rear, at a small angle with the river. But this was prevented by a quick movement of the howitzer and Gatling guns to a second bluff in that direction, beyond a deep and rocky transverse ravine, almost at right angles to the cañon.

Beyond the second bluff, Joseph and his warriors were quickly dismounted and in position, awaiting the approach of the troops, and lost no time in despatching about forty or fifty mounted Indians to annoy the left flank of the approaching column. At this moment Colonel Mason, the Department Inspector-General, appeared, with Burton's and Farrow's companies of infantry, which deployed, stretching off to the right, with Winter's cavalry on his right. All now pressed forward, in open line, under a hail of fire.

The line of troops was rapidly extended to the left by the cavalry, and to the right by the infantry and artillery battalions, gradually refusing the flanks until the bluff was entirely enveloped. Four hundred men thus held a line about two and one-half miles in extent. The main pack had passed by this position, but a small train was still on the road near the line of battle. The Indian flankers, by rapid movement, struck the rear of

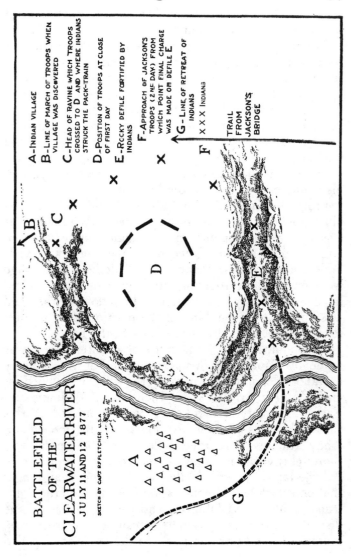

BATTLEFIELD
OF THE
CLEARWATER RIVER
JULY 11 AND 12 1877

SKETCH BY CAPT. R.F.FLETCHER U.S.A.

A - Indian village

B - Line of march of troops when village was discovered

C - Head of ravine which troops crossed to D and where Indians struck the pack-train

D - Position of troops at close of first day

E - Rocky defile fortified by Indians

F - Approach of Jackson's troops (2nd day) from which point final charge was made on defile E

G - Line of retreat of Indians

X X X Indians

TRAIL FROM JACKSON'S BRIDGE

this train, killed two men and disabled two packs loaded with howitzer ammunition.

The steep and high banks of the river are roughly cut with numerous most rugged transverse ravines. The Indian camp, from which the hostiles emerged on the approach of the troops, yet hidden from view, was beyond the river, and hundreds of ponies and horses were herded in the ravines near this camp. The warriors, finely mounted, had forded the river under cover of the bluffs and were racing up a transverse ravine, endeavoring to cut off the trains and stampede the cavalry, then dismounted and on the firing-line.

From this moment the Indians manifested remarkable quickness and boldness, planted sharpshooters at every conceivable point, made terrific charges on foot and on horseback to the accompaniment of savage yells and demonstrations. Many remarkable feats of courage were noticeable throughout the engagement, all calculated to encourage the warriors to follow in the bold attempts to turn the flank of the position. All these attempts were resisted at every part of the line.

At about four P.M. a spirited countercharge was made by Capt. Evan Miles, commanding the infantry battalion, down into a ravine on the right. Captain Bancroft, Fourth Artillery, and Lieutenants Williams and Farrow, Twenty-first Infantry, were wounded at this time. This was a desperate but successful movement, many Indians were then killed and the ravine was thoroughly cleared of a murderous enemy at short range. A little later, Captain Miller led a second charge near the center, while a demonstration was made on the right, using artillery and infantry, and thus was secured the disputed ravine near Winter's position. Further spasmodic charges by the Indians on the left were repelled by Perry's and Whipple's cavalry and Morris's artillery. At dark the Indians still held the only spring or water-supply, in spite of many successful charges made by the troops.

During the night, additional rifle-pits and barricades were constructed by both the troops and Indians, each party still hopeful of a final victory. Firing was kept up throughout the night, every flash drawing return fire. Under cover of darkness, all available canteens and buckets were filled at the spring, in the midst of flying bullets, and taken to the thirsty men on the firing-line. As promptness and courage had saved the ammunition and supplies, so gallant exposure during the darkness saved the water-supply.

At daylight of the 12th every available man was on the line. By a magnificent feat, executed with great spirit by Miller and Perry, with Otis's howitzer, the spring of water was captured from the Indians and brought within the lines. This enabled the famished troops on the firing-line to have a taste of coffee, and consequent new life and energy. The artillery battalion was then withdrawn from the lines and held as a reserve force for any offensive movement that might become necessary.

The firing was rapid throughout the day, the Indians from time to time threatening to force the weaker parts of the line and fighting at very close range. About three P.M. a dust appeared in the distance, toward the South, beyond the Indian position. This proved to be an approaching pack-train, escorted by Captain Jackson's company of cavalry. The artillery battalion under Captain Miller was immediately sent out to meet it, and after considerable skirmishing, brought it safely in. Captain Miller, instead of returning with the train and reinforcements, marched slowly by the right flank toward us, and when crossing the Indian line, faced to the left and quickly and rapidly moved in line for nearly a mile across our front, and repeatedly charged the Indians' positions.

The Indians made a desperate effort, by ferocious charges, to turn his left flank; this, however, failed as Rodney's reserve company in the rear quickly deployed and flanked the flankers. There was a most stubborn resistance at Joseph's barricades for a while, when suddenly the whole Indian line gave way, and the Indians, closely pursued, rushed down the cañons and crossed the south fork of the Clearwater.

The infantry pressed them to the river opposite their main camps and there awaited the cavalry, which slowly worked its way through the ravines, over rocks and down precipices over steep and craggy trails. The Indian camp was taken, after the Indians had hurriedly left it, and were fleeing in all directions up the heights and going to the left of Cottonwood Creek. The Indian camp so hastily abandoned had the lodges still standing filled with blankets, buffalo robes, cooking utensils and plunder of all descriptions. The many dead and wounded horses in the camp and along the trails leading to it indicated the great damage done by the troops in this desperate engagement.

General Howard had four hundred fighting men in this two days' engagement, and it is remarkable that only thirteen were killed and twenty-two wounded. The Nez Percés fought with great skill and obstinacy and were more than five hundred strong, not including the squaws or women, who assisted in providing spare horses, and doing all manner of things, while acting as a substantial reserve.

III. Letter from Maj. H. L. Bailey, United States Army,
Regarding the Battle of the Clearwater

I believe our present excellent Quartermaster-General,
Gen. Charles F. Humphrey, got his Q. M. appointment
and later a brevet for gallant services in the battle of
Clearwater, July 11 and 12, 1877, in the Nez Percés
Indian War. He was a first lieutenant, Fourth Artillery
at the time. He was awarded a medal of honor March 2,
1897, for most distinguished gallantry in action at the
Clearwater, Idaho, July 11, 1877, where he voluntarily
and successfully conducted, in the face of a withering fire, a party which recovered the possession of an
abandoned howitzer and two Gatling guns lying between the lines and within a few yards of the Indians,
while serving as a first lieutenant, Fourth United States
Artillery.

On the morning of the 12th, General Humphrey and
myself found ourselves apparently the only officers on
the outer line where the men had dug a line of detached
holes or trenches during the night. We were very thirsty
and hungry, and the fire from the Indians having slackened considerably, in their preparations for some new
attacks and tricks, we insisted on each other going back
to the central rendezvous where General Howard had
his headquarters and supplies, to get water or coffee and
some bacon. Finally, we drew cuts and I won, taking
first turn. I found most of the officers at the headquarters.

I was given an order to execute upon my return to the
long section of line where Humphrey and I had met.

I relieved him and then, alone, walked along the lines some hundreds of yards, getting the men placed at proper intervals for a grand or general charge to be made later. I had a task, as you may imagine, as many men would run back to the holes or trenches as soon as I had gone a few rods farther along, but I got them into place. Away to the left I found Capt. James A. Haughey, Twenty-first Infantry, and Lieut. F. E. Eltonhead, Twenty-first Infantry (now both deceased), lying flat behind small head shelters with dusty sweat streaks down their faces, dodging bullets. They yelled at me to "get down" as I was "drawing fire." I was careless until two bullets tipped the earth between their heads and my ankles, when I thought it fair to squat till I got away from them again. I left to them the arranging of the men to their left and returned to where I had left Humphrey.

Later the final, beautiful charge was made, full of interesting details, for which I have not now space. Humphrey was as cool as though at a parade or drill. Col. M. P. Miller (then Captain Fourth Artillery, now Brigadier-General, retired) was also as cool under fire as though taking a summer stroll. The latter was also brevetted for gallant service in this battle. When he took his company to a point where a gap in our line permitted the Indians to climb up the river bluff and enfilade us, he was smoking a short stem pipe which good luck kept the bullets from knocking from his mouth.

When placed, his men faced so that their backs were toward my company (B, Twenty-first Infantry). It was while I was back at the center for cartridges and hospital men that his men took the men of my company for Indians, all being in the prone position in rocky, grassy ground, and as I was returning the artillery company and the infantry company were bobbing up and down firing at each other at a lively rate.

Lieut. Peter Leary, Fourth Artillery, commissary officer, rushed out with a carbine flourishing in the air, shouting: "Packers to the rescue, packers and scouts to the rescue." I saw and knew the situation at a glance, as I had seen Captain Miller lead his men out, and I passed Leary, rushing between the two lines, yelling: "Cease firing, you're firing into your own men."

The trouble was quickly ended, though at least one poor man (Winters of my company) always believed his dreadful hip wound was by a friendly bullet. This was during the first day of the battle. It was Captain Jocelyn (now Colonel-General Staff, and I hope soon the next Brigadier-General), who got General Howard to send Captain Miller out to that vital part of our lines.

CHAPTER TEN

The Battle of the Big Hole *

By G. O. Shields (Coquina)

BRAVE old General Gibbon, the hero of South Mountain, was on the war-path. On receipt of General Howard's despatch that the Nez Percés were coming his way, he hastily summoned Company F, of his regiment, from Fort Benton, and D from Camp Baker, to move with all possible speed to his post. Meantime, he gave orders that Company K and every man that could be spared from Fort Shaw should prepare at once for the field. When Companies F and D arrived there, he took the field at their head, with the troops detailed from his own post, and moved rapidly toward Fort Missoula, crossing the Rocky Mountains through Cadotte's Pass, carrying a limited supply of provisions on pack-mules. The distance, one hundred and fifty miles, over a rough mountainous country, was covered in seven days, the command reaching Fort Missoula on the afternoon of August 3rd.

On the 4th, with his command reinforced with Captain Rawn's company, and Company G of the Seventh

---

* This vivid and dramatic sketch is reprinted, after some slight abridgment, from the book of the same name with the kind permission of the author, and Rand, McNally & Co., the publishers.— C. T. B.

from Fort Ellis, General Gibbon left Fort Missoula in pursuit of the Nez Percés. His command now numbered seventeen officers and one hundred and forty-six men. A wagon-train was taken from Missoula, wherein the men were allowed to ride wherever the roads were good.

General Gibbon moved as rapidly as his means of transportation would permit, covering thirty to thirty-five miles per day. In his march through the valley he was joined by thirty-six citizens. Gibbon ascertained that he was covering two of their daily marches with one of his, and the question of overtaking them became, therefore, merely one of time.

When the command reached the foot of the mountains and learned that the Indians had already crossed, a number of the citizens became discouraged and hesitated about going farther. But the General, appreciating the importance of keeping these hardy frontiersmen with him, besought them to keep on a few days longer.

He assured them that he was in earnest, and should strike the Indians a terrible blow as soon as he could overtake them. He told the volunteers that they should have an honorable place in the fight, if one occurred; that they might have all the horses that could be captured, save enough to mount his command, and that, meantime, his men would divide their last ration with their citizen comrades. This announcement created great enthusiasm among the soldiers and volunteers alike, and the latter at once decided to follow their gallant leader until the Indians should be overtaken, no matter where or when that might be.

Lieutenant Bradley, with eight men of the Second Cavalry, and all of the mounted volunteers, was now ordered to push on, strike the Indian camp before daylight the next morning, if possible, stampede the stock and run it off. If this could be done, and the Indians set on foot, then their overwhelming defeat would be certain. Lieut. J. W. Jacobs asked and obtained permission to go with Bradley and share in the hazardous undertaking. This detachment, amounting, all told, to sixty men, made a night march across the mountains, while the main command camped at the foot of the divide on the night of the 7th, and at five o'clock the next morning resumed the march.

The road up the mountain, a steep and difficult one at best, was seriously obstructed at this time by large quantities of down timber that had to be cut out or passed around, so that the ascent was very slow and trying to men and beasts. The wagons were but lightly loaded, and by doubling teams and using all the men at the drag ropes, the command succeeded in reaching the summit, a distance of three miles, in six hours, and by the performance of such labor and hardship as only those can realize who have campaigned in a mountainous country.

From the summit the road leads down a gentle incline for a mile, when it reaches the head of Trail Creek, and follows down that stream a distance of ten miles into the Big Hole basin. It crosses the creek probably fifty times, and the banks being abrupt, and the road obstructed in many places by down timber, the progress of the command was extremely slow and tedious.

While ascending the mountain on the morning of the 8th, General Gibbon received a courier from Lieutenant Bradley, with a despatch stating that, owing to the difficult nature of the trail and the distance to the Indian camp, he had been unable to reach it before daylight, and that the Indians had broken camp and moved on. Later in the day, however, another courier brought news that they had again gone into camp, after making but a short march, at the mouth of Trail Creek, and that, not deeming it safe to attack in daylight, Bradley had concealed his command in the hills, and was now awaiting the arrival of the infantry.

Upon receipt of this information, Gibbon took his men from the wagons (leaving twenty men to guard the train), gave each man ninety rounds of ammunition and one day's rations, and pushed on on foot, having ordered that the wagons should come up as fast as possible. The gallant General with his faithful little band moved quietly but rapidly forward, but owing to the bad condition of the trail, it was nearly sundown when they reached Bradley's camp.

Bradley informed his chief that he believed the Indians intended to remain in their camp several days, for he had secretly observed their movements from the top of a neighboring hill, and found that the squaws were engaged in cutting and peeling lodge-poles to take with them for use on the treeless plains of the buffalo country.

On arriving at Bradley's camp, the men filed into the gulch, ate a scanty supper of hard-tack and raw pork, and without camp-fires or blankets, lay down to rest. Having conferred with Lieutenant Bradley and his scouts as to the best disposition of the proposed attack, General Gibbon ordered his adjutant to call him at ten o'clock at night, and lying down under the spreading branches of a pine-tree, slept as peacefully as a child.

Lieutenants Bradley and Jacobs did a piece of reconnoitering on this day for which they deserve great credit. Having failed to reach the Indian camp during the previous night, when it would have been safe to undertake to capture or stampede the pony herd; and knowing it would be rash to attempt it in daylight, it then became important to learn the exact situation of the village, in order that the commanding General might be given the most minute information concerning it when he came up.

Having secreted his command in the woods, therefore, Bradley sent out scouts in different directions with instructions to proceed cautiously and stealthily about the valley and ascertain, if practicable, the actual whereabouts of the Indians.

In about two hours these men returned and reported numerous fresh signs of Indians in the immediate vicinity, while one of them, Corporal Drummond he said, had, standing in the timber some distance to the east, heard voices and other sounds that evidently came from a busy Indian camp near by, but, fearing he might give an alarm, he had not gone near enough to the camp to see it.

Lieutenant Jacobs asked Bradley to let him take Drummond, return to the spot and verify such important information. Bradley replied that they would both go, and, leaving Sergeant Wilson in charge of the camp, both officers started with Drummond on foot.

They proceeded with the greatest caution a distance of about a mile and a half, when the corporal whispered to Lieutenant Bradley that they were near the place where he had heard the voices. They were surrounded by a thick growth of small pine-trees, through which it was impossible to see to any distance. Moving slowly forward, they soon heard the sound of axes, and inferred that the squaws were cutting lodge-poles in the very body of the woods they were then in.

Creeping along with bated breath, on the alert for every sound or sign, fearful lest they should make known their presence to the Indians, bring on a skirmish, and thus avert the purpose of the General, they scarcely dared breathe.

They finally caught the sound of voices and stopped. Here the officers held a whispered consultation which resulted in their crawling ahead to a larger tree that stood about eighty paces in front of them. Still they could see nothing of the camp, although the sounds came plainer, and all were impressed with the knowledge that they were treading on the very crest of a volcano, as it were. Jacobs suggested that they climb the tree, arguing that as it was taller than those about it, they might be able to see something interesting from its top.

To this Bradley readily assented, and leaving their rifles with the corporal and cautioning him to keep a sharp lookout for any possible intruders, both officers climbed cautiously and stealthily into the topmost branches of the pine-tree. When they had gained this position, they halted for a moment in a crouching posture, and then, cautiously straightening themselves up, found that they were well above the surrounding foliage, and were thrilled at seeing hundreds of Indian horses quietly grazing in a prairie almost beneath them, for the tree stood on top of a high hill.

Several herders sat on their ponies in and about the herd, while others lounged lazily on the ground under the shade of neighboring trees. A few hundred yards beyond, they saw the Indian camp where hundreds of warriors were resting and chatting, while squaws were pitching tents, making beds, carrying in poles, and cooking the noon-day meal.

A brief look was all these brave officers dared risk, for they feared detection, and hastily lowering themselves to the ground, they lost no time in regaining their own camp.

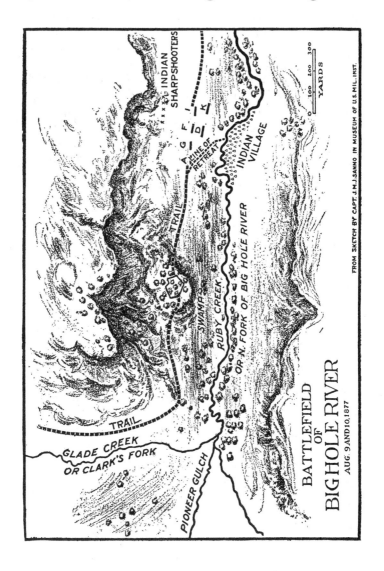

BATTLEFIELD
OF
BIG HOLE RIVER
AUG. 9 AND 10, 1877

FROM SKETCH BY CAPT. J. M. J. SANNO IN MUSEUM OF U.S. MIL. INST.

A brief despatch was sent off to the General, the receipt of which by him has already been referred to, advising him of their discovery, and the remainder of the day was spent in impatient awaiting his arrival.

At ten o'clock at night the officer of the guard spoke to the General in a whisper, and he arose with the alacrity of a youth who goes forth to the sports of a holiday. The men were called at once, and in whispered orders the line of march was speedily formed. All were instructed to preserve the most profound silence from that moment until the signal should be given to open fire on the enemy, and, under the guidance of Joe Blodgett and Lieutenant Bradley, the little band filed silently down the winding trail, threading its way, now through dark groves of pine or fir; now through jungles of underbrush; now over rocky points; frequently wading the cold mountain brook, waist deep, and tramping through oozy marshes of saw-grass; speaking only in whispers; their rifles loaded, eyes peering into the starlit night, and ears strained to catch the slightest sound that might indicate the hiding-place of any lurking foe who might perchance be on an outpost to announce to his followers the approach of danger.

Five miles were thus stealthily marched without giving an alarm. Then the valley in which the troops had been moving opened out into what is known as the Big Hole, that is, the valley of the Big Hole River. This is a beautiful prairie basin, fifteen miles wide, and sixty miles long, covered with rich bunch-grass and surrounded by high mountains. In the edge of this valley the soldiers saw the smoldering camp-fires of the enemy; heard the baying of his hungry dogs responding to the howls of the prowling coyotes, and saw, by the flickering lights, the smoky lodges of the warriors. The men crept up to within a few hundred yards of the slumbering camp, when they again crossed the creek down which they had been marching, and ascended its eastern bluff. Here they encountered a large herd of ponies, some of whom neighed anxiously as the strange apparition filed past them, but luckily did not stampede.

Down the side of this steep bluff, thickly overgrown with sage-brush, mountain laurel and jack pines; over rocks and through break-neck ravines and washouts, the soldiers and citizens picked their way with all the skill and adroitness of trained hunters, until at last they reached a position overlooking the Indian camp, and within one hundred and fifty yards of the nearest tepees. The camp was pitched on the south bank of the Wisdom or Big Hole River, which is formed by the confluence here of Trail and Ruby Creeks. It was in an open meadow, in a bend of the river, and was partially surrounded by dense thickets of willows. There were eighty-nine lodges pitched in the form of a V, with the angle up the stream, and below the camp four hundred or five hundred ponies grazed peacefully, tethered to stakes and willows. The Indians had evidently secured them there in order to be prepared, ready for any emergency. The command halted here, and lay down to await the coming of daylight, but not to sleep.

It was now two o'clock in the morning, and the men suffered with cold, for even the summer nights are cold in these mountains, and they had neither overcoats nor blankets, having left all these with the wagons. The smoldering camp-fires flickered fitfully in the pale star-light, and the smoky lodges of the savages presented a most fantastic picture, as the dying lights blazed with ever-changing weirdness upon them. Eagerly the soldiers watched the scene, and with bated breath thought of the awful tragedy that the rising sun would look upon in that now peaceful valley.

"They have no idea of our presence," said Bostwick, the half-breed scout. "After a while you will see some fires built up if we remain undiscovered."

Sure enough, in the course of an hour squaws began to come forth from their lodges, and replenish their waning fires.

As these blazed up they stood about them, jabbered, turned, and warmed themselves, yawned, and then one by one returned to their skin couches and betook themselves again to sleep. And again the soldiers and their citizen allies were left to meditate, and in whispers to commune with each other.

As soon as it was light enough to see to move advantageously the little army was again astir; but its movements were yet as silent as the grave. Under whispered orders and with stealthy tread Sanno's and Comba's companies, deployed as skirmishers, descended the bluff into the valley, groped their way through the willow thickets, waded the icy river, the water coming nearly to their armpits. Logan, Williams and Rawn, with their companies, were sent to the extreme right to cross and attack the camp near Ruby Creek, while Lieutenant Bradley, with his handful of soldiers and citizen scouts, was sent down the stream with orders to cross and strike the camp lower down.

As the light increased the troops were advancing cautiously, when an Indian, who had crawled out of his lodge and mounted a horse, rode out of the willows directly in front of Bradley's men and within a few feet of them. He was *en route* to the pony herd on the hillside above, and so quietly had the advance been made that even he had not heard or seen the men, and was within a few feet of them when he emerged from the thicket of willows. He and his horse were instantly shot down.

The order had been given:

"When the first shot is fired charge the camp with the whole line."

And most eagerly was this order obeyed. Volleys were fired into the tepees, and with an eager yell the whole line swept wildly into the midst of the slumbering camp. The surprise was complete. The Indians rushed from their lodges panic-stricken by the suddenness and ferocity of the attack. They ran for the river-banks and thickets. Squaws yelled, children screamed, dogs barked, horses neighed, snorted, and many of them broke their fetters and fled.

Even the warriors, usually so stoical, and who always like to appear incapable of fear or excitement, were, for the time being, wild and panic-stricken like the rest. Some of them fled from the tents at first without their guns and had to return later, under a galling fire, and get them. Some of those who had presence of mind enough left to seize their weapons were too badly frightened to use them at first and stampeded, like a flock of sheep, to the brush.

The soldiers, although the scene was an intensely exciting one, were cool, self-reliant and shot to kill. Many an Indian was cut down at such short range that his flesh and clothing were burned by the powder from their rifles. Comba and Sanno first struck the camp at the apex of the V, and delivered a melting fire on the Indians as they poured from the tepees. For a few minutes no effective fire was returned, but soon the Indians recovered in a measure from their surprise and, getting into safe cover behind the river-banks, and in some cases

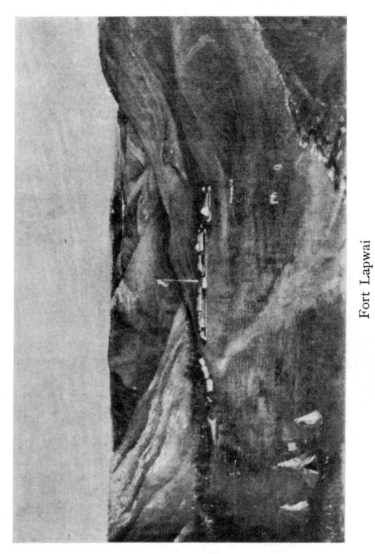

Fort Lapwai

From a painting by First Lieutenant Robert H. Fletcher, U. S. A., retired, and reproduced by his permission

in even the very bed of the stream, opened fire on the soldiers, who were now in the open ground, with terrible effect.

The fire was especially destructive on the right or upper end of the line where the river made a short bend As Logan, with a valor equal to that of his illustrious namesake, swept forward, he and his men found themselves directly at the backs of the Indians hidden in this bend, who now turned and cut them down with fearful rapidity. It was here that the greatest slaughter of that day took place. Logan himself fell, shot through the head, and at sight of their leader's corpse his men were desperate. Regardless of their own safety, they rushed to the river-bank and brained the savages in hand-to-hand encounters, both whites and Indians in some cases falling dead or wounded into the stream and being swept away by its current.

In twenty minutes from the time the first shot was fired the troops had complete possession of the camp, and orders were given to destroy it. The torch was applied with a will, and some of the canvas lodges with the plunder in them destroyed, but the heavy dew had so dampened them that they burned slowly, and the destruction was not as complete as the men wished to make it. Many of the lodges were made of skins, and these would not burn at all.

Though the Indians were driven from their camp they were not yet defeated. Joseph's voice and that of his lieutenants, White Bird and Looking Glass, were heard above the din of the battle, rallying their warriors and cheering them on to deeds of valor.

"Why are we retreating?" shouted White Bird. "Since the world was made, brave men have fought for their women and children. Shall we run into the mountains and let these white dogs kill our women and children before our eyes ? It is better that we should be killed fighting. Now is our time to fight. These soldiers cannot fight harder than the ones we defeated on Salmon River and White Bird Cañon. Fight! Shoot them down! We can shoot as well as any of these soldiers."

Looking Glass was at the other end of the camp. His voice was heard calling out:

"Wal-lit-ze! Tap-sis-il-pilp! Um-til-ilp-cown! This is battle! These men are not asleep as those you murdered in Idaho. These soldiers mean battle. You tried to break my promise at Lo-lo. You wanted to fire at the fortified place. Now is the time to show your courage and fight. You can kill right and left. I would rather see you killed than the rest, for you commenced the war. It was you who murdered the settlers in Idaho. Now fight!"

Thus praised and railed at by turns, the men recovered their presence of mind and charged back into the camp. The fighting was now muzzle to breast. This deadly encounter lasted for some minutes more, when the Indians again took to the river-bank and delivered their fire with great precision and deadliness on the troops in open ground.

In the hottest of the fight, Tap-sis-il-pilp was killed. Wal-lit-ze, upon being told of his companion's death, rushed madly upon a group of soldiers and was shot dead in his tracks. Thus did two of the three murderers, who were said to have brought on the war, pay the penalty of their crimes with their own blood. The implied wish of their chief that they might be killed was realized.

Before these two men were killed, so says a surviving Nez Percé, an almost hand-to-hand fight occurred between an officer and an Indian.

The Indian was killed. His sister saw him fall, and springing to his side, wrenched the still smoking revolver from his hand, leveled it at the officer and shot him through the head. The Indian who described the event did not know who the officer was, but every soldier in the Seventh Infantry knows and mourns the squaw's victim as the gallant Captain Logan. Another Indian, named "Grizzly Bear Youth," relates a hand-to-hand fight with a citizen volunteer in these words:

"When I was following the soldiers through the brush, trying to kill as many of them as possible, a big, ugly ranchman turned around swearing and made for me. He was either out of cartridges or afraid to take time to load his needle gun, for he swung it over his head by the barrel and rushed at me to strike with the butt end. I did the same. We both struck at once and each received a blow on the head. The volunteer's gun put a brand on my forehead that will be seen as long as I live. My blow on his head made him fall on his back. I jumped on him and tried to hold him down. He was a powerful man. He turned me and got on top. He got his hand on my throat and commenced choking me.

"All turned dark and I was nearly gone. Just then a warrior came up. This was Red Owl's son. He ran up, put his gun to the volunteer's side and fired. The ball passed through the man and killed him. I had my arm around the waist of the man when the shot was fired, and the ball, after going through the volunteer, broke my arm."

Some of the Indians had, at the first alarm, mounted their horses, and rode rapidly to the hills on either side and to depressions in the open prairies of the valley. From these positions, as well as from the thickets and river-banks, now came a most galling fire, which the soldiers were kept busy replying to. Although much of this shooting was at long range it was very deadly, and at almost every crack of their rifles a soldier, an officer, or a scout fell. General Gibbon, Lieutenant Woodruff, and both their horses were wounded by these sharp-shooters.

Gibbon formed his troops in two lines back-to-back, and charged through the brush in opposite directions for the purpose of driving out the Indians who remained there, but they simply retreated farther into the jungle, ran by the flanks of the assaulting parties, and kept up their fire at short range. In this part of the action Lieutenant Coolidge was shot through both thighs. Lieutenant Hardin and Sergeant Rogan carried him into a sheltered spot near where the body of Captain Logan lay.

By this time Coolidge had recovered from the shock of his wounds sufficiently to be able to walk, and, although weak from the loss of blood, picked up a rifle that had belonged to a fallen comrade and again took his place at the head of his company. While in this enfeebled condition he attempted to wade the river, but getting into water beyond his depth was compelled to throw away his rifle and swim. His failing strength now compelled him to seek shelter and lie down.

It soon became evident to General Gibbon that it would be unwise to hold his position on the river bottom, where there was no adequate cover for his men, and he reluctantly ordered them to fall back up the hill and take cover in the mouth of a gulch since known as "Battle Gulch." They withdrew through the willow thickets to a position under the hill, gallantly carrying their wounded comrades with them, and then made a push for the timber. It was held by about twenty of the

Indian sharpshooters, who were killed or driven from it only at the muzzles of the soldiers' rifles. On the approach of the troops these Indians took shelter in a shallow washout, not more than a foot deep and two or three feet wide. Some of them were behind trees which stood beside this trench.

One had a few large rocks piled about the roots of his tree, and from a loophole through these he picked off man after man, himself secure from the many shots aimed at him at short range by the soldiers. Finally, however, a soldier, who was an expert marksman and cool as a veteran, took a careful aim and sent a bullet into this loophole which struck the rock on one side, glanced and entered the Indian's eye, passing out at the back of his head — a veritable carom shot. This tree was girdled with bullets, and the plucky Indian who lay behind it is said to have killed five of the soldiers before the fatal missile searched him out.

While the main body of troops were clearing out this clump of woods, the valiant band of regulars and volunteers, who had been sent down the river under Lieutenant Bradley to strike the lower end of the camp, now turned and fought their way up through it; through the willow thickets; through the sloughs and bayous; through the windings of the river; killing an Indian and losing a man at every turn, and finally joined the command in the woods.

But the gallant young leader of the band was not there. He had fallen early in the fight; in fact, the first white man killed. He was leading the left wing of the army in its assault on the camp. General Gibbon had cautioned him to exercise great care going into the brush at that point, and told him to keep under cover of the brush and river-bank as much as possible, but the brave young man knew no fear and bade his men follow him. One of them called to him just as he was entering a thicket where a party of Indians were believed to be lurking, and said:

"Hold on, Lieutenant; don't go in there; it's sure death."

But he pressed on, regardless of his own safety, and just as he reached the edge of the brush an Indian raised up within a few feet of him and fired, killing him instantly.

The Indian was immediately riddled with bullets, and then the men charged madly into and through the brush, dealing death to every Indian who came in their way, and the blood of many a redskin crimsoned the sod, whose life counted against that of this gallant young officer. Thus he, who had led the night march over the mountains; who had by day, with his comrade, crawled up, located and reconnoitered the Indian camp, and sent the news of his discovery to his chief; who had on the following night aided that chief so signally in moving his command to the field and in planning the attack; who had gallantly led one wing of the little army in that fierce charge through the jungle and into the hostile camp, had laid down his noble life, and his comrades mourned him as a model officer, a good friend, a brave soldier.

Soon after the assault was made on the camp a squad of mounted warriors was sent to round up the large herd of horses, some fifteen hundred in number, on the hillside, half a mile away, and drive them down the river. General Gibbon saw this movement and sent a small party of citizen scouts to turn the horses his way and drive the herders off. A sharp skirmish ensued between the two parties, in which several whites and Indians were wounded, but the Indians being mounted and the citizens on foot, the former succeeded in rounding up the herd and driving it down the river beyond the reach of Gibbon's men.

During the progress of the fight among the tepees, the squaws and young boys seized the weapons of slain warriors, and from their hiding-places in the brush fought with the desperation of fiends. Several instances are related by survivors of the fight, in which the she devils met soldiers or scouts face to face, and, thrusting their rifles almost into the faces of the white men, fired point blank at them. Several of our men are known to have been killed by the squaws, and several of the latter were shot down in retaliation by the enraged soldiers or citizens.

A scout who was with Bradley states that, while they were fighting their way up through the willows, he passed three squaws who were hidden in a clump of brush. Knowing their bloodthirsty nature, and that several of his comrades had already been killed by this class of enemies, he was tempted to kill them, but as they seemed to be unarmed and made no show of resistance, he spared them and passed on.

Two days later, however, while out with a burial party, he found these same three squaws all dead in their hiding-place. One of them now had a Henry rifle in her hands, and beside another lay a revolver with five empty shells in the cylinder. He thought they had recovered the weapons from slain bucks after he passed and, opening fire on some soldier or scout, had met the fate to which their conduct had justly subjected them.

All through the fierce struggle on the river bottom, officers fought shoulder to shoulder with their men; some of them with their own rifles, some with rifles recovered from killed or wounded comrades, and some with revolvers. Even General Gibbon himself — who, by the way, is an expert rifle shot — from his position on the bluff, devoted all his spare moments to using his hunting-rifle on the skulking redskins, and more than one of them is said to have fallen victim to his deadly aim.

Lieut. C. A. Woodruff, his adjutant, dealt shot after shot into the foe, as he rode from point to point, carrying the orders of his chief. Captains Comba, Williams, Browning, and Sanno used their Springfields with telling effect and put many a bullet where it would do the most good. Lieutenant Jacobs was as swift as an eagle in search of his prey, and, with a revolver in each hand, dashed hither and thither hunting out the murderers from their hiding-places and shooting them down like dogs.

Lieutenants Jackson, Wright, English, Van Orsdale, Harden, and Woodbridge were all at their posts, and none of them lost an opportunity to put in a telling shot. Lieut. Francis Woodbridge was the youngest officer in the command, then a mere boy but a few months from West Point, yet he was as cool as any of the veterans and displayed soldierly qualities that endeared him to every one who participated in that day's work.

Captain Rawn was at all times in the thickest of the fight, and was admired alike by officers and men for the alacrity with which he shared in every danger. His conduct in that fight gave the lie to the carpers who had accused him of cowardice in the affair in Lo-lo Cañon. In short, every officer, every enlisted man, and every citizen volunteer, fought as though the responsibility of the battle rested solely with him, and all acquitted themselves most nobly.

As soon as the command abandoned the camp, the Indians reoccupied it, and under the fire of the sharpshooters, hauled down several of their tepees; hastily bundled together the greater portion of their plunder; packed a number of horses with it, and, mounting their riding ponies, the squaws and children beat a hasty retreat down the valley, driving the herd of loose horses with them. They had hot work breaking camp, and several of them and their horses were killed while thus engaged. Two of Joseph's wives and a daughter of Looking Glass were among the slain, who were believed to have been killed at this time.

When the command retired into the timber, the Indians followed and surrounded them, taking cover along the river-banks below, and behind rocks and trees on the hillsides above. The men dug rifle-pits with their trowel bayonets and piled up rocks to protect themselves as best they could, and a sharpshooting fight was kept up from this position all day. At times the Indians' fire was close and destructive, and here Lieutenant English received a mortal wound. Captain Williams was struck a second time, and a number of men killed and wounded.

Two large pine-trees stand on the open hillside some four hundred yards from the mouth of the gulch. Behind one of these an Indian took cover early in the morning, and stayed there until late in the afternoon. He proved to be an excellent long-range shot, and harassed the troops sorely by his fire until a soldier, who had crawled up the gulch some distance above the main body, and who was equally expert in the use of his rifle, got a cross-fire on him and finally drove him out. He went down the hill on a run and took refuge in the willows, but with one arm dangling at his side in a way that left no doubt in the minds of those who saw him that it was broken.

A large number of Indians crawled up as close to the troops as they dared, and the voices of the leaders could be heard urging their companions to push on. A half-breed in the camp, familiar with the Nez Percé tongue, heard White Bird encouraging his men and urging them to charge, assuring them that the white soldiers' ammunition was nearly gone. But he was unable to raise their courage to the desired point, and no assault was made. The troops held their ground nobly, wasting no ammunition, and yet returning the fire of the savages with coolness, accuracy, and regularity; and from the number of dead Indians and pools of blood found on the hillside the next day, learned that their work here had not been in vain.

During the afternoon of the 8th the wagon-train and howitzer had been brought down to within five miles of the Indian camp, parked, and fortified by Hugh Kirkendall, the citizen wagonmaster in charge, aided by the few men who had been left with him as train-guard.

An amusing incident occurred that night, and yet one that came near costing Kirkendall his life. Among the men left with the train was William Woodcuck, Lieutenant Jacob's servant. He was armed with a double-barreled shot-gun and ordered to take his turn on guard.

During the still hours of the night the wagonmaster was making the "rounds" to see if the men were on the alert. As he approached William's post the latter called out to him to halt; and without waiting to learn whether his challenge had been heeded, blazed away at the intruder, whom he took to be a prowling redskin. The charge of buck-shot tore up the ground and cut down the brush about the wagonmaster, but fortunately none of them hit him. William showed himself to be a vigilant sentry, but a poor shot, and it is supposed that he will never hear the last of "Who goes there? — bang!" while there is a survivor of the expedition.

At daylight on the morning of the 9th three non-commissioned officers and three men started to the front with the howitzer under the direction of Joe Blodgett, the scout. They succeeded in getting it up to within half a mile of the scene of action a little after sunrise. They took it across Trail Creek and up on the bluff, where they were in the act of putting it in position to open fire, when a body of about thirty mounted Indians saw it, and ascertaining that only a few men were with it charged with the intention of capturing it. Two of the soldiers who were with the piece became panic-stricken and fled when they saw the Indians coming, and did not stop until they reached the settlement a hundred miles away, where they spread the news that Gibbon's whole command had been captured and massacred. So far as is known, this is the only instance in which cowardice was shown by any man in the command.

The remaining four men stood bravely by the gun, however, loaded and fired it twice at the assaulting party, and then, as the Indians closed around it, used their rifles on them. When they saw that they could not successfully defend the piece, they threw it off the trunnion and retreated. Corporal Sayles was killed and Sergeants Daily and Fredericks wounded at their posts. The horses that were hauling the piece were both shot down. Private Bennett, the driver, was caught under one of them in its fall, and pretended to be dead until the Indians withdrew, when he took out his knife, cut the harness, and then prodding the animal, which was still alive, made it move sufficiently to release him, and he retreated and reached the wagon-train, where Sergeants Daily and Fredericks also arrived later in the day.

The Indians, finding the howitzer useless to themselves, took the wheels off the trunnion, hid them in the brush, and, taking a pack-mule that had been brought up with the howitzer and which was loaded with two thousand rifle cartridges, returned to their camp.

The loss of the cannon was a serious blow to the command, for, could it have been gotten into position and held, it could have done excellent service in shelling the Indians out of their strongholds, whence they so annoyed the troops. The piece could not consistently have been more strongly guarded, however, than it was, for every available man was needed in the assault on the camp. The loss of the two thousand rounds of rifle cartridges also weakened the command seriously, for it compelled the men to reserve their fire all day, in order to make the supply taken into the action with them hold out. Had this extra supply reached them, they could have killed many more Indians during the day than they did.

Meantime the fight continued to rage at the mouth of the gulch, with varying fortunes and misfortunes on either side. Late in the afternoon a smoke was seen rising from beyond the brow of the hill below Gibbon's position, and the cry went forth that the Indians had fired the grass. A wind was blowing the fire directly toward the beleaguered band, and all were greatly alarmed. The General had feared that the Indians would resort to this measure, for he knew it to be a part of the Nez Percés' war tactics, and he believed that they intended to follow up the fire and assault his men while blinded by the smoke. Yet he was not dismayed. He urged his men to stand firm in the face of this new danger.

"If the worst comes, my men," said he, "if this fire

reaches us, we will charge through it, meet the redskins in the open ground, and send them to a hotter place than they have prepared for us."

The fire burned fiercely until within a few yards of the intrenchments, and the men were blinded and nearly suffocated by the smoke. But again the fortunes of war were with the beleaguered band, for just before the fire reached them the wind shifted squarely about, came down off the hills from the west, and the fire, blown back upon its own blackened embers, faltered, and died out. At this lucky turn in their fortunes the soldiers cheered wildly, and the Indians cursed savagely.

The men had left the wagons in the forenoon of the previous day with one day's rations, but in the charge across the river many of their haversacks had been filled with water, and the scant supply of food that remained in them was destroyed. Others, more fortunate, had divided their few remaining crackers with their comrades who were thus deprived, so that all were now without provisions and suffering from hunger.

The gulch in which they had taken cover was dry and rocky, and as the August sun poured his scorching rays upon the men they suffered for water. True, the river flowed within a few hundred yards of them, but the man who attempted to reach it did so at the risk of his life, and there were no more lives to spare. Not until nightfall did the commanding officer deem it prudent to send out a fatigue party for water. Then three men volunteered to go, and under cover of darkness, and of a firing party, they made the trip safely, filling and bringing in as many canteens as they could carry.

The men cut up Lieutenant Woodruff's horse (which the Indians had conveniently killed within the lines), and as they dared not make camp-fires, devoured full rations of him raw. The night was cold, and again the men suffered greatly for bedding. The Indians kept firing into the woods occasionally, even after dark, so that the soldiers were unable to rest. Once or twice they charged up almost to Gibbon's lines and delivered volleys on the men, but were speedily repulsed in each case by a fusillade from the intrenchments.

General Gibbon had heard nothing from his wagon-train since leaving it, and the fact that mounted parties of Indians were frequently seen passing in his rear made it extremely dangerous to attempt to pass to or from it. Indeed, he feared the train had been captured, for it was but lightly guarded, and during the night he started a runner to Deer Lodge for medical assistance and supplies. This man, W. H. Edwards by name, succeeded in making his way out through the Indian lines under cover of darkness, and walked or ran to Frenche's Gulch, a distance of nearly sixty miles, where he got a horse, and made the remaining forty miles during the following night, arriving at Deer Lodge on the morning of August 11th.

On the morning of the 10th a courier arrived from General Howard, informing Gibbon that he (Howard) was hurrying to his assistance with twenty cavalrymen and thirty Warm Spring Indians. On being questioned as to the supply-train, this courier reported that he had seen nothing of it, which statement greatly increased the fear of the men that it had been captured and destroyed.

Later in the day, however, a messenger arrived from the train, bringing the cheering news that it was safe. The Indians had menaced it all day, but the guard in charge of it had fortified their position and fired upon the savages whenever they came in sight with such telling effect that the latter had made no determined attack. Howard's messenger had passed the train in the night without seeing it.

Early on the morning of the 10th Serg. Mildon H. Wilson, of Company K, with six men was sent back to bring up the train, and later in the day Captain Browning and Lieutenant Woodbridge, with twenty men, all of whom had volunteered for the service, were sent to take charge of it. They met the train on the way in charge of Sergeant Wilson, and with it succeeded in reaching the command just at sundown, bringing the blankets and provisions so much needed by the men.

This detachment performed a hazardous and meritorious piece of work in thus rescuing and bringing up the train, for large parties of Indians were still scouting through the woods and hills watching for opportunities to cut off any small body of troops who might be found away from the main command and with whom they might successfully contend.

In the face of this danger, Browning and Woodbridge, with their few supporters, marched nearly ten miles through the swampy, brush-lined ravine, and succeeded in moving the train over roads that were wellnigh impassable under the most favorable circumstances. The wagons had to be literally carried over some of the worst places, the mules having all they could do to get through without pulling a pound.

As soon as the train had been safely delivered to the command, General Gibbon asked for a volunteer messenger to go to Deer Lodge with additional despatches, fearing that Edwards might have been killed or captured *en route*, and Sergeant Wilson, the hero of so many brave deeds, promptly volunteered for this perilous service. He started at once, rode all night, and reached his destination only a few hours behind Edwards.

The last party of Indians withdrew about eleven o'clock on the night of the 10th, giving the soldiers a parting shower of bullets, but it was not known until daylight on the morning of the 11th that all had really gone.

From the time the last shots were fired, as stated, all was quiet, and the men got a few hours of much-needed rest, such as it was, for they had slept but two hours in the past forty-eight. The fight was over; the enemy was gone. The sun that rose on the morning of the 11th shone brightly over as beautiful a valley as the eye of man ever beheld, and the blackening corpses that lay strewn upon the field were the only remaining evidences of the bloody tragedy that had so lately been enacted there.

CHAPTER ELEVEN

The Battle of Camas Meadows*

By H. J. Davis, formerly Sergeant Second Cavalry,
United States Army

URING the memorable campaign against
the Nez Percé Indians, in the year 1877,
there were many stirring incidents that have
never been given to the public, and notably
among these is the Camas Meadow fight of Capt. Randolph Norwood's Company L, of the Second Cavalry.

In the early part of the summer we had assisted the
Fifth Infantry, under Col. Nelson A. Miles, in rounding up and capturing the remnant band of Cheyenne
Sioux, under Lame Deer, and bringing them into the
cantonment at the mouth of Tongue River. Shortly
after arriving there, Gen. W. T. Sherman and staff,
and the General's son, Thomas, came up the Yellowstone on a tour of inspection, and we were ordered
to escort them to Fort Ellis, which was our home station. Arriving there, a portion of the company was
detailed to accompany our distinguished visitors on a
trip of sight-seeing to the Yellowstone Park. They had
scarcely departed when despatches arrived telling of
a disastrous engagement of Col. John Gibbon's troops

* By kind permission of the Journal of the Military Service Institution.

with the Nez Percés at Big Hole Pass, something like one hundred and sixty miles away; saying he was in desperate circumstances and in danger of annihilation, and ordering us to hasten with all speed to his relief.

Our company was depleted, by various details, to about fifty men, and with this force we started within the hour, which was already late in the day. Virginia City, sixty miles, was made on the night of the following day; the next ninety miles were made without halt, except for coffee for the men and short rests for the horses. It was a tedious ride; all day, all night and all day again, the steady plod, plod of the horses broken at night by the occasional smothered exclamation or oath of some trooper who had dropped asleep and nearly fallen from his horse.

On the second night out from Virginia City we went into camp late, moved early the following morning, and had not been on the road long before we met a wagon and travois train bringing wounded from the battle-field. They told us that they had been soundly whipped, with great loss, and that the Indians, unable to dislodge them, had, after a three days' siege, departed, taking a southeasterly course and following the main range of the Rocky Mountains.

They would, without question, have killed or captured every man of Gibbon's force, had they not been apprised of a large force of soldiers coming from the West. This was Gen. O. O. Howard's command, consisting of two companies of the First United States Cavalry, two or three batteries of the Fourth United States Artillery, and the Twenty-first United States Infantry. The artillery was equipped as infantry. This force we joined, and then began a stern chase which proved to be the traditional long chase.

Our course was the same as the Indians had taken. But with our heavier impedimenta the best we could do was to keep from fifteen to twenty miles behind them. We crossed to the south side of the main range, and for seven nights we slept booted and spurred. We were following the trail, which, after crossing the mountains, led through a good grazing country, and from the numerous carcasses of cattle which lined the trail we knew that the Indians were well sustained. An interesting fact, to those not acquainted with Indian ways, is that these dead steers were disemboweled and the bulk of the internal arrangements had disappeared, while the loins, rump, and, in fact, all choice parts, from a white man's point of view, had not been disturbed.

The trail was easily followed, as it was from fifty to one hundred and fifty feet wide, and the vegetation was almost entirely obliterated by the tramping of their several hundred ponies and the dragging of scores of travois poles. At their halting-places we found many freshly made graves, showing that their wounded list was rapidly growing smaller. We also noticed, at such resting spots, numbers of conical piles of pony droppings, evidently built by hand, which our scouts told us were constructed by the young bucks to show their contempt for us.

When we struck Camas Creek, General Howard decided to give the men and horses a chance to rest, as our march had been arduous, and the Indians seemed about to strike for the headwaters of Snake River, and from there enter the then almost wholly unexplored Yellowstone Park. We camped on the east bank of Camas Creek, on open ground. Opposite, and above the camp, the creek was fringed with cottonwoods and alders, and below, the banks were clear and the stream flowed over a natural meadow to "The Sink" a few miles below, where it disappeared. The creek was literally alive with trout from twelve to twenty inches long, and offered the finest sport I have ever seen. With only a small portion of the men fishing, enough were taken to feed the entire command. In the immediate vicinity of that camp ground there is now a company, with a capital of two hundred thousand dollars, engaged in raising trout for market, and they supply Ogden, Salt Lake City, and even San Francisco; the waters are ideal for the purpose. At night guards were posted, and a picket post was established some five hundred yards up stream, near the creek and on a rocky knoll, and two at other points. The mule herd was turned loose to graze in the space between the camp and the principal picket post mentioned above.

Some of the men slept under the wagons and others pitched shelter tents; I chose the latter method, and with Private Monaghan for a "bunky" was soon in a state of "innocuous desuetude." Either our pickets fell asleep or the Indians were very astute, for during the dark half hour that generally precedes daylight we were awakened by a disconcerting concert of demoniacal yells and a cracking of rifles, while the whizzing of bullets could be heard well overhead. Every one was out in a minute, and all we could see was a magnified imitation of a swarm of fireflies flittering in the alders as the rifles spoke; while the tramping of hundreds of hoofs added to the din.

We had no sooner sent them "a Roland for their Oliver" than the fireflies ceased winking, and, except the noise we were making ourselves, nothing could be heard but receding hoof-beats and faint yells, as the enemy returned from whence they came, taking with them, as a souvenir, about one hundred and fifty mules, our pack-train. Our company horses had pulled one picket-pin, and had them milled 'round and 'round and twisted themselves into a grotesque puzzle.

Orders came quickly for the three companies of cavalry to saddle, pursue and try to recapture the pack-train. One company of the First Cavalry was to make a detour to the right and the other to the left, and our company was to follow the trail. The morning air was extremely chilly and crisp and the horses rank, so that what was an orderly gallop, at first, soon developed into a race. After half an hour of this we approached a ridge, which was the first roll of the foot-hills. The first ones to make the summit of the ridge suddenly stopped and then quickly returned to the foot; as the rest of us came up we soon learned that the Indians had made a stand just over the ridge.

We dismounted, and the Number Fours, each holding four horses, being unable to fight, left about thirty-five of us to meet the Indians. Crawling to the top we saw a line of dismounted skirmishers, standing behind their ponies, on open ground and about a thousand yards away. We deployed along the ridge and for twenty minutes or so exchanged shots with them with but little damage on either side, as the range was long for our Springfields and longer for their Winchesters.

Lieutenant Benson of the Seventh Infantry, who was attached to our company for the day, standing up for an instant, just at my side, received a bullet which entered at the hip-pocket and went out at the other, having passed entirely through both buttocks; this, while we were facing the enemy, caused us to realize that we had no ordinary Indians to deal with, for, while we had been frolicking with the skirmishers in front, Chief Joseph had engineered as neat a double flank movement as could be imagined, and we were exposed to a raking fire coming from right and left.

The horses had been withdrawn, more than five hundred yards, to a clump of cottonwoods; and when we turned around there was no sight nor sign of them. For a brief period there was a panic, and then we heard the notes of a bugle blowing "Recall" from the cottonwood thicket. The race to that thicket was something never to be forgotten, for a cavalryman is not trained for a five hundred yard sprint. Luck was with us, however, and no man was hit in that mad race for safety. I had a horse's nose-bag slung over my shoulder containing extra cartridges, and a bullet cut the strap and let it fall to the ground. A hero would have stopped, gone back and recovered that bag, but not I.

We all reached the horses and found the place an admirable one for defense; it was a sort of basin, an acre or so in extent, with a rim high enough to protect our horses, and filled with young cottonwoods in full leaf. It was oval in shape, and we deployed in all directions around the rim. For two hours it was a sniping game and our casualties were eight. The Indians crawled very close, one shooting Harry Trevor in the back at about fifteen feet, as we knew by the moccasin tracks and empty shells found behind a rock after the engagement. Poor Trevor's wound was mortal as was that of Sam Glass, who was shot through the bladder; a bullet hit Sergeant Garland's cartridge-belt and drove two cartridges from it clear through his body; his wound never healed and he blew out his brains a few years later. Will Clark had his shoulder partly torn away by an explosive ball; Sergeant Wilkins, a head wound, and Farrier Jones, a "busted" knee; a citizen attaché, a bullet through the foot, and the lieutenant, wounded as told above. This was the amount of damage done to us, and what we did to the Indians we never knew, as they retreated in good order taking their dead or injured with them, after they found they could not dislodge us. Three dead ponies and some pools of blood were all the records we found of their casualties.

The real hero of the occasion was Sergeant Hugh McCafferty, who climbed a cottonwood tree, and in short range of every Indian and only concealed by the foliage, kept us posted on their movements by passing the word to a man stationed under the tree. For this act he was given a certificate of merit and a medal by Congress. It should have been mentioned that we recovered twenty mules that were dropped by the Indians about midway between the camp and battle-ground. The others were never retaken, but were worn out or died before the final surrender of the few survivors to Colonel Miles.

We took up the trail the next day, after our wounded had been started for the post under escort. I could never understand how those two companies of the First Cavalry could have missed the Indians and gotten entirely out of touch with us, when we started together and we were fighting within half an hour and kept it up for nearly three hours. More could be told of our chase through forest and cañon, over mountains and across gorges, where wagons had to be let down almost perpendicular walls by hand, for two hundred feet. But that is another story.

CHAPTER TWELVE

Story of Bugler Brooks

By Col. J. W. Redington

United States Scout and Courier in Campaigns Against
Hostile Indians in the Pacific Northwest *

MORN amid the mountains, cold's the hour
before the dawn; also dark. So it was that
autumn night on Camas Meadows, away
up in Idaho, under the sentinel shadows
of the great peaks of the Three Tetons.

How still the cavalry camp, with its tired troopers,
snatching what sleep they can before beginning another
day's pursuit of Chief Joseph's hostiles.

A shot! Another! A dozen! A regular rattling volley!

A bugle blast — Brooks' bugle, always musical, now
stirringly imperative in its call to arms — the cool, firm
orders of Major Jackson — and, above all, the Indian
yells of defiance to the entire white race.

And all in the chill, intensified darkness that precedes the dawn. Shots in all directions.

Very suddenly had the hostiles attached the sleeping
soldiers and cleverly stampeded the pack-mules grazing
within the lines. Carefully, in columns of fours, personally conducted by Joseph, had they advanced toward the

* From *Sunset Magazine* by permission of the author.

watchful picket, and in the uncertain starlight made him think they were Bacon's troopers returning. But answering not his challenge, they received the contents of his carbine.

A few Indians had skilfully crept in between the sentries, and mingling with the mules, had removed the hobbles from the bell mares. The sentry's shot, the shrill signal yell, the buffalo robes flaunted in their faces — and the herd made a wild dash for freedom.

It lay in the course shaped by the Indians.

Strenuous seconds now, with only a few of them consumed while General Howard and Lieutenants Fletcher, Wood and Howard rolled out of their blankets and arranged for pursuit. Decamped had the hostiles, with the hundred mules they were after, and the bullets, in darkness sent, found few the marks their senders meant.

There was no stuttering in the hurry-up calls that came from Bugler Brooks, and the mountain spurs and neighbor cañons caught up the notes and echoed and reëchoed them as only cañons can.

How realistic it all was! And how the horses of the Montana volunteers, commanded by Captain Clark, now United States Senator, went wild and dashed away to join the stolen mules. And how Jackson, the veteran of many wars, talked to his horses, plunging at the picket rope, and quieted them down.

Boots and saddles! and away went the troopers of the dashing Norwood, Carr, Sanford, Jackson and Bendire, and in an hour they were in a hot engagement with double their number of Indians. They recaptured half the stolen stock, but the frantic animals broke away and dashed back into the enemy's lines.

No amateurs at war were these Nez Percés. Their ambuscade was a success, and it soon became a case of the troopers holding their own. And when the day's battling was over and Lieutenant Benson and the rest of the wounded had had their misery eased as much as was possible away out there in the then wilderness, there was one dead.

That was Bugler Brooks.

When the boy, for he was scarcely more than that, was shot out of his saddle, he tried at once to spring up on to his feet again, but only succeeded in getting to his knees. His horse, a very intelligent animal, went back to his fallen master, nickered, and edged up alongside of him. Brooks caught the stirrup strap and tried to lift himself back into the saddle, but just then death came. The horse whinnied and champed and stood around Brooks, plainly urging him to remount. It was a snap-shot scene that did not last long, but was quite pitiful while it was passing.*

The heroic rescue under a fierce fire of his slender and suddenly lifeless form, by Major Jackson, eventually brought that officer a medal of honor from Congress. Boy that he was, full of life and enthusiasm, it seemed singularly sad that fate had selected him to fill the shallow trench scooped out by his comrades.

Brief was the service read by Colonel Mason, touching the remarks by General Howard, heavy the hearts of those who stood by. And as the little mound was rounded up and the farewell volleys rang out on the evening

---

* Just after the youngster died, Charles Gibbons shot an Indian, and his body came rolling down from the rocks above. It was thought that that Nez Percé was the one who had shot Brooks, so Gibbons was called the Long-Haired Avenger. He had not had a chance to cut his own hair for several months, as the butcher-knife he packed in his boot had become pretty dull from slicing hard-tack. Please remember, Doctor, that on those rough campaigns the cavalry did not carry any cheese-knives (sabres), and the officers carried no swords (or toad-stickers). It was tough service on the horses, and every ounce taken off of them counted big.—J. W. R.

air, the setting sun slanted its shadowing shafts against the soaring summits of the Snake River sentries, the Three Tetons, the wondrous western clouds took on their fairy forms and tints of rose and amber and purple, the stars let down their hanging lamps, and the rising autumn moon saw soldiers resuming the stern realities of wicked war, with Trumpeter Sembower sounding the calls.

Miles from human habitation, what a lonely place it was to bury the boy. How tender the termination of the camaraderie. And how would weep the mother who tended his infant footsteps could she have seen through the shadows that shroud the to-morrow, and viewed the ending of the life she gave.

With such sacrifices have Western trails been blazed.

Alone with nature and nature's God Bugler Brooks' grave will remain for many a year, but the Bannock women will come to dig the camas and the cowse among the near-by knolls, and superstitiously point out the mound to their little ones. And every winter, with its deeper snows, will surely bring a spring, with meadow-larks' sweetest songs, and every early June these mountain glades will be fragrant fields of beautiful blue blossoms of the camas, and the wild timothy and the red-top will dip and wave in the summer breezes, and the lupine and fire-pink will illume the smiling slopes.

And later on, some day, the settler will come, and the district school, and the teacher will tell her little pupils the tradition of the lonely grave. While down the spectral aisles of thought, the termination of whose windings we do not know, will come glintings of day through the darkness, arc lights of heaven in the dusk, and on the far-off morn — the resurrection morn — the reveille bugle-call of Brother Trumpeter Gabriel will find

202 Northwestern Fights and Fighters

young Brooks among the good and true, in his faded blouse of blue, ready to join his scattered comrades of the gallant old First Cavalry, with Colonel Jackson at the head of the column, his favorite bugler again at his elbow, and riding along with their troops General Boutelle, and Captain Bendire, and Lieutenant Bacon and Major McGregor, and Col. John Green, and Captain Winters, and Colonel Parnell, and Major Trimble, and Captain Forse, and Colonel Bernard, and Majors Pitcher and Wainwright, and Sergeants McCarthy and Burkett and Wooten and Hanvey, with Col. Rube Robbins and Capt. S. G. Fisher leading on as chiefs of scouts, and the rest of the veteran troopers who put in the best years of their lives paving the way for the prosperous civilization that now blesses the Pacific Northwest.

CHAPTER THIRTEEN

The Seventh Cavalry at Cañon Creek

By Theodore W. Goldin

THE winter of 1876-77, following the "Little Big Horn" campaign, was spent by the Seventh Cavalry very quietly in posts along the Missouri and vicinity, resting, reorganizing and awakening to a realizing sense of what the previous season's campaign had meant to us. Early in the winter rumors reached us that the regiment was to take the field in the early spring, so that when orders reached us in early April for eleven troops of the regiment to move out under Colonel and Brev. Maj.-Gen. Samuel Sturgis, we were not at all surprised.

On April 30th eleven troops of the regiment were reunited a short distance below Bismarck, and on May 2nd we took up our line of march for Fort Buford. Owing to the early season and the incessant rains our progress was slow and practically void of incidents of interest to the general reader. After a brief halt in the vicinity of Buford we were ferried across the river, and in the weeks that followed spent the time in scouting the valley of the Yellowstone, remaining not far from the cantonment at Tongue River.

From time to time rumors reached us of an uprising

of the Nez Percés in Oregon. This did not cause us any uneasiness, as the scene of war was too far removed, apparently, to bring it within the limit of possibilities of our being called upon to participate in the campaign against them.

We were therefore somewhat surprised one pleasant afternoon, while we were enjoying a somewhat lazy existence along the banks of the Yellowstone some twelve miles from Miles City, to hear "Officer's Call" sounding from headquarters, followed a few moments later by the "General." We rushed out of the quarter-master's tent where we were on guard to see every tent in the regiment down and the men packing up with orders to march at once for the Tongue River canton-ment. On arriving there with the wagon-train about midnight, we learned that the Nez Percés had eluded General Howard and were making their way across the divide, and that eight troops of our regiment were to take the field, the remaining three troops, A, D, and K, being left at the cantonment under General Miles. Our destination was the old Crow Mission away up on the Stillwater.

With five days' rations in our wagons we broke camp the following morning and pushed ahead up the valley of the Yellowstone, passing on the way our old camp where General Custer's fatal march began the pre-ceding summer. The following day a courier overtook us from Tongue River with the news that the steamer on which were our extra rations was hard aground on the Yellowstone, with no immediate prospect of getting up until there was an improvement in the stage of the water. This raised serious complications, as by this time we only had about one day's rations in the wagons. Lieutenant Fuller had already started for Fort Ellis and Bozeman, Montana, to arrange to have rations and forage forwarded to us from there, and Lieutenant Varnum, regimental quartermaster, with his orderly and chief clerk, had pushed on ahead of the command to intercept the steamer at Terry's Landing, expecting there to unload sufficient rations to carry us to the Mission.

A hurried consultation was held, and couriers sent forward to overtake the quartermaster, in order that he might make such other arrangements as seemed possible under the circumstances. He lost no time in pushing forward a courier to Fort Custer and we secured from that post a supply of flour, but no hard bread and no forage to speak of. Leaving one troop to bring forward such rations as were secured, the balance of the command pushed forward to the Mussel Shell River where we overtook them a couple of days later. While here we learned that General Gibbon had run up against the Nez Percés near Big Hole, Montana Territory, and had been quite roughly handled. With this news we pushed forward as rapidly as possible for the Mission.

The ride, particularly on our last day's march, was a very interesting one, the country was new to us and the scenery most beautiful, indeed. Leaving a detachment at the crossing near the mouth of the Stillwater the balance of the command marched on to the Mission. The following day a small wagon-train arrived at the crossing, but to our regret we found they had nothing but forage for our command. Loading up with this we rejoined the command at the Mission and spent several days resting, fishing, and becoming acquainted with the Crows.

After remaining here several days a detachment was sent back to the crossing to meet a wagon-train reported to be on its way from Fort Ellis, and again we were doomed to disappointment; not a pound of rations, nothing but corn and oats. During the absence of the train the command had left the agency, and crossed the Red Rock. There we were at last overtaken by the wagon-train in the vicinity of Clark's Fork, and orders were at once issued placing the command on half rations as we did not know when we were likely to see anything of the missing supplies.

Leaving Clark's Fork we marched toward the mountains, passing through the valley of the Stinking Water, and finally went into camp under the lee of Old Heart Mountain on the middle branch of Clark's Fork. Here we rested for a day, spending the time between fishing and manufacturing our limited supply of flour into biscuit, not knowing how soon we might have to make a hurried dash after the enemy.

While we were resting at the Mission, General Sturgis had hired a couple of prospectors and sent them into the mountains ahead of us with instructions to report to him in this vicinity. Hearing nothing from them the general became anxious and two scouting-parties, under Lieutenants Hare and Russell respectively, were ordered out to scout the vicinity of our camp and locate the prospectors, if possible. After their departure the remainder of the command spent the day in fishing, writing letters or scaling the adjacent peaks.

In company with Mr. Dubray, the civilian clerk in the quartermaster's department, some of us started to make the ascent of Heart Peak. Just as we reached the base of the peak, Dubray called attention to a thin, curling cloud of smoke arising apparently from the summit. We were somewhat surprised at this, but finally decided that it must come from a fire started by some of our

U. S. Scouts during the Wars with the Nez Percé
Indians in 1878

From left to right: upper row—Andrew McQuaid, George Banks,
Colonel Morton, John Campbell; lower row: Charles Adams,
Rube Robbins, Chief, Henry Pierce

From the collection of J. W. Redington

people who had started earlier in the day to make the ascent. Thus disposing of the matter we sought a convenient place and began the ascent.

After a half hour's hard climbing we came out on the face of the mountains some distance above the camp, and sat down to rest and smoke. We were just about to proceed when our attention was attracted to a considerable dust cloud moving rapidly down the valley. Unslinging our field-glasses, it took but a moment to decide that it was a party of horsemen. A few moments later we discovered another dust cloud still farther to the right, again caused by mounted men. A careful examination satisfied us they were soldiers, undoubtedly our scouting-parties. Judging from the way they rode that there was something in the wind, we at once abandoned our idea of scaling the peak and made our way back to camp as rapidly as possible.

Both details had reached the camp before we did, and on our arrival we found the officers clustered around the tent of the Colonel, and we had only barely reached headquarters when the "General" sounded, followed a moment later by "Officer's Call" to bring in those who were fishing and mountain climbing. Orders were issued to pack everything not absolutely necessary in the wagons, which were to return to the agency and await further orders. In the rush of preparation, we had no time to make inquiries as to the reasons for this sudden move, and it was after eleven o'clock, when we went into camp again and I found myself on guard, that we learned the reason for our haste.

After leaving us in the morning, the party under Lieutenant Hare pushed ahead up the valley without seeing anything out of the ordinary. Some distance above the site of our present camp they suddenly came upon fresh pony tracks and evidences of a recent struggle, and a few moments later discovered the body of one of the prospectors, stripped and bristling with arrows, stretched dead on the hillside. All around him were ample evidences of the recent presence of Indians.

Pausing for a few moments to give him as decent a burial as circumstances would permit, some of the detachment scattered and began searching the adjacent territory. A few moments later a loud "halloo" from down near the banks of the stream sent the whole party scurrying in that direction. There they found one of the sergeants bending over the still breathing body of the second prospector. Stimulants were speedily administered, and in a short time the man had so far recovered as to be able to tell his story.

It seems that after leaving the Mission he and his partner had pushed in to the foot-hills and mountains for several days without discovering any signs of Indians. They had turned back for the purpose of rejoining the command and had just forded the little creek on which the detachment was now gazing, when, without a moment's warning, they were fired upon from an ambush. His partner was killed early in the fight, and a few moments later he, too, was forced to succumb, grievously wounded. For some unknown reason the Indians made no effort to find him, but jumped on to their ponies and hurried away up the valley. He said that he only caught a glimpse of two of them, and that he was sure they were Nez Percés; that it seemed almost certain that the main body could not have been at any great distance.

After hearing the story, Lieutenant Hare at once determined to return to the command and report. There was no possible way of taking with them the wounded prospector in his enfeebled condition; so, after dressing his wounds as best they could, they carried him down near the banks of the creek, erected a temporary shelter, and leaving him well supplied with water and such food as they had, the command swung into the saddle and made for camp in a hurry.

The second detachment under Lieutenant Russell, after leaving camp, followed for several miles the same general direction taken by Lieutenant Hare's column, then branching off to the right, they pushed their way up into the foot-hills, scouting in and out among the valleys and peaks, but without discovering any traces of the enemy. They had about determined to return when one of the scouts, who had crawled to the top of a little ridge beneath which they had halted for a moment, called to Lieutenant Russell. The lieutenant crept cautiously to the scout's side, together with one or two of the veteran sergeants. Peering over the divide they discovered, not more than a couple of miles away, a large herd, apparently, of ponies. Judging from what they could see the herd had been driven down to water and was then returning up one of the countless ravines, or cañons, with which the hillsides were seamed, urged on by a dozen or more half-naked Indian boys.

There appeared to be no thought of danger in the minds of the herd boys, for no apparent effort at concealment was made. For some time the soldiers watched them; in fact, until the herd had disappeared up the cañon, then they scrambled down, clambered into their saddles and made a hurried dash for the command. This, then, was what had routed us out of our pleasant camp and sent us wandering through the darkness into the foot-hills, at least this was the story told us by one of the sergeants who had accompanied the scouting-party. It was evident that somewhere in the hills ahead of us there was, or had been, a considerable body of Indians, and without doubt our efforts were now to be directed to rounding them up.

While we had been listening to this story of the scout, we had allowed our pipe to go out, and knocking the ashes from the bowl we stowed the pipe away, told the men not on post to go to sleep, and leaning up against a stump we began to think over the story we had heard, and were just putting on our belts preparatory to making the rounds of the picket posts.

"Bang, bang, bang!"

"What the devil was that?"

"Bang, bang, bang!"

"There it goes again!"

An instant later and the officer of the day dashed past, scurrying and stumbling through the darkness in the direction of the shots. In a moment the whole camp was astir, the voices of the first sergeants could be heard calling out:

"Fall in there lively, men."

The stable guard and some of the men previously instructed hurried about among the horses, quieting and securing them against a stampede. A hasty dash through sage-brush and over boulders brought the officer of the day and the sergeant of the guard to one of the most distant of the outposts, where they found the corporal in charge and his men, carbine in hand, stretched on the ground and peering grimly into the darkness.

In response to the query, "Who fired that first shot?" one of the men, a veteran of a dozen campaigns, rose to his feet and said:

"I did, sir."

"What was it you fired at?" was the next question.

The old soldier hesitated for a moment and then replied that he could not tell for certain, but that it looked very much to him like a mounted man. He further reported that he had gone on post at twelve o'clock and for some time walked up and down, but that it finally occurred to him that the country in his front was, or might be, much lower than his post, so that any one approaching from the outside could discover him before he could even hear or see him. With this thought in mind he hunted up a convenient sage-bush and squatted down behind it.

Just how long he had been in this position he could not say, but all at once he heard a sharp sound as of metal striking against a rock somewhere out in his front. Reaching back he woke up the corporal, who crept to his side and the two listened intently. Suddenly they both heard the sound again, apparently closer than at first. The men on this outpost were all wide-awake by this time and all heard the sound not only once but several times, each time nearer than before. He was just thinking about challenging when right in front of him, apparently not twenty yards away, he caught sight of a dark moving object. He challenged and fired almost at the same instant. The corporal and one of the men of the guard saw it and fired, too. When the smoke cleared away they could see nothing, but could hear what sounded like hoof-beats off to their right, but before they had time to challenge again three shots were fired from the next post to them.

There was no use to make a search at this time, so the officer of the day returned to camp and quietness again reigned. With the first rays of the coming daylight the officer of the day and his non-commissioned officer of the guard accompanied by a couple of Crow scouts crept out to the front of the post from which the shot was fired, and sure enough, not thirty yards from the post they found the tracks and could follow them around the line of bluffs until they became intermingled with horse and mule tracks in the rear of our camp.

Leaving camp early the following morning we soon reached the place where the wounded prospector had been left. He was as comfortable as could be expected. Here we slackened girths and allowed our horses to graze while the surgeons redressed the poor fellow's wounds. Some of the men busied themselves in building a rude travois or stretcher on which he could be transported to the Mission, for it was the Colonel's determination to push ahead and attempt to overhaul the enemy. There were several prospectors with our party, and in their charge we left their wounded comrade. Half an hour later he passed rearward past our line and was on the back trail while we recinched our saddles, filled our canteens and advanced into the mountains.

That night we made our camp in a broad valley surrounded on every side by towering hills. Early the following morning we were in the saddle and away, and about noon we in the advance were surprised at discovering wheel tracks apparently leading farther into the mountains. They were evidently made by a two-wheeled cart of some sort! At a loss to understand the presence of a wheeled vehicle of any kind in this wilderness we pushed, rolled, stumbled and clambered over a spur of the divide, slid down on the other side, wandered in and out among the valleys for an hour or two and suddenly came upon a broad beaten trail, apparently not many hours old.

We followed this trail as fast as the exhausted condition of our horses would permit, and that night went into camp in a grove of scrub pines at the very top of the range and right alongside the trail. Daybreak the next morning found us in the saddle, and all day long we clambered up one side of a mountain only to slide down the other. The trail was growing fresher every hour and we lost all sense of fatigue and hunger in the excitement of a prospective fight.

Late in the afternoon the trail landed us at what seemed to be a veritable "jumping-off place." On all sides of us were towering mountains; in our front a deep, precipitous cañon, leading apparently into the very bowels of the earth. But down there lay the trail and down there we were bound to go, so swinging from our saddles, we grasped our bridle reins, and slipping, sliding and stumbling we made the dangerous descent and finally reached what appeared to be the bottom. There before us winding in and out beneath the overhanging cliffs was the now narrowed trail. On we went and half a mile further to our utter surprise we came upon an abandoned government horse, the saddle marks scarcely dry on his back. There was only one solution of this: General Howard was in close pursuit of the Indians, and his command had passed through this "devil's doorway" only a short time ahead of us. An hour later we emerged from the mountains about three miles above our old camp at Heart Mountain.

It was verging on twilight, and after a half hour's march down the valley we sighted a large fire. Fifteen minutes later General Howard rode up to our column, talked for a few moments to our Colonel, and then our command swung off to the left of the trail and we were soon in camp. After our very frugal supper we sought the camp of the other command, and from some of the scouts we learned that the Indians were supposed to be at least fifty miles ahead of us, apparently fleeing for the British Possessions, and that the horses of General Howard's command were so badly exhausted that he had almost determined to abandon the chase. We knew our old Colonel was hopping mad that the savages had outwitted him, and as we returned to camp we heard the old veteran, with many an explosive adjective, declare that he would overtake those Indians before they crossed the Missouri River if he had to go afoot and alone. He wound up his impromptu oration with an order for reveille at half past three and an advance at five o'clock.

We were not long in making up our minds that we were in for some hard times, but, soldier-like, with the prospect of a fight ahead, we didn't care. In fact, we were glad of the chance to get at Joseph's band. During the night General Howard selected from among his troops such men as were best mounted and attached to them a battery of mountain howitzers, or a "jackass" battery as we were wont to call them, and ordered them to push forward with us.

Half past three found us up and stirring. We swallowed our cup of weak coffee and a couple of flapjacks, tightened our belts a hole or two, and "hit the trail." Hardly were we in the saddle when it began to rain, not a good hard rain, just a miserable drizzle, drizzle, drizzle. But the Colonel's blood was up and on we went, hour after hour, with only the briefest halts to allow our horses a breathing spell. Morning merged into afternoon, afternoon into evening, evening into darkest night, and still we marched. About three o'clock the preceding afternoon we caught a last glimpse of General Howard's detachment several miles in our rear. Nine o'clock, ten o'clock, eleven o'clock, and still no signs of a camp.

Almost twelve o'clock and the old Colonel swung himself from the saddle with the remark:

"Well, men, we will camp right here."

Five minutes later our horses were unsaddled and picketed out in the deep grass and we started a fire at the foot of a cottonwood log, wrapped ourselves in our wet blankets with our feet to the fire and tried to sleep. As we dropped into a doze we heard the adjutant say:

"Sixty miles since five o'clock, pretty good for played-out horses."

At daybreak the camp was astir, the men were stiff and tired, rations were mighty scarce, and the men not in the best of humor. Making the best of it, however, we saddled up, and half an hour later we followed the Indian trail across the ford, halted on the bank and threw ourselves on the ground, where the sun soon thawed us out.

A few moments later word was passed down the line:

"Unsaddle where you are and put your horses on lariat."

So the chase was over; the Colonel had given up. Springing to their feet, the men began to unsaddle. In fact, some of the companies were already leading out to herd when we heard a shout from the lower end of the camp. Looking up we saw Pawnee Tom, one of our best scouts, coming down the valley at a wild gallop, yelling "Indians! Indians!" at the top of his voice.

Just in the rear, although apparently some distance down the valley, we could see a huge column of smoke rolling skyward. In an instant all was excitement. Officers and men were on their feet, horses were hurried back from the herds, saddles were thrown on, and in a very few moments the first and second battalions under

Lieutenant Colonel Otis and Major Merrill, respectively, were hurrying off down the valley.

Pausing only long enough to see that our pack-train was ready, the third battalion under Captain Benteen sprang into saddle, and taking a direction almost at right angles with that taken by the other two, we were all racing madly away for the front. Apparently by intuition, Captain Benteen divined that the Indians were making for what was known as Cañon Creek.

Ten minutes' ride and we popped over the top of the divide, and there, sure enough, were the Indians. They seemed to be bunched together a mile or two away, and were pushing forward as fast as they possibly could for the mouth of the cañon. It did not take an expert strategist to decide that unless we reached the cañon in advance of them, they would escape us entirely. Slacking only long enough to close up his command, Captain Benteen moved forward, flankers were thrown out toward the bluffs and the race was on in earnest.

On we went at a mad gallop. The Indians seemed to divine our purpose and redoubled their efforts. For a few moments it was doubtful which would win. An instant later and our flankers were assailed with a murderous fire from the bluffs, and we realized that an advance-party of the Indians were in the cañon ahead of us. The fire was so fierce that our men were compelled to draw away from the hills and rejoin the main body of the battalion. It was apparent, now, that our only hope lay in heading off the main body, which was by this time dangerously near the entrance to the pass.

On we galloped and a little later, sheltered from the enemy on the bluffs, we were dismounting in a deep ravine. Our loss so far had been only two men. Leaving our horses in charge of the horse holders, we scrambled up the bank, deployed as skirmishers and were soon hotly engaged. In the meantime, so far as we could see, the other two battalions, as dismounted skirmishers, were moving up the valley, keeping up a running fight with the Indians. Just about this time up came Lieutenant Otis with his "jackass" battery. Pushing well out to the front he opened fire on the enemy, apparently doing considerable damage. By this time the first and second battalions had joined us and the fight was raging fiercely, the Indians gradually drawing into the cañon in spite of our efforts to restrain them. The first and second battalions had been pushed out toward the hills, and from the incessant firing in that direction we knew they had their hands full.

A flank movement was ordered and the men of the third battalion hurried to their horses, mounted and moved out of the sheltering ravine. Urging their tired steeds into a gallop they pushed up the valley at right angles with the old line of battle and toward a narrow cañon, the plan being apparently to push through this, swing around to the right, and then coöperate with the other battalions in checking the advance of the enemy into the cañon. Strange to say not a shot was fired at us.

On we went at a swinging gallop and in a few moments entered the mouth of the cañon and were just at its narrowest part when, without an instant's warning, a dozen or more rifle-shots rang out from the cliffs on our right, and the bullets zipped madly past our ears and buried themselves in the banks on the farther side of the cañon. We at the head of the column put spurs to our horses and were soon out of range.

For a short time the men in the rear, taken unawares, came near losing their heads; in fact, one or two of the recruits did make a mad dash for the shelter of a ravine, but Captain French coming up with M Troop checked any disorder, and with a mad cheer the men rushed up the steep hillside, some mounted, some dismounted, in a wild effort to reach the enemy. The head of the column soon rejoined the charging lines, and a few moments later we stood on the top of the plateau, but not an Indian was in sight.

We remained here for a few moments to regain our breath and permit the men to bring up their horses from below. To our unbounded surprise, when we "took stock" of our casualties, we found that, aside from one man severely wounded and one horse killed and another stampeded, no damage had been done.

Reforming ranks, we moved cautiously across the plateau where, leaving our horses, we crept forward through the grass and sage-brush until we could peer down into the valley below us. In a ravine some three or four hundred yards from where we were we could see some thirty or forty Indians huddled together, evidently in a conference of some sort. To bring our carbines to the front, draw bead on the nearest savage and blaze away was but the work of an instant. When the smoke cleared away all we could see were two flying Indians galloping madly down the valley, their moccasined heels playing a lively tattoo on their ponies' ribs. Down in the ravine we could see a number of inanimate forms and struggling ponies, showing that our aim had not been altogether faulty.

Our horses were now brought up, and with skirmishers thrown forward and well out on either flank we made our way cautiously down the steep hillside. Scarcely were we in the valley when the Indians again opened fire on us from the bluffs on the opposite side of the valley and rendered our position open to decided objections. Moving up the valley some distance we dismounted behind the shelter of a projecting ledge and engaged the enemy whenever opportunity offered.

Being desirous of ascertaining more regarding the movements of the Indians a non-commissioned officer and a couple of men were instructed to creep to the top of the bluffs and secrete themselves as best they could, keep a sharp lookout for the enemy and report any decided advance. Very reluctantly, apparently, the men turned their horses over to their comrades, and, carbine in hand, left the shelter of the friendly ridge, and dodging, creeping and running they made their way across the narrow valley and clambered up the sides of the steep bluff.

It was now late in the afternoon, and the chill September winds were whistling across the bleak hilltops in a manner suggestive of warm fires and overcoats. Sheltered from sight by a friendly rock or two the men crouched there in the cold, every eye intently scanning the surrounding country for a sign of the approach of the enemy, every nerve on the alert for the faintest intimation of danger, and though an occasional redskin could be seen on the distant hilltops and an occasional bullet would go whizzing past or flatten itself on the rocks in front of them, the enemy did not seem disposed to make a closer acquaintance.

Soon the sun sank behind the adjacent hills; a few moments later the bugles sounded the "Recall," and the men of the battalion were hurrying to their horses. The way the little detachment slid down the hill to join them might not have been strictly tactical, but it accomplished the desired result. Half an hour later we were in camp near the first and second battalions. We unsaddled and tried to make out a meal on the scrapings of our haversacks, but the results were far from satisfactory. Over at the hospital the surgeons were busy at their tasks, and the camp was soon quiet and peaceable.

We had learned that there was to be an advance in the morning, so that we were not surprised when at half past four a large detachment of Crows, who had joined us during the night, saddled and soon disappeared up the cañon. In a short time the camp was astir, and leaving our wounded in care of General Howard's division, which was to remain behind, we went up the valley in the wake of the Crows. For a mile or more our way lay up the gradually narrowing valley, then the trail turned abruptly to the right and soon disappeared midst the gullies, ravines and cañons with which the hillsides were seamed. The farther we advanced, the more clearly we realized that it would have been utterly impossible for us to have forced our way through here against even fifty well-armed Indians. The narrow trail surrounded by overhanging ledges, flanked by deep gorges, towering peaks and bottomless gullies, made a passage almost impassable in face of a determined enemy.

After an hour or so of hard climbing, the summit was reached, and before us, stretching away for miles, was the broad, rolling prairie. Far away on the horizon we could catch an occasional glimpse of the Crows, who were apparently eager for a fight. All through the long afternoon we pushed forward with scarcely a halt. Shortly after noon a courier came back with word that our allies were engaged with the enemy some miles ahead. Our jaded horses were spurred on, a gleam shot across the bronzed faces of the troopers as their carbines were swung within easy reach. But it was no use, our horses were not equal to the strain, and after a few miles were suffered to resume their old gait.

Late in the afternoon we came up with our Crows, who with some Shoshones and Bannocks of Howard's command, had kept up a running fight with the enemy most of the day, and several scalps and a considerable number of ponies attested the fact that they had not had entirely the worst of it.

Tired out and hungry, we at last went into camp on the banks of a small creek. Our rations were exhausted and none in sight; still men must eat to live, but what? Evidently the men were not long in making up their mind. A visit to a neighboring ravine, two or three muffled shots, a rush of soldiers, and fifteen minutes later hundreds of tiny camp-fires were blazing along the banks, and the men with much joking and laughter were making themselves acquainted with good grass-fed pony steaks and rib roasts. Terrible! Well, perhaps it would seem so now, but at that time we thought we had never tasted sweeter meat.

The following morning we made a breakfast on the remainder of our pony meat, and after a hard day's march went into camp on the banks of the Mussel Shell. Our stock of pony meat was exhausted and that night we made a supper on "choke cherries" and the red, tart "buffalo berries" which lined the banks of the river in every direction. Hungry, tired and discouraged, it was not a good-natured crowd to say the least, but officers and men were on an equal footing. As time went on conditions did not improve at all. For several days we pushed ahead on the trail until we reached a point where it divided into innumerable smaller trails and there, so far as our regiment was concerned, the pursuit was abandoned and the command headed for Carroll on the

Missouri River, to replenish our supplies from the boats that had succeeded in making their way to that point.

Scarcely had we reached this point when news came that the Indians had crossed the Missouri at or near Cow Island and were advancing to the British line as fast as their ponies could take them. Leaving behind all dismounted men and men with unserviceable horses, the regiment was put across the river and hurried off on the trail of the enemy. General Howard's command was rushed on board waiting steamers and pushed up the river for the purpose of following the trail of the Indians wherever it might lead.

CHAPTER FOURTEEN

Anecdotes of Chief Joseph taken from the *New York Sun* of September 24, 1904

WITH the death of Chief Joseph, the famous leader of the Nez Percés, the United States has lost its most celebrated Indian. Joseph, since the death of Red Cloud and Sitting Bull, has been the most discussed American Indian. He was the last of the great warrior chiefs. Descendant of a long line of fighters, chieftain, since early manhood, of the Nez Percé tribe, and followed with constant devotion by his dwindling people, Chief Joseph was the last Indian leader who dared to put up a real fight against civilization; and in his desperate Waterloo he put up a fight that gave Gen. Nelson A. Miles and Gen. O. O. Howard all they could do to nab him and crush him till he grimly buried the hatchet. Chief Joseph it was who, when the United States took away the reservation given him and his people by grant, brandished a defiant fist and after years of peace dragged the Government into one last fierce struggle between red and white, and the old chief came out of it blue, but silent. When he took up the cause of his little band again it was with the diplomacy of a vanquished man, beaten by a civilization which finally landed him in a half-dollar show at Madison Square Garden. This was a year ago, after New

York society had fondled the old chief without awakening in him any enthusiasm. Now that Chief Joseph is dead, the mantle of his diluted power falls to his son, Flo-Cut, of a generation which knows little of the old-time warfare.

Red Cloud, perhaps, was the most famous of latter-day Indians. From the time of Red Cloud's death Joseph typified the Indian nation, for he was the last of the really great chiefs. No one knows how old he was, but he is believed to have approached fourscore. He died near Spokane, in the little reservation set by for his tribe after his Waterloo in the Bear's Paw Mountains, in the Yellowstone, in 1877.

For twenty-five years Chief Joseph stayed among his people quietly, living peacefully in the reservation mapped out for them near Spokane, and making only one long journey away, when he visited New York at the time of the Grant celebration in 1897. To General Miles, who afterward became his close friend, and who always calls him "The Napoleon of Indians," Joseph had said: "From where the sun now stands I fight no more against the whites." And his word was kept.

But a little over a year ago the Indians grew suspicious of the near-approaching homes of the whites, and the old chief, stung by the fear of another order to "move on," journeyed to Washington to petition the President to regrant them the Wallowa Valley in Oregon. But official deeds of right and the long unquestioned holding of property by white settlers in the Oregon Valley made intricate difficulties loom up on the legal horizon, and Chief Joseph finally dropped his plea. It is thought that General Miles, his victor and his champion, was chiefly instrumental in persuading the old chief that he and his people would be safe in their Washington home, where he died Thursday, September 22, 1904.

The chief's first visit to New York, in 1897, was in the nature of a tribute to the man who had granted his tribe the reservation afterward wrested from them. Joseph had gone to Washington on business, and General Miles suggested to him that he go to New York and join the Grant celebration. The old chief, however, was too poor to take the additional trip, though he said he would like to, and when he did come it was as the guest of Colonel Cody, or, as he was invariably known to the chief, Buffalo Bill.

Chief Joseph participated in the parade at the dedication of Grant's Tomb, and at this time much discussion was caused by a report that he had refused to ride near General Howard. In line with the talk caused by this alleged action there was a revival of the controversy in regard to the amount of credit relatively due to Miles and Howard for the victory over the chief in the Yellowstone so many years before.

While in New York on this visit the big chief stayed at the Astor House, and he appeared there in full regalia, shortening the breath of the less *outré* guests. He wore his enormous head-dress, his most astonishing mark of distinguishment, and it caused more craning of Astor House necks than anything else about him. Joseph, however, wasn't at all daunted, and had his own opinion about some New York arrangements of the head, though he didn't say anything to indicate this until one afternoon in an Indian exhibition camp in South Brooklyn, where he had gone to rest after he had looked at New York till he was tired.

Here he was visited by a young woman who was dressed to impress and had a store of slated questions to ask.

"Did you ever scalp anybody ?" she inquired. Chief Joseph pondered a moment and then turned to the interpreter. "Tell her," he said, pointing at the combination aviary and garden on her head, "that I have nothing in my collection as fine as that."

When he returned to New York again he took a trip to the Fifth Avenue Hotel with two or three of his admirers and had his first experience with a modern bar. A fat whisky glass was procured and filled to the brim. The chief, with his usual taciturnity, lifted the glass and swallowed its contents with one wonderful gulp.

When, a year ago, he came East for the second time, he was entertained at the White House and also in the Washington home of General and Mrs. Miles, and a little later he came on to New York. His utter taciturnity always made it impossible to know whether he was pleased with anything or not, but his voluntary trip to the metropolis on this visit seemed to indicate that he had enjoyed his first experience. Now he was made a temporary pet in society, and later astonished his entertainers by consenting to join Cummins's Indian Congress and Life on the Plains during that show's exhibition at Madison Square Garden. After it was over he returned to his reservation, and remained on it till he exchanged it for the happy hunting-grounds.

Chief Joseph was famous for his face and figure. He was tall, straight as an arrow and wonderfully handsome, his features being as clear-cut as chiseled marble. He never spoke a word of English, but some of his sayings, translated, have become famous. He used to say: "Look twice at a two-faced man"; "Cursed be the hand that scalps the reputation of the dead"; "The eye tells what the tongue would hide"; "Fire water courage ends in trembling fear"; "Big name often stands on small legs"; "Finest fur may cover toughest meat"; "When you get the last word with an echo you may do so with a squaw."

Part II

The Modoc War

CHAPTER ONE

In the Land of Burnt Out Fires

A Tragedy of the Far Northwest

By Dr. Brady

THE most costly war in which the United States ever engaged, considering the number of opponents, occurred in the winter of 1872–73 in the lava-beds of Oregon. Fifty Modoc * Indians, under the leadership of one Kientpoos — commonly known as Captain Jack, held that pedregal against overwhelming numbers of regular soldiers upon whom they inflicted defeat after defeat with little loss to themselves. They were not captured until treachery had played its maleficent part. To understand this tremendous drama a knowledge of the first act is essential.

In September, 1852, an emigrant train, comprising sixty-five men, women and children, was making its way northward into the lake region of southern Oregon.

The California-Oregon trail led between Lower Klamath and Tule Lakes. Huge bluffs several hundred feet high approached nearly the shore of Tule Lake, leaving a narrow road between the cliffs and the water. There the emigrant party mentioned was overwhelmed by Modoc Indians led by old Schonchin. The Modocs

* According to some etymologies, the word means a stranger.

closed both ends of the trail and attacked from the bluffs. The settlers fought bravely, but to no avail. Those not killed were captured and tortured to death with every device of savage malignity. One man, desperately wounded, and left for dead, escaped to tell the tale. Two girls of twelve and fourteen were spared. The massacre of Bloody Point long remained a ghastly memory on the frontier.

This affair was the culmination of a series of unparalleled atrocities. The magnitude of this latest massacre, however, begot stern determination for revenge. One Ben Wright, a man of influence and standing in California, led a body of volunteers in pursuit of the Modocs. The Indians eluded him, and he was unable to bring them to a stand in order to crush them. Failing that he resorted to a stratagem — which was treachery of the deepest dye. He sent messengers to the Modocs with propositions of peace. They agreed to his proposition, that Schonchin and his principal warriors should meet the settlers for a peace conference at a point on the shore of the lake across from Bloody Point, both sides being unarmed. There was to be an armistice, each party was to come and go freely, unharmed of the other. It is alleged that Wright mixed strychnine with food which he prepared for a peace feast, hoping to poison the whole party. Two reasons are given for the failure of this enterprise. One, the Modocs refused to eat; two, the strychnine proved to be innocuous.*

At any rate, out of conflicting stories one thing is clear. Some forty-six Modocs attended this conference. Schonchin was kept from it by illness, but his sub-chiefs and principal men were present. Wright's men were

* Perhaps the person who sold it may have tricked the purchaser, being unwilling to further such wholesale assassination.

Modoc Braves on the War Path

From the collection of J. W. Redington

armed, the Modocs were not. Giving a signal, Wright whipped out his pistol and shot the nearest Indian dead. In five minutes after the firing began forty-one guests of this Red Abencerrages feast lay dead. Five escaped, among them the younger brother of the chief, named Schonchin John.

It is true the Modocs had been guilty of numberless outrages. They had waged war in a cruel and unjustifiable manner, from the civilized standpoint, although quite in consonance with their savage customs. The settlers were justly exasperated, yet there was no excuse for the ineffable treachery of assassination under a flag of truce. Yet public opinion, highly wrought as it was, fully sustained Wright and his men. The chief murderer was acclaimed a popular hero and was subsequently made Indian Agent — for having shown that he possessed qualities which enabled him to deal successfully with the red men, I presume! He was killed by the Indians a few years later.

The lesson was a severe one to the Indians. The power of the Modocs was broken. They remained defiant, but their capacities for further mischief were greatly impaired. They remembered the transaction, however, and it bore bitter fruit in the end.

In 1864 a treaty was made with the Modocs by which they agreed to go upon the reservation, which had been set apart for the La-la-kes, or Klamaths, and themselves. The treaty was not ratified by the United States Senate until 1869. One or two minor alterations were made in it before the ratification, and the Modocs saw in these changes an excuse for complying with its provisions. The main body of them under old Schonchin finally accepted the treaty and went on the reservation. Captain Jack, one of the head chiefs, with a band numbering about a score of warriors with their women and children, Curly-headed, Doctor, one of his sub-chiefs, Hooker Jim, and others, with small groups of followers, proved recalcitrant. They were finally induced to go on the reservation, there to meet with bitter persecution from the malicious and overbearing Klamaths who greatly exceeded them in numbers.

Jack protested to the Indian agents who, instead of requiring the Klamaths to leave the Modocs in peace, moved them from one part of the reservation to another. This happened several times until the Modocs finally grew desperate. They refused to stay on the reservation any longer and migrated to their old home in the Lost River region, a country teeming with game and fish. Having accepted the treaty they had no right there, of course, and the section was rapidly filling with settlers who resented their presence. But they had been hardly dealt with; the Government had given them no protection on the reservation. They had been moved from pillar to post, and had never remained long enough in one stay to make a crop — even the poor crop of the Indian. Wherever they had been sent the Klamaths had followed them and had made life a burden for them. No other reservation was proposed to them. They naturally went back to the land of their fathers.

It cannot be denied that they were a drunken, dissolute, disreputable lot. Just a sordid, squalid, degraded band of homeless, wretched Indians. They frightened the women and children, and worried and annoyed the settlers, although there is no evidence that they resorted to open violence. The situation, however, was plainly impossible. Something had to be done.

The commander of the Department was Gen. Edward S. Canby, a soldier of forty years' experience, distin-

guished in three wars, familiar with Indian affairs,
well-disposed toward his red brethren, a just and
upright man of the highest qualities. The matter could
not have been committed to better hands. Asserting that
the Modocs had been unjustly and harshly treated, he
deprecated the employment of force against them. He
hoped to effect a settlement of the difficulties by peaceable methods. In spite of every effort the trouble grew,
until it culminated in a formal request from the local
Indian Agent upon Maj. John Green of the First Cavalry, who commanded at Fort Klamath, made at the
instance of the Interior Department, that the Modocs
be put on the reservation, "peaceably if you can, forcibly
if you must." Major Green despatched Capt. James
Jackson with some forty troopers to Jack's camp on
Lost River, a few miles above Tule Lake.

Jackson had orders to arrest Captain Jack and several
of his companions for the murder of an Indian medicine-man whom Jack had shot on the reservation because he had failed to cure the chief's ailing children
— a summary way to pay a doctor's bill! Jack and
Schonchin John with fourteen men and their women and
children were encamped on the west side of the river, a
deep, rapid stream some three hundred feet broad. On
the other side were Hooker Jim and Curly-headed
Doctor, with fourteen warriors and others. Twelve
citizens had been apprised of Captain Jackson's movement, and they came down on the east side to intercept
any Indians who might retreat across it, thus cooperat-
ing with the soldiers. Leaving Fort Klamath on the
morning of November 28, 1872, after a hard all-night
march through a pouring rain, Jackson reached the
Indian camp at daybreak on the morning of the 29th.

In his own expressive language he "jumped the

camp." The Indians, unsuspicious, knew nothing of his presence until they were ordered to surrender. They all came out of their tepees except Jack, and a parley began. The soldiers ordered the Modocs to disarm. One particularly bold savage, named Scar-faced Charley, whose father had been killed by the whites — lassoed and hung before his son's eyes — refused to give up his weapon, and others followed his example. Jackson ordered Lieutenant Boutelle to take a squad of men and arrest him. Boutelle started toward the Indians and the battle began. It is asserted that Scar-faced Charley fired first, but it is probable that the officer and the savage fired simultaneously. At any rate, the soldiers poured in a volley, the Indians snatched up their guns and returned it, and then ran to the hills seeking concealment in the timbers and undergrowth on the bank of the river, from which they stoutly engaged the soldiers.

At the first shot Captain Jack came out of his tent and took charge of the defense. Meanwhile, the citizens engaged the party on the other side of the river and were badly worsted. Captain Jackson lost one man killed and seven wounded. Three citizens were shot down. In all fifteen Indians were killed, some of them being women and children. After fighting for about an hour, Jackson became convinced of the impossibility of whipping the Indians with his small force. Boats were at hand and the troops withdrew across the river. Leaving his wounded under a strong guard at Crawley's Ranch, Jackson recrossed, found the Indians gone, burned their camp and retired. Meanwhile, Hooker Jim's band had also escaped.

Jack retired post-haste to the lava-beds. He molested no one on his retreat. Hooker Jim and his followers killed everybody they met, in all some seventeen settlers. They did not molest any women. After this bloody

Attack on Modoc Camp by Major Jackson—First Blow

raid they joined Captain Jack in the lava-beds. Col. Frank Wheaton, commander of the district, repaired to the scene of the action at once. The nearest available troops (detachments of the First Cavalry and Twenty-first Infantry) were sent to him together with two companies of Oregon militia and one from California. In all, his force numbered over four hundred men.

On Hot Creek, an affluent of Lower Klamath Lake, another band of Modocs dwelt. Some of these broke away and joined the defiant in the lava-beds, so that Jack's force was increased to fifty warriors and about one hundred and fifty women and children. They were well supplied with ammunition and food. They boasted that with the natural advantages of the lava-beds they could whip a thousand soldiers, a statement which was literally true, but which was laughed to scorn at the time. The fight they put up, whatever be their character, awakened the admiration of the world.

These lava-beds are among the most peculiar natural formations on the continent. They are a mass of volcanic débris included in a territory about eight miles long and four miles wide. The formation is thus described by Captain Lydecker of the United States Engineers, who surveyed and mapped it.

"They present the appearance on first view of an immense sage-bush plain, with no obstructions to easy movement in every direction. A closer examination, however, develops the fact that the plain is broken at irregular intervals by sections of low, rocky ridges. The ridges are not isolated, but occur in groups, and form a perfect network of obstructions, admirably adapted to a defense by an active enemy; they seldom rise to a height of ten feet above the bed, and are, as a rule, split open at the top, giving thus continuous cover along their crests."

Transversal crevices furnished excellent communication through which the Indians were enabled to pass from one ridge to another without the least exposure. Only a few of these cross passages and unseen positions, sufficient to satisfy the requirements of free communication, were left open by the Indians in that series of ridges which made up "Jack's Stronghold." The rest were in all cases blockaded by rolling in heavy stones.

The Modocs were familiar with every foot of it. None of the soldiers and few of the settlers had ever entered it; certainly, none of them had explored it. The ridge formation was not continuous. It broke out in spots separated by wide open places comparatively level, although the ground was everywhere terribly rocky and uneven. These open places, however, were cut up by deep, impassable ravines and pitted with holes or pockets. There was no way to tell the existence of a ravine or pocket, until one stood on the very brink of it.

During the campaign there were numerous small skirmishes for the description of which space is lacking. On the morning of January 17, 1873, a heavy fog lying low on the pedregal, the first effort at dislodgment began. The troops started out gleefully, shouting that they would have "Modoc steak" for breakfast. "A more enthusiastic, jolly set of regulars and volunteers I never had the honor to command. If the Modocs will only try to make good their boast to whip a thousand soldiers all will be satisfied," wrote Colonel Wheaton, two days before.

The soldiers fought all day and scarcely saw a Modoc. They stumbled blindly forward over rocks, ranging in size from a cobble to a church, with points like needles and edges like razors. From the most unexpected places would come a spit of fire, followed by the crack of a rifle or musket. Somebody generally received the bullet. The soldiers fired volleys at the ridges and did not hit a single Indian. Their courage was of the highest order. They scrambled forward over the rocks, blazing away at every rifle flash, fearlessly exposing themselves, traversing impassable ravines, in a desperate endeavor to come at close quarters with the enemy, and all to no avail. The Modocs had made good their boast!

When evening came the troops withdrew to their camps on the shores of the lake — they had attacked the stronghold from both sides — utterly discomfited, with a loss of nine killed and thirty wounded. The infantry battalion under Major Mason lost nearly one-fourth of its strength, the loss among the volunteers was trifling. Captain Perry and Lieutenants Kyle and Roberts were wounded. If the Modocs had been better shots the loss would have been vastly greater. Thereafter, Colonel Wheaton stated that he would require at least a thousand men with mortars and other artillery to dislodge the little Modoc band from its position. He and other experienced officers declared that they had never seen a position so thoroughly defensible, so impossible of successful attack, as the lava-beds. The soldiers, no longer cheerful, were in a state of complete exhaustion. Their shoes were cut to ribbons, their uniforms in rags, their ammunition expended, their spirits depressed by the hardships and struggles of the long and fruitless day. Wheaton had done his best with the means at his command. Neither he nor his men had dreamed of the difficulties of the situation.

He was superseded, however, and Col. A. C. Gillem, First Cavalry, was ordered into the field. Reinforcements were hurried to him until the thousand men required were present. General Canby then took command in person. It was thought best, before proceeding further, to try the effect of negotiations. A Peace Commission was created charged with their conduct. From a humanitarian standpoint there can be no question as to the propriety of this course. To the Indian an offer to negotiate is a confession of weakness. The Modocs concluded that the white soldiers were afraid of them.

The United States demanded that the Indians go back on the reservation and that the men, headed by Curly-headed Doctor and Hooker Jim, who had killed the settlers after Captain Jackson's unsuccessful "jump" of the Modoc camp, should be surrendered for trial as murderers. It is true they had shot down inoffensive men, yet the first act of hostility had come from the soldiers and the little band of settlers who had attacked them on Lost River. Jack had not participated in this slaughter, yet to have given up these men would have been a lasting disgrace in his eyes. He refused to surrender them, naturally. He demanded a complete amnesty and the withdrawal of the troops as his conditions of peace. He professed willingness to go upon the reservation, but he wanted to choose his own. Several localities that he suggested were regarded as impracticable. Finally, he proposed the lava-beds. Such a thing could not be thought of. The United States was not ready to name any definite reservation. They offered to place Jack and his people on Angel Island in San Francisco Bay, and thereafter to transport them to some suitable reservation as might be desired.

Jack promptly refused this proposition. The Lost River country was his home and he wanted to stay there. For one thing the wily chief was playing for time. The negotiations were terribly protracted. Meanwhile, he had tried in vain to induce the other Indians to join forces with him, especially the main body of the Modocs on the reservation under old Schonchin. Failing in that, he was inclined toward peace, ultimately, if he could get it on his own terms. The majority of his warriors were clamorous for war. Boston Charley professed to be able to make medicine which would protect the Modocs from the soldiers' bullets. He pointed out the fact that none of them had been killed in the recent attack as proof of his claims. Jack was a man of much native shrewdness and he realized what the end of the little handful of Indians would be. He stood out for a settlement as best he could. There were scenes of intense dramatic interest in the lava-beds. Finally, the warriors put a woman's hat and shawl on their chief and called him a squaw. This insult, and his inability to agree upon anything definite with the commissioners, broke down his determination. He tore off the offensive garments and declared that if the band wanted war they should have it with a vengeance.

The first step resolved upon was the murder of the commissioners and the commanders of the soldiers. The commission had been variously constituted at different times, but at present included General Canby, whose function was of an advisory nature; Colonel Gillem; the Rev. Dr. Eleazer Thomas, a Methodist minister, a man of the deepest piety and widely known as a friend of the Indians; the Hon. A. B. Meacham, formerly an Indian Agent, who was also famed for his just treatment of these very Modocs who knew him well, and Mr. L. S. Dyer, another Indian Agent of character and standing.

The Modoc stronghold was in the center of the north line of the lava-beds, about three-quarters of a mile from

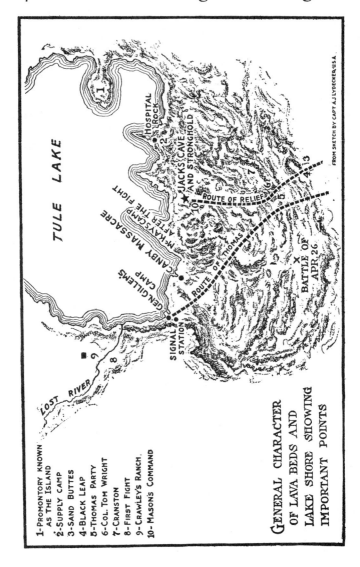

GENERAL CHARACTER
OF LAVA BEDS AND
LAKE SHORE SHOWING
IMPORTANT POINTS

1-PROMONTORY KNOWN
   AS THE ISLAND
2-SUPPLY CAMP
3-SAND BUTTES
4-BLACK LEAP
5-THOMAS PARTY
6-COL. TOM WRIGHT
7-CRANSTON
8-FIRST FIGHT
9-CRAWLEY'S RANCH.
10-MASON'S COMMAND

TULE LAKE

LOST RIVER

FROM SKETCH BY CAPT A.J.LYDECKER.U.S.A.

HOSPITAL ROCK

JACKS CAVE AND STRONGHOLD

ROUTE OF RELIEF

McKAYS CAMP
AFTER THE FIGHT

CANBY MASSACRE

GEN GILLEM'S CAMP

ROUTE OF THOMAS

SIGNAL STATION

BATTLE OF
APR 26

Tule Lake. Jack had roughly fortified his position by joining several ravines by rudely made stone walls, and by filling some of the exits and entrances with huge boulders, rolled into the crevices with prodigious labor.

On the east side of the lava-beds near the lake front, about two miles from the stronghold, Major Mason's men were posted. About the same distance on the west, General Canby had his headquarters with the main body under Colonel Gillem. About three-quarters of a mile from headquarters the peace tent had been pitched under the shadow of a bluff, a short distance from the lake shore. Meacham and others had visited Jack in the lava-beds during the negotiations, and various Modocs had returned these visits to Gillem's and Mason's camps. There had been a rather free exchange of courtesies and calls.

After he had decided upon treachery, Jack requested that the five commissioners with Riddle, a squaw-man, who had married a Modoc woman named Toby, and who acted as interpreter, should meet an equal number of the Modocs at the council tent for final conference, both parties to come unarmed. The meeting was agreed upon, but before it took place it was reported from the signal-station on the bluffs back of Gillem's camp, from which the peace tent was in full view, that, in addition to the six Modocs who were of the council party, some twenty armed warriors were concealed in near by ravines. The commissioners refused to go to the meeting. They were not surprised at this evidence of bad faith.

Undeterred by this another meeting was arranged under the same conditions. So confident was Riddle, an unusually intelligent man, that treachery was intended, that he remonstrated personally with each member of the commission. Meacham and Dyer agreed with him that the meeting should be declined, and urged the two officers and Dr. Thomas to refuse it. General Canby realized the danger. He did not doubt that the Indians desired to murder the commissioners. He did not believe, however, that they would be so short-sighted as to commit an act which would inevitably bring summary punishment upon them. In any event he felt that it was his duty to leave no stone unturned to bring about a peaceable solution of the difficulty. In this conclusion Dr. Thomas agreed. He said the whole matter was in God's hands and that, if necessary, he would go alone to the meeting.

Meacham was chairman of the commission. Since the others looked at it in that way, he bravely decided against his better judgment and agreed to go. He felt that without its chairman the conference would be a failure. It was his duty to accompany the others; his honor would not permit him to withdraw from danger that they were willing to face. Like considerations influenced Dyer. Therefore, the meeting was arranged for eleven o'clock on the morning of April 11, 1873.

Riddle demanded that the commissioners go with him to the bedside of Colonel Gillem, who was too ill to go with them, and he there made a formal protest. He, too, would have backed out except for an unwillingness that any man should say that he was afraid to go where other men went.

Jack had sent two Indians, Bogus Charley and Boston Charley, to make the final arrangements. Dr. Thomas had entertained these Indians at his tent the night before. Piloted by them, he and General Canby on foot started for the peace tent. A short distance behind them Meacham, Dyer, and Riddle followed on horseback with the faithful Toby. The signal-station reported that

Colonel John Green, U. S. A.

Colonel W. H. Boyle, U. S. A.

General E. R. S. Canby

General Frank Wheaton,
U. S. A.

Officers of the Modoc War

there were no warriors concealed in the vicinity and that the only persons present were Jack and five other Indians and that they had no rifles with them. These Indians were Schonchin, Black Jim, Hooker Jim, Ellen's Man and Shacknasty Jim.*

A fire had been built and stones piled around to form a council ring. It was noticed that the tent was between the council ring and the signal-station on the bluffs, concealing the council from the observation of the officers. The commissioners, to their great dismay, at once saw that the Indians were armed with revolvers. Beneath coats and shirts which they wore, the butts of the weapons were plainly visible. But two of the commissioners were armed. Before they started Meacham had suggested that each of the commissioners carry a concealed weapon.

General Canby and Dr. Thomas positively refused. Each had given his word of honor to come unarmed and that word he would not break. They pointed out that the suspicions of the Indians were highly excited and that the least evidence of bad faith would probably result in breaking off the negotiations. Mr. Meacham then proposed that in case affairs looked threatening they should immediately agree to any propositions made by the Indians in order to get away. General Canby and Dr. Thomas again refused. They declined to promise anything which they could not perform. Dr. Thomas said, "I will be a party to no deception under any circumstances; this matter is in the hands of God." General Canby said, "I have dealt with Indians for thirty years. I have never deceived an Indian and I will never

* The curious names of these Modocs were given them by white men for various trivial reasons: Jack was called Captain because of a fondness for brass buttons and uniforms, Hooker Jim had worked for a man named Hooker, Boston Charley was very light colored, like the "Bostons," *i. e.*, the soldiers, etc.

consent to it — to any promise that cannot be fulfilled." Meacham and Dyer gave up after that. Before they started some one gave each of these two a small derringer pistol, single shot, which they slipped in their pockets.

General Canby passed cigars to the savages and then the speech-making began. The council was short, but full of excitement. The Indians were insolent in their behavior and extravagant in their demands. In spite of the endeavor of the commissioners so to group themselves that they were mingled with the Indians they found the Modocs gathered on one side of the fire and themselves on the other. During the council another white man approached, but at Jack's request he was sent back. At one period Hooker Jim got up and took Mr. Meacham's overcoat from the pommel of his saddle and put it on with an insulting remark. Thinking to pacify him, Meacham gave him his hat also with a careless jest.

Everybody knew now what were the intentions of the Indians. There was nothing then to be done but brave it out. No one exhibited the least sign of fear. After perhaps an hour's conference the demands of the Indians culminated in a peremptory request for the immediate removal of the soldiers, which was proffered by Schonchin John. Captain Jack had withdrawn from the council fire a moment or two previously. He came back just as Schonchin John finished his speech and Canby rose to reply. The General's answer was a prompt, unqualified negative. The soldiers were there and there they would stay until the thing was settled one way or the other. Schonchin John again began speaking vehemently. Before he had finished two Indians, Barncho and Sloluck, suddenly appeared from the cover of the rocks, each with his arms full of guns. At this Jack stepped from behind Dyer's horse, pistol in hand. He spoke one guttural word, "At-tux!" (All ready!) and as he did so snapped the pistol in Canby's face. The revolver missed fire. The General started toward the Modoc, but Jack recocked the pistol with the barrel almost touching the old soldier and pulled the trigger. The bullet struck Canby under the eye. Dazed, he staggered back.

Dr. Thomas had been kneeling on one knee, his hand on Meacham's shoulder. He had just made an eloquent plea for peace. Boston Charley deliberately shot him through the breast. Schonchin shot Meacham while the others opened fire upon Dyer and Riddle. To each Indian had been apportioned a victim. Dyer had risen and was standing some few feet away from the fire. He and Riddle ran for their lives, hotly pursued by the Indians. Bullets cut the air about them. One grazed Dyer. Hooker Jim drew near to him. His pursuit was checked by a shot from Dyer's derringer. He and Riddle succeeded in escaping. Meacham snapped his pistol at Schonchin, wounding him slightly. He was instantly shot by half a dozen Indians, receiving five wounds.

Canby was shot twice more, once by Ellen's Man. Toby was knocked over by the butt of Sloluck's rifle and would have been killed had it not been for a threat of Scar-faced Charley, who said that he would shoot the first man who touched her. He was attached to Toby for some reason and was watching the scene from a hiding-place in easy range. General Canby had gone but a short distance when he was shot dead. Dr. Thomas, unable to move, raised himself on one arm, and put out his hand in faint protest, exclaiming:

"Don't shoot again, Charley. I am a dead man already."

"Damn ye," returned the Indian, who spoke English, "may be you believe next time what squaw tell you." He shot the dying man again and again until life was gone.

The Indians stripped Canby, Thomas, and Meacham, and Boston Charley started to scalp the latter who was thought to be dead. He had made a long cut in the head and prepared to tear away the scalp when Toby, to whom Mr. Meacham had been very kind, raised herself from the ground where she had been lying tremblingly awaiting her doom, and shouted with quick wit, "Soldiers are coming!" The murderers fled instantly to the lava-beds. The tragedy was over.*

While all this was going on another band of Indians had approached the camp of Colonel Mason on the east side and had requested a parley with him. The officer of the day, Lieut. Walter Sherwood, met them with

---

* In writing about the Modoc War I hope you will not get the two Thomases mixed. The other Thomas was Dr. Thomas, the Methodist preacher from Petaluma, who had been appointed a member of the Peace Commission of which Meacham was chairman, and who was butchered at the council tent. He made the mistake, in the absence of the chairman, of promising a committee of Modocs that the commission would go out and hold a talk with them the next day. Toby Riddle, the Modoc wife of Frank Riddle, warned them that they were to be killed, and from what I have heard from soldiers I should judge that Meacham did all he could to prevent the commission going out. When Meacham was superintendent of Indian Affairs for Oregon and Washington, he issued an order compelling all white men living on reservations with squaws either legally to marry them or get off the reserves. This resulted in Toby being made a legal wife and she always felt grateful to Meacham for it. Everybody said she made a good wife. She saved Meacham from being completely killed.

They used to illustrate the strength of commissary whisky in the army by telling that when Dr. Cabiness, contract surgeon and a very brave man, was reviving Meacham with the whisky, the latter refused to take it and said that he was a teetotaler and had taken the pledge. Cabiness replied, "Damn it, if that's the case, pry his teeth apart and pour canteen and all down him," which was done as nearly as possible. That kind of whisky is said to have had sufficiently strong reviving qualities to set equestrian statues of General Jackson cavorting around single-footed on their pedestals.— NOTE BY J. W. REDINGTON.

Tule Lake, Camp South, from the Signal Station, Tule Lake in the Distance

The Peace Commission's Tent, and Stone on which General Canby was Sitting when Shot

From the collection of General C. P. Egan

Lieut. W. H. Boyle. The Indians opened fire upon them at once. Sherwood was mortally wounded and Boyle escaped by the skin of his teeth. The plan had been for the Indians to kill all the commissioners and ranking officers in the belief that by so doing the soldiers would withdraw and their freedom would be achieved.

The cowardly attack on Lieutenant Sherwood was signaled from Mason's camp to the station on the bluff. Scarcely had the message been received when the officers there discovered that the peace commissioners had been attacked. Scrambling down the bluffs they burst into Colonel Gillem's tent with the dire news. The sound of the firing had been heard throughout the camp. The soldiers, without orders, sprang to arms, yet there were moments of unaccountable delay. The advance was not made promptly. There was some question as to Gillem's course later on. Finally, the several companies and troops went forward on the double quick. Sergeant Wooten, with twenty men of K Troop, First Cavalry, led the advance without orders. They arrived too late, of course. There was nothing to be done but bring back the dead bodies and the wounded Meacham. His life was despaired of, but he finally recovered.

It was plain now to every one that the Modocs must be subdued at whatever cost. Colonel Gillem and Major Mason attacked the lava-beds on the 14th. There were three days of fierce fighting exactly of the character of Wheaton's battle. This time the soldiers were reinforced by several mortars, which finally got the range of Jack's Stronghold and threw shell after shell into it. One of the shells did not explode. The Indians seized it and, their curiosity excited, tried to open it and find out what it was. One Indian attempted to draw the plug with his teeth. The shell blew up and killed several of the Indians. Convinced that his lair had become untenable on account of the artillery, Jack withdrew. For three days he had been cut off from the lake which was his only water-supply, the lava-beds being as dry as a bone.

The troops had surrounded the place, and on the morning of the 17th they moved forward to the final attack. There was some skirmishing by a rear-guard of Modocs, but the soldiers at last rushed the ridges that had been so gallantly defended against such heavy odds. They found the place deserted. An underground passage connected with the distant ravines had afforded the Modocs a way of escape. They were still somewhere in the maze of the lava-beds, but just where no one knew. The troops had lost eight killed and seventeen wounded. They found the bodies of three men and eight women in the Modoc stronghold.

On the 21st of April a party of soldiers with fifteen Warm Spring Indians, auxiliaries, eighty-five in all, under the command of Capt. Evan Thomas, with Lieuts. Albion Howe, Arthur Cranston, G. M. Harris, all of the Fourth Artillery, and Lieut. T. F. Wright of the Seventeenth Infantry, with Act.-Asst. Surg. B. G. Semig, was sent to the lava-beds to discover the location of the Indians. They were instructed to proceed cautiously and to avoid an engagement. These soldiers were from the Twelfth Infantry and the Fourth Artillery, the latter being used as infantry in the lava-beds and sometimes as cavalry in the open country, in this campaign.

They proceeded carefully with skirmishers thrown out on both sides, the Warm Spring Indians far on the flanks. By this time the soldiers had conceived a wholesome respect for their antagonists which almost amounted to fear. The ground was admirably adapted for surprise, and it was with difficulty that the flanking parties could be kept to their proper distance. They were constantly shrinking in toward the main body. They were not molested in their advance, however, and at noon halted for dinner.

They had stopped at the base of a sand-hill in comparatively open ground, with lava-beds several hundred yards distant on either side, and were quietly eating when a rifle-shot from one of the ravines, which two men had been directed to reconnoiter, gave the alarm. This shot was followed by a volley from the hidden enemy and a number of men fell. The officers, the non-commissioned officers and some of the veteran privates coolly ran to cover to some of the pits and ridges before mentioned and returned the fire. The sand-hill in front was charged by a detachment which occupied it, only to find that it was commanded by another hill to which the unseen enemy had retired. The place was a regular death-trap, and the Modocs got on both sides of the soldiers and coolly shot them down. The plain was alive with fire.

A panic took possession of some of the men, a panic which is remembered with shame by the Army of the United States to this day. Half of them turned and fled headlong, abandoning their officers and their braver comrades who disdained to fly. Every officer was killed or mortally wounded except the surgeon, who was desperately wounded in two places. The total loss was twenty-two killed and eighteen wounded. The cowards who fled reached the camp in safety. The Warm Spring Indians were scouting at the time, and being mistaken for Modocs by the troops, they were unable to succor them. These all escaped. Fortunately for some of the wounded who remained on the field, the nature of the ground was such that the Modocs could not come at them. They were found still alive by the rescuing party, which reached them from the main camp late in the evening. The Modocs had but twenty-one men in the field. None of them was hit.*

In the meantime Col. Jefferson C. Davis, a brilliant and energetic old soldier with a distinguished record, was appointed to the command with instructions to prosecute the campaign vigorously until it closed. He restored Colonel Wheaton to his place at once. He also set about restoring the somewhat shattered morale of the soldiers. He reorganized the troops, brought up supplies and reinforcements, and prepared to force the fighting.

The Indians finally separated, roughly speaking, into two bands. A portion remained with Captain Jack and the rest under Hooker Jim, and others withdrew. By a series of scientific and gradual approaches, by occupying the lava-beds just as the Indians had done, General Davis constantly tightened the cordon around the Modocs. The situation of the Indians had become exceedingly difficult. They had been forced away from their water-supply; their provisions and ammunition were running low; they were practically surrounded in the lava-beds with little hope of escape. Dissensions arose, as was natural in a body so loosely coherent and comprised of so many diverse and mutually

* General Davis thus comments on the battle in his report:

"An error was made by the officer in command in not pushing his skirmish-line further to the front and on the flanks before halting, but this mistake could have been easily and quickly remedied had the men, as a few did, stood by the officers and obeyed orders. This they did not do. The result was conspicuous cowardice on the part of the men who ran away, and conspicuous bravery and death on the part of the officers and men who stood. The lesson taught by this affair is that a great many of the enlisted men here are utterly unfit for Indian fighting of this kind, being only cowardly beef-eaters. My recommendation is, however, that they be kept here, trained, and made to fight. I shall take such steps while here as I think will insure this training."

independent elements. Finally, they decided to leave the lava-beds.

On the morning of the 10th of May Hasbrouck's light battery of the Fourth Artillery, mounted as cavalry, and two troops of the Fourth Cavalry were encamped on Sorass Lake on the west side of the pedregal. The Indians, who seemed to have temporarily reunited, made an attack upon this force. Captain Jack, clad in General Canby's uniform, led a company of thirty-three Modocs in a charge on the camp, while a detachment was absent for water. They succeeded in stampeding the horses and mules and for a time things looked serious. Hasbrouck, however, rallied his men, checked the advance, and, by a series of brilliant charges directly upon the lines the Modocs had established in the surrounding hills, cleared them out of the country, killed one man and — most important of all—captured twenty-four pack-animals, carrying most of the Indians' ammunition, all with a loss of but two killed and seven wounded. This was the first clean-cut defeat the Modocs had sustained, and proved conclusively that they could not fight the troops in the open.

After this the differences between the two parties of Modocs became permanent. They separated, left the vicinity of the lava-beds, and fled. A vigorous advance all along the line disclosed the fact that the Indians had abandoned their stronghold and were at last in the open. A hot pursuit was instituted in every direction. The first large party, numbering about a hundred, was captured on the 22nd of May after some hard marching, but Jack and his immediate following were still in the field.

Davis determined to use the leaders of the first party to effect the capture of the remainder. These Modocs saw the game was up and were willing to save their own lives by betraying the others. Hotly pursued by the soldiers, who were guided by the traitors, the remaining Modocs were gathered up in little bunches here and there, and on the 1st of June Jack was captured in Willow Creek Cañon by Captain Perry's troop. He had been literally run to earth by the cavalrymen. As he came out of the cañon and surrendered his gun, he sank to the ground exhausted, with the remark that his legs had given out.

General Davis made preparation to hang Jack and the other murderers of the commissioners out of hand. He was stopped by an order from Washington, and after considerable discussion as to the legality of the proceedings, upon the opinion of the Attorney-General, Captain Jack, Schonchin, Boston Charley, Black Jim, Barncho, and Sloluck were ordered for trial before a military commission. Hooker Jim, Bogus Charley, and Shacknasty Jim turned State's evidence. Ellen's Man had been killed. The charge was violation of the laws of war, attacking a peace commission under cover of a flag of truce. The prisoners were not represented by counsel. As Jack remarked, they had been unable to obtain any. The trial was fairly conducted, nevertheless. The testimony of the witnesses, both white and Indian, was strong against the prisoners. The captives asked these witnesses no questions. They called a few witnesses to the stand in their turn, and these only with the apparent object of establishing the fact that the Klamaths, their hereditary enemies, had urged and incited them to war, and had furnished the weapons and supplies to enable them to carry it on, all of which may possibly have been true, but none of which was material.

Jack made a speech, pitiful in its futility, in which he brought out one point that hostilities had commenced

Modoc War—Major Thomas's Command Defeated in
Lava Beds

by Captain Jackson's attack on his camp on Lost
River. Jack also stated that the Modocs who had betrayed him and turned State's evidence were the very
Modocs whom he had refused to surrender at the beginning of the war, and if he had done so there would
have been no trouble. It was also shown that these men
were the most guilty and that it was their insistence in
their desperation which had induced him and others to
commit the murders.

In closing, the Chief Advocate specifically acquitted
the prisoners of any participation in the murder of the
citizens after Captain Jackson's attack. The verdict was
guilty, and the punishment death by hanging.

Peace societies and earnest, intelligent, but misguided
individuals, some of them of great eminence, all over
the country, pleaded with the Government for a suspen-
sion or commutation of the sentence. Public agitation
rose to fever heat. The Government, however, declined
to interfere and stood firm in the case of the greater
culprits.

It was shown that Barncho and Sloluck were merely
tools of the others. President Grant, therefore, commut-
ed their sentences to imprisonment for life, but that was
all. In the case of the other four the sentence was carried out with due solemnity and all the forms of the law
at ten o'clock in the morning of Friday, October 3, 1873.

They were hanged in full view of the Klamaths and
their own women and children, who, from the stockade
in which they were confined, saw all that happened. The
prisoners met their death with calm fortitude. A wail of
anguish rose from the stockade, in which even the
stoical Klamaths joined when the trap was sprung and
the men swung in the air. Justice had had her innings.
The murder of the great general and of the devoted

missionary had been avenged. The dignity of the United States had been upheld.

It was right that Jack should die, but what might he not have said had he possessed the fluent tongue of some of his race, as he stood on that scaffold, looking southward toward that point where but twenty-one years before, when he was scarcely fourteen, Ben Wright had violated a flag of truce in the same way as that for which he was being punished, only to receive reward and promotion thereafter from his fellow-citizens? What must Schonchin John, who had escaped from that catastrophe, have felt as the noose was placed about his neck?

The history of the Modocs thereafter is unimportant. To the number of thirty-four men who had been in the lava-beds, five other men who had joined them, fifty-four women and sixty children, they were translated to a reservation at Baxter Springs, Kansas. To-day a handful survives.

In the war the Modocs lost twelve killed, four executed, one a suicide — all warriors, and an unknown number of women and children. The total loss of the white settlers and soldiers was one hundred and sixty-eight, of whom eighty-three were killed. The cost of the war was over half a million dollars. They say it takes a ton of lead to kill one soldier in battle: to put down these fifty Modocs about twelve hundred men were employed. Each Modoc accounted for three men and cost the United States Government over ten thousand dollars before he was himself killed or captured — a fearful price, indeed.

Insignificant people they were, but in their brief hour they managed to stamp themselves on the pages of history. The name of Captain Jack will not be forgotten, and the defense of which he was the central figure, in spite of his treachery, together with the desperate campaigning of the soldiers in the land of burnt out fires, is a story that will long be related. With all his faults, the rude Modoc chief had some of the high qualities that go to make a man. We can bury his vices in his unmarked grave and remember his virtues and his wrongs.

Note on the present status of Modocs furnished by the Department of the Interior.

This office is in receipt of your communication of the 10th instant, in which you state you are anxious to know the present status of the Modocs who were translated from California and Oregon to Baxter Springs, Kansas, in 1873; and you ask if these Indians are still at Baxter Springs, and if they still retain their tribal existence. You further inquire as to their number and their temporal condition.

The Modoc reservation embraces a tract of land about two and one-half miles square, and is situated about one and one-half miles northeast of the Quapaw Agency. It was formerly a part of the Shawnee Reservation and contained in round numbers about 4,000 acres, equally divided as to timber and prairie land. The reservation was obtained for them by agreement with the Eastern Shawnees, made June 23, 1874, which was confirmed and ratified by Congress in an Act approved March 3, 1875 (18 Stats. 447): 3,976 acres were allotted to sixty-eight Indians, 8 acres being reserved for church and cemetery purposes, 2 acres for a school, and 24 acres were set aside as a timber reserve to supply timber to allottees living on the prairie.

The last annual report of Mr. Horace B. Durant, Superintendent of the Seneca Indian Training-school (address at Wyandotte, Indian Territory), and in charge of the Modocs, gave the following statistics concerning the Indians under consideration:

Population 54
Males 25
Females 29
Males over eighteen 17
Females over fourteen 16
Males under eighteen 8
Females under fourteen 13

Children between six and sixteen 11
Number of allotments 68
Acres in each allotment 48
Indians of one-half Indian blood and over 40
Indians of less than one-half Indian blood 14
Living out of the Agency, inclusive of children in non-
    reservation schools 15
Males over eighteen who are farmers 4
Children in non-reservation schools 1
Children attending all other schools 5

He further reported that all of the Modocs wore citizens' clothes and that all were engaged in civilized pursuits and were living in very poor houses of mainly one room each and with dirt floors.

From the above you will see that the Indians practically no longer sustain their tribal relations, they having received their allotments of land in severalty; that they all wear citizens' clothes and that they are still near Baxter Springs.

CHAPTER TWO

The First Blow

Jackson's Expedition *

THE Modoc Indians belong generally to the races known as "Digger Indians" — from living largely upon esculent roots which the squaws dig, dry and cache for winter subsistence, — but they are much superior to the average Digger Indian, and are more nearly allied in character — and by intermarriage — to the "Rogue Rivers," a warlike tribe, now about extinct, inhabiting at one time the western slope of the Cascade Mountains in Oregon.

Schonchin was chief of the tribe when the treaty was made with the Klamaths, Modocs and Yainaskin Snakes, by which these tribes, for the consideration offered by the Indian Bureau, agreed to live upon the Klamath Reservation, then just established.

The Indian title to the Lost River and Tule Lake country was thus extinguished, and the land thrown open to settlement.

The Klamath Reserve proving to have a much colder climate than the Modocs were accustomed to, and the Klamath Indians, their ancient foes, taunting them

---

* Abridged from the account of the war by Col. James Jackson, U. S. A. (Retired), in *The United States Service Magazine*, July, 1892, by permission of the publisher.

with living on "their" land, catching "their" fish, and killing "their" game, the Modocs became discontented.

The governing chief, "Old Schonchin," with a large part of the tribe, got as far away from the Klamaths as he could, and lived up to the terms of the treaty; but the restless and desperate spirits of the tribe, under the leadership of the Indian afterward widely known as "Captain Jack," and John Schonchin, a brother of the hereditary chief, left the reservation and returned to the Tule Lake basin, declaring that they would live in their old home and nowhere else.

It is with this band of desperadoes that history has to deal when treating of the Modoc War, though subsequently to the breaking out of hostilities they were joined by the Hot Spring and Rock Modocs, making a fighting force of about one hundred and twenty warriors. Many of these Indians were what would be called "half-civilized." A number of them had been born and reared near the outlying California settlements, and had worked for white men on their ranches and cattle-ranges.

They dressed like the frontier white men, talked some English, and were familiar with the ways of white people, including all their vices.

They were well armed with breech-loading and other rifles, which, by constant practice at game and water-fowl, they had learned to handle with skill and precision. The settlers in the country thrown open to settlement by the treaty soon began to complain of Captain Jack's band of desperadoes, charging them with killing cattle and abusing the settlers' families when their men were absent.

The Indian Agent of the Klamath Reserve made repeated efforts to induce them to return to the reservation; but every effort was met with contemptuous refusal and the declaration that they would fight rather than leave their present location.

The home of these Modoc Indians was in a district of country just east of the Cascade Mountains and lying on both sides of the boundary line between Oregon and California: a rocky, broken, sage-brush region containing a number of alkaline lakes, some fertile valleys, and a few mountain streams, but covered for the most part by volcanic scoria.

Their principal habitat was the valley of Lost River and the basin of Tule Lake, into which the valley opens.

The rivers and lakes abounded in fish and were the resort of vast numbers of water-fowl; game was plentiful in the adjacent mountains, the bunch-grass was luxuriant, the climate mild, snow seldom fell and never remained long in the valleys. Taken altogether it was a paradise for nomadic Indians.

At the southern extremity of Tule Lake basin was a district of country known as the "Lava-Beds," which at the outbreak of hostilities was, to the white man, a *terra incognita*, being for miles each way a confused jumble of lava, which had in some prehistoric period rolled down the slopes of volcanic peaks on its eastern border, and, lashed into furious foam and toppling waves by the obstructions in the lake valley, had — apparently while at the height of the disturbance — solidified into a hard, blackish rock, honeycombed by bursting air bubbles, caught in the lava flow, leaving a surface over which no white man ventured of his own accord, and whose intricate passages and cavernous retreats were known only to this tribe of Indians and the mountain-lion as he stalked them in search of prey. The ocean breakers as they dash on a rocky coast, suddenly petrified in all the wildness of their fury, would give some idea of the character of a portion of this lava surface and induce a realizing sense of the difficulty of carrying on military operations in such a country.

Along a mile or more of the lake front, the molten lava had poured over the abrupt and irregular bluffs, forming, as it cooled, a rock-wall whose almost vertical face was impossible of direct ascent. On the crest of this wall the lava, in cooling, had broken away from the horizontal flow, forming a deep crevice which in an irregular line followed the indentations of the lake shore and, curiously enough, made almost as perfect a defensive work as a military engineer could have laid out.

There was no part of this abrupt rocky glacis that was not covered by a line of fire from the natural rifle trench, while at the angles masses of rock had fallen forward, forming lunettes, covering the receiving lines and affording loop-holes or windows through which all approaches could be observed, and serving as admirable picket or lookout stations for a defending force.

Where the line of crevice had been broken through, or failed to give sufficient defense, the Indians had supplemented it with a double wall of broken lava, carried to and around the caves used for sleeping purposes, affording a continuous channel of unexposed communication from one flank to the other, completing and making impregnable, against a small force, this Modoc stronghold.

In the fall of 1872 the settlers in southern Oregon procured an order from the Interior Department for the removal of Jack's band to the Klamath Reservation, "peaceably if possible, forcibly if necessary." The Superintendent of Indian Affairs, Mr. Odeneal, visited their village and tried to induce them to comply with

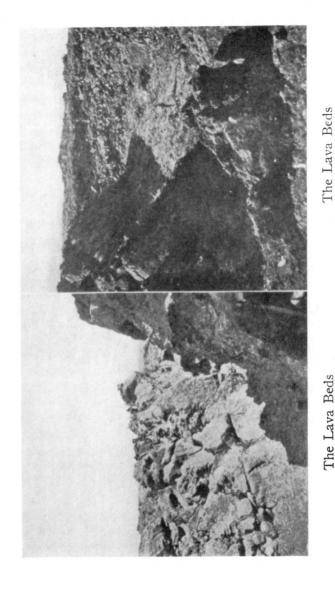

The Lava Beds   The Lava Beds

From the collection of General C. P. Egan

the orders he had received, but failed in his attempt; and while negotiations were still pending, but with no uncertainty as to the result, turned the matter over to the military authorities, sending his agent, Mr. Ivan Applegate, to Fort Klamath to request the commanding officer there, at that time Col. John Green, Major First Cavalry, to send a force to the Modoc camp to compel their compliance with the orders from the Department of the Interior, and insisting upon it that only a "show of force" (about twelve or fifteen men was mentioned) was necessary to accomplish the object.

Colonel Green directed Major Jackson to take all available men of his troop (B, First Cavalry) and proceed by forced march to the Modoc camp, and induce them to comply with the orders given by Superintendent Odeneal, or, failing in this, to arrest the leaders.

Major Jackson with thirty men, and accompanied by Lieut. F. A. Boutelle and the post surgeon, Dr. H. McEldery, who had volunteered to go with the command, was soon on the march.

Mr. Ivan Applegate, in the capacity of interpreter, and a few citizens joined the column while *en route*. These citizens were detached at the ford on Lost River to take post at Crawley's Ranch to protect the family there and prevent an attack on the rear of the troops, the ranch being situated between the two Modoc villages or camps, which were about a half-mile apart on opposite sides of Lost River, a deep, sluggish stream with abrupt banks, that could be crossed only by boat.

Marching continuously day and night, the troops arrived at the Modoc village about daylight and formed line among the tepees, taking the Indians completely by surprise. Had they been undoubtedly hostile there would have been no Modoc War. The chiefs and leaders were called for, particularly Captain Jack, but he did not put in an appearance, and, so far as is known, took no part in the subsequent fight. Some of the sub-chiefs gathered around and the orders of the Indian Superintendent were explained by the commander of the troops to such Indians as could understand English, and to all of them by Mr. Applegate, who visited both villages to carry out his instructions.

The time given to parleying was used by the Indians to recover from their surprise, and to get ready for the resistance which they had previously determined upon. While some talked to gain time, the boldest spirits disappeared in their tepees and soon came out painted, stripped to the buff, and carrying from one to three rifles.

The interpreter, after using every effort to persuade the tribe of the folly of resisting United States authority, gave it up, and, convinced that no compliance with the orders of the Indian Superintendent could be obtained, so informed Major Jackson.

It was then determined to carry out the second part of the instructions before alluded to and "arrest the leaders."

A squad of the best known warriors having taken position near some tepees about thirty yards in front of the line of dismounted cavalrymen, — seventeen men in skirmish order, — Lieutenant Boutelle was directed to advance some men from the left and secure these Indians.

At the order to move forward all of the Indians aimed their rifles at the line and one of them fired, apparently at Lieutenant Boutelle.

The troops instantly returned the fire, pouring volley after volley in and through the tepees, behind which the Indians had taken cover, and from which they were rapidly firing at the soldiers.

This fire beginning to weaken the line, a charge was ordered, which drove the Indians from cover of the tepees into the surrounding brush and left in the village only a few squaws bemoaning their dead and wounded.

The Indians continuing the fire from distant cover, a line of pickets was thrown around the captured camp, in such shelter as could be found or improvised, while the wounded were being cared for by the surgeon and then transported across the river, by canoe, to Crawley's Ranch.

This done, an advance was ordered, when the owner of the ranch came galloping up on the other side of the river, imploring assistance to protect his family and the wounded men at his house from a threatened attack on that side of the river, the citizens stationed there having left to notify the settlements of the breaking out of hostilities. He was told to hold the place at all hazards, and the troop, carrying its dead, moved quickly up the river to the ford, Lieutenant Boutelle with a small skirmish-line protecting the rear and keeping the Indians at a respectful distance.

The command arrived at the ranch in time to prevent any catastrophe there.

The Indians lingered around until sundown, burned a few haystacks and then retired to the "rock fort," which, they had told the settlers, was to be their refuge and stronghold.

What this "rock fort" was no one knew, further than that it was a place in the lava-beds which Jack had boasted he could hold against any number of white men, and where he had cached the possessions of the tribe and a sufficiency of dried roots and jerked beef to last his people a year.

Thus commenced the Modoc War.

CHAPTER THREE

Major Boutelle's Account of His Duel with Scar-faced Charley in the First Engagement

By Maj. F. A. Boutelle, United States Army (Retired)

IN the latter part of November, 1872, Mr. Odeneal, Superintendent of Indian Affairs for the State of Oregon, appeared upon the scene and sent word to Captain Jack of the Indians that he was at Linkville and to meet him there. Jack not responding, he was informed that Odeneal would be at Lost River two days later to talk to him. Instead of making preparations for his suggested meeting he despatched Mr. I. D. Applegate to Fort Klamath asking that troops be sent to move the Indians.

Mr. Applegate arrived at Fort Klamath about five o'clock in the morning of November 28th, and was brought by the sergeant of the guard to my quarters, I being Officer-of-the-Day. He told me his errand and asked if I thought Colonel Green would send troops. I told him to make himself comfortable until later as I knew Colonel Green would not send troops, that he had been informed if troops were used enough men should be sent to place the result "beyond peradventure."

About eight o'clock, I was amazed at receiving orders from Major Jackson to make ready for a trip to Lost River; that we were ordered to move the Modocs. Soon after I was called to the adjutant's office to prepare an order for the move. When the command was ready, or about half after eleven, I met Colonel Green and took occasion to call attention to the copy of General Canby's letter to the commanding-officer, District of the Lakes, which had been furnished him for his guidance, and to suggest to him that there was no reason to believe these Indians would not fight, and that the command he was sending was, in my judgment, altogether inadequate — just enough to provoke a fight in fact. His reply was:

"If I don't send the troops, they (the citizens of Klamath Basin) will think we are all afraid."

The command, consisting of Maj. James Jackson, First Cavalry, in command, Asst.-Surg. Henry McEldery and myself, both of us being second lieutenants at that time, and thirty-five enlisted men, followed by five other enlisted men with pack-train, left Fort Klamath about noon in a cold rain and sleet-storm. We arrived at a point near Linkville in time to cook supper and feed the animals. Here the Major found Superintendent Odeneal and had a talk, the character of which I cannot relate. As soon as possible after supper we were in the saddle and *en route* to the Modoc camp. We were accompanied a part of the way by a party of citizens, who next morning engaged the Indians on left bank of Lost River.

The heavy roads made the ride an unusually hard one, and when daylight appeared it found a very tired lot of soldiers about to attempt a very disagreeable task. We halted about a mile from Jack's camp, dismounted to adjust saddles. I took off my overcoat, saying to Major Jackson that if I was going into a fight I wanted my deck cleared for action. Most of the men, seeing my movement and hearing my remark, followed suit, notwithstanding the fact that the temperature had fallen and that the wet coats were partly frozen. We strapped the coats on the cantles of our saddles. Mounted again, we rode at a rapid rate and came into the Indian camp before many were out of bed. An Indian who was out fishing saw us crossing and ran down the river-bank crying:

"Soldiers! Soldiers!"

Soon after our arrival Scar-faced Charley crossed the river in a canoe and as he came up the bank of the river fired a shot. He told me after the surrender that it was an accidental discharge. I believed him.

As soon as we were formed in the Modoc camp Major Jackson, through Applegate, who knew the Indians individually, attempted to summon Captain Jack; but could neither get a talk with, nor a sight of, the chief. While these attempts at parley were going on, the Indians, under the influence of Scar-faced Charley and others, were undoubtedly preparing for combat. Applegate saw that there was trouble brewing as fast as possible. Scar-faced Charley had withdrawn to one end of the camp and was talking in a very excited manner with a number of other Indians. He had one rifle in his hand which he waved defiantly, and three or four lay on the ground at his feet.

Major Jackson finally rode over to me and said:

"Mr. Boutelle, what do you think of the situation?"

"There is going to be a fight," I replied, "and the sooner you open it the better, before there are any more complete preparations."

He then ordered me to take some men and arrest Scar-faced Charley and his followers. I had taken the situation in pretty thoroughly in my mind, and knew that an attempt to arrest meant the killing of more men than could be spared if any of the survivors were to escape. I was standing in front of the dismounted men of the troop. I called out to the men, "Shoot over those Indians"; and raised my pistol and fired at Scar-faced Charley. Great minds appear to have thought alike. At the same instant Charley raised his rifle and fired at me. We both missed; his shot passing through my clothing over my elbow. It cut two holes through my blouse, one long slit in a cardigan jacket and missed my inner shirts. My pistol bullet passed through a red handkerchief Charley had tied around his head; so he afterward told me. There was some discussion after the close of the war as to who fired the first shot. I use a pistol in my left hand. The track of Scar-faced Charley's bullet showed that my arm was bent in the act of firing when he fired. We talked the matter over, but neither could tell which fired first.

The fight at once became general. Shots came from everywhere, from the mouths of the tepees, from the sage-bush on our left, from the river-bank and from the bunch of braves in which Scar-faced Charley was at work. As soon as I had time to see that I had missed as I supposed I fired another shot at Charley, at which he dropped and crawled off in the bush. Just then an Indian dropped on his knees in the opening of a tepee a few yards from our right and front and let slip an arrow at me. This I dodged and the subsequent proceedings interested him no more.

The men of the troop were tired as well as exhausted by the ride of fifty-six miles in a terrible storm; and when the firing had knocked out eight of the twenty-three men in action, the line began to give way. I saw that to retreat meant death, and calling on the men to charge, we rushed right at the main body. We were white and they were red. There was the almost invariable result. The dark skin gave way.

We had the camp and everything in it, women and children included. It was believed by all that we had killed very many Indians; so many that there would be no further resistance if the women and children were permitted to go to the men. This was allowed and the camp destroyed.

As soon as the fight was over, Major Jackson crossed the wounded over the river and sent them to Crawley's Ranch about half a mile beyond. About the time this work was accomplished a messenger came flying from Crawley's Ranch with the information that the Indians were making a demonstration upon that point.

I failed to mention that the party of citizens who accompanied us from Linkville had had a brush with a small party encamped on the left bank of the river below Crawley's Ranch and had not been successful. The river was not fordable at this point. Major Jackson then took all sound men except about ten left with me and started for a ford seven miles up the river where he crossed and came down the other bank of the river to Crawley's Ranch.

As soon as the Indians, who had retreated to the foot-hills, saw Jackson leave me with a small party they came on and made a futile attack. They had had enough and did not want any more. I followed Jackson, reaching Crawley's Ranch late in the afternoon with the dead strapped on horses.

A dreadful mistake had been made; yes, more than

one, but I shall not treat of matters previous to the
attempt to move the Indians. In the attempt the greater
sin lies at the door of Mr. Odeneal, who would not
trust his precious skin to a council on Lost River; but
preferred treacherously to send troops with guns in
place of an agent of the Indian Department with an
olive branch. He was sadly mistaken in believing that
the Indians would not fight. He was dealing with desperate men. When the troops were sent "a boy was sent
to the mill." The heroes of the so-called outbreak do
not diminish with years. I believe Superintendent Odeneal still lives. If he failed to send any word to the settlers
on the north side of Tule Lake that troops were coming,
he has more to think of than I should care to have. Of
such failure he was freely charged in those dreadful
days.

You may in your work have seen a book written by
A. B. Meacham, at one time Superintendent of Indian
Affairs for the State of Oregon. I do not know where
he got the information upon which he based his description of the first fight with the Modoc Indians. I
remember seeing it years ago and that he represents me
as advancing upon Scar-faced Charley, uttering vile and
insulting epithets. I did not move forward a foot when
I received Major Jackson's order to disarm the party,
but commanded the men to fire and fired myself. I did
not address a word to an Indian that morning. Meacham attempted to get an account from me and was referred to Major Jackson's official report. Hence his insults to me. Meacham made the battle last three hours,
and that we were whipped. Rot! It did not last much
more than so many minutes. We drove the Indians
across the sage-bush plain and burned their tepees.
Left when called to the other side of the river for the pur-

pose of protecting our wounded and citizens threatened by Indians from camp on left bank of river.

The citizens who attacked the Indian camp on the left bank of Lost River were there without order or authority, and had no more right for their attack than if it had been made on Broadway, New York. The Indians, who repulsed them and afterward made such dreadful killing, were called treacherous murderers and were indicted in the Oregon courts, Scar-faced Charley, among others, who I have ample reason to believe was on our side of the river.

In contrast with the action of this civilized party may be noticed the "brutal" conduct of some of Jack's people who saw two cow-boys, whom they knew, approaching their assemblage. They went out to meet them, telling of the occurrences of a few hours previous, and advising them to go away while they were at war with the soldiers, as they did not want to hurt them.

Of the fight in the lava-beds chapters might be written by the participants in explanation of why so many men were not able to dislodge so small a number of Indians. The newspapers frequently asked why some officer experienced in such work was not sent to command. There was no officer experienced in such work; he did not live.

The popular impression of the Modoc was that he was a dreadful savage, a wild Indian. As a matter of fact, all of them wore white men's clothing. Nearly or quite all had cut off their hair, and many were in the habit of working for the neighboring stockmen or farmers. Nearly all understood English and many spoke it as well as many white men. As an instance: I had encamped just across Lost River from Jack's camp a few months before the war, and had talked enough with the

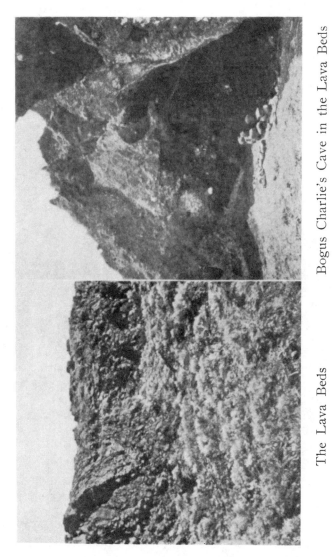

The Lava Beds   Bogus Charlie's Cave in the Lava Beds

From the collection of General C. P. Egan

Indians to recognize Bogus Charley's voice. In the early morning of January 17th, as the two lines, one on each side of the stronghold, were closing in on the Indians, I heard a voice calling out to Colonel Bernard's command:

"Don't shoot this way. You are firing on your own men."

Colonel Bernard commanded "Cease firing," and was surprised to hear me bawl out:

"Look out, Colonel Bernard, that is Bogus Charley talking!"

Bogus talked a great deal, and when on April 1st I told people that at last Bogus Charley was dead, I was rallied a good deal and asked how I knew. I replied that I had not heard him and knew he could not keep his mouth shut. It transpired that Bogus had left the Modocs the night before the investment and could not get back.

As an indication of the disposition of the Modocs, with relation to learning the ways of the white men and not asking for assistance from the Government provided they were allowed to remain on Tule Lake, in one of the peace talks Bogus Charley offered as proof or reason why he should want a cessation of hostilities that he had "lost his whole winter's work."

CHAPTER FOUR

The Initial Shot

A Civilian's Description of the First Battle of the Modoc War *

By Ivan D. Applegate

PERHAPS few places on earth, of like area, have cost so much in blood and treasure as Klamath land, and yet it may be worth the price, dear as it was, for it is one of nature's brightest gems. The native possessor held it with a tenacity which compels us to admire his patriotism, his reverence for the land of his ancestors, while we deprecate the methods of his warfare. As he would put it: "Here is the dust of my fathers. Better for me to die here than to be removed to any other country. If I die here I go down to dust with my father and my people. If I die in some other land I shall be lost forever."

The Modocs stood as bloody sentinels along the line of the emigrant road. As far back as 1852 they began the work of ambush and slaughter, and Modoc land was for a quarter of a century the scene not only of savage treachery and cruelty, but of heroic deeds and tragic incident. Weary immigrants toiling onward toward the

* From the souvenir edition of *The Klamath Falls Express*, January 10, 1895.

setting sun — no record tells how many — were here sacrificed almost on the very threshold of their land of promise.

Later, when the enterprising white man, having seen and appreciated this land of green meadows, silvery lakes and crystal streams, determined to possess it, brave settlers, representing that hardy race of men and women who have led the hosts of civilization across the continent, planted settlements here; but a band of about three hundred renegade Modocs, under the leadership of Captain Jack, renouncing the authority of brave old Schonchin, the rightful chief, inaugurated a reign of terror throughout the lake country.

During the summer of 1872 many petitions were forwarded through the Indian Department, asking the authorities at Washington to order the removal of Captain Jack's band from the vicinity of Tule Lake, their ancient home, to the Klamath Reservation, and to keep them there. Orders were finally received by the Superintendent of Indian Affairs in Oregon, Hon. Thos. B. Odeneal, to secure their removal, peaceably if possible, but by force if necessary.

On his arrival from Salem, Mr. Odeneal, having by messenger called upon the Modocs to return to the reservation without avail, determined to place the matter in the hands of Capt. James Jackson, of the United States Army, an officer of well-known discretion and courage. At noon, on the 28th day of November, 1872, Captain Jackson, with thirty-five men of Company B, First United States Cavalry, left Fort Klamath and arrived at the pioneer town of Linkville at a little after dark. Here he met Superintendent Odeneal and received instructions as follows:

"When you arrive at the camp of the Modocs, request an interview with the head men and say to them that you did not come to fight or to harm them, but to have them go peaceably to Camp Yainax on Klamath Reservation, where ample provision has been made for their comfort and subsistence, and where, by treaty, they agreed to live. Talk kindly but firmly to them, and whatever else you may do, I desire to urge that if there is any fighting let the Indians be the aggressors. Fire no gun except in self-defense, after they have first fired upon you. I. D. Applegate will accompany you as my representative; will also act as guide and interpreter."

During that dark rainy night we made our way from Linkville down the Klamath Valley toward the stone bridge on Lost River, where Captain Jack was encamped on the west side of the river. About a third of his forces, under Hooker Jim and the Curly-headed Doctor and some other of his trusty lieutenants, were encamped on the east side of the river near the Dennis Crawley cabin.

We found it very difficult in the darkness to make our way through the heavy sage-brush, for we had to leave the road in order to avoid being discovered by the wily Indians who, doubtless, were observing as closely as possible every movement. We followed along the foot of the chain of hills west from Lost River, and at daylight we were about one mile west of the Modoc camp, which was at that point on the river-bank where Dan Colwell's residence now stands.

The company was formed into two platoons, and we rode directly through the village and halted upon the river-bank, facing the encampment. As we came near the river, Scar-faced Charley, who had crossed just before we came up, fired at us from the other side of the river, shouting at the same time to arouse the sleeping

Indians. In a moment there was great excitement and commotion.

As soon as the men were dismounted and advanced in line, standing at order arms in front of the horses, I was directed to enter the camp to see Captain Jack and inform him of our friendly mission and assure him that no harm was intended, but that he would be required to remove with his people to the reservation. Going from camp to camp I was not able to find Captain Jack.

As I came out of one of the huts I saw Scar-faced coming up the river-bank. As he passed Major Jackson, who was still mounted, the Major ordered him to halt, at the same time drawing his revolver. To this Scar-faced paid no attention, but came on into the village, all the time haranguing his people and demanding that they fight to the death; telling them that if they would be quick enough they could kill every soldier without the loss of a man. With an oath, he rushed past me and went into Bogus Charley's tent, and in a moment both Scar-faced and Bogus appeared with their guns drawn, and called to the women and children to throw themselves flat on the ground. Then I knew they were going to fire upon us. I immediately started toward our men saying, "Major, they are going to fire!"

At this, the Major ordered Lieutenant Boutelle, who stood in advance of the line, to take four men and arrest the two Indians who had guns in their hands. As Boutelle stepped forward with the four men, the two Indians fired. The warriors in the camps and in the heavy sagebrush in the rear of the village fired almost simultaneously. Then all was din and commotion; men were falling in the line, the riderless horses were dashing here and there and kicking among us, but instantly came the order from the brave Major, "Fire!"

The attack was so sudden and desperate, the Modocs rushing onto us with demon-like yells, that the men were forced back a step or two, and it seemed for a moment that the thinned line would yield and break. But immediately came the order "Forward!" and it was like an inspiration. The men sprang forward, under the leadership of the brave Boutelle, delivering a deadly fire, and the Indians were forced back.

Scar-faced's first shot struck Boutelle's revolver, disabling it, and cutting through the sleeve of his blouse, passed through the clothing on his right shoulder. Scar-faced was knocked down by a bullet which cut through the handkerchief he had tied around his head, and Watchman, Captain Jack's most daring lieutenant, fell, riddled with bullets, almost at our feet. Boutelle's calmness saved us. Speaking to the men coolly and confidently, he led the charge into and through the village, driving the Indians out, advancing his skirmish-line far beyond into the heavy sage-brush.

O. C. Applegate, who was to take charge of Captain Jack's band in case they came onto the reservation, rode from his station at Yainax on November 28th, reaching Linkville (Klamath Falls) late in the evening. Superintendent Odeneal informed him of the movement on foot and requested him to be present to assist in securing, if possible, a peaceable removal of the Modocs. With the Klamath scout, Dave Hill, and five trusty citizens, he forded Lost River near the Lone Pine that night and reached the Crawley cabin, near Hooker Jim's camp, about daylight on the morning of the 29th, finding there Messenger Brown of the Indian Department, Dennis Crawley, Dan Colwell and a few other citizens. When daylight revealed the presence of the cavalry in Captain Jack's camp, Hooker's men made a rush for their canoes, evidently to reinforce Captain Jack, but were prevented by the citizens. The object of the authorities was explained to the Indians, and a few of them were in the act of giving up their arms when the firing began at Captain Jack's camp.

Instantly the Modocs fired on the citizens and a fierce fight at close range took place, so that, looking across the river during the fight with Captain Jack, we could see another battle going on almost opposite to us. Two citizens, Jack Thurber and William Nus, were killed and Joe Penning was maimed for life, and the Indians, securing their own horses, which were near at hand, escaped to the long rocky ridge east of where the Frank Adams' farm is now located; while the citizens rallied at the Crawley cabin.

Captain Jack, with most of his best and most desperate men, had made good his escape, though at the time both he and Scar-faced were reported among the killed, even by the prisoners. We had lost Sergeant Harris, killed, and as nearly as I can remember, six men were mortally wounded, and several others painfully though not dangerously hurt. Among the Indians killed were Watchman and We-sing-ko-pos, leading warriors, and Black Jim, Long Jim and Miller's Charley were among the wounded. The loss on our side amounted to fully a third of the military force then in the field, and was quite sufficient to disable Captain Jackson's small force for the time being.

After the fight Captain Jackson sent his wounded across the river in a canoe, Dave Hill being the oarsman; Surgeon McEldery and a few more as a guard were also taken over and the men were conveyed to the

Crawley cabin. The remaining troopers mounted their jaded horses and, as there was no ford in the vicinity, hastily rode up toward the Stukel Ford seven miles distant. Before arriving at the ford word reached them that Jack and his infuriated men had renewed the fight. Looking toward Tule Lake great volumes of smoke could be seen arising from burning buildings. Dashing through the rapid ford, the poor horses seemed to realize the awful situation as they put forth renewed effort down the river with utmost speed on the east side, and soon the cavalry rode onto the ground where the citizens and Hooker's men had so lately fought, but the wily savage was already wreaking vengeance on the inoffensive settlers, beyond the ridge on the plains at the head of Tule Lake.

The butchering and devastation on Tule Lake had already begun, and eighteen settlers were added that day to the long list of Modoc victims.

On that fateful day, a few miles below the scene of the fight, a mule team was seen coming toward the Boddy residence, but no driver held the reins. Mrs. Boddy secured, unhitched and stabled the team. Very uneasy, she called to her married daughter, Mrs. Schira, and hastily the two women started toward the woods where the men had gone that morning to their accustomed work. They had not gone far when they saw the Indians not far away and heard the awful war-whoop. Soon they came upon the stripped and mutilated body of Mr. Schira, and soon after those of Mr. Boddy and his older son.

The younger boy who had been on the plain below herding sheep could not be seen, and the sheep were wandering at will among the sage. The heroic but horror-stricken women knew that all were killed; that nothing remained for them but to seek their own safety in flight, to hide themselves among the juniper and mahogany, in the almost trackless and, to them, unknown woods. Struggling onward, they knew not whither, only that they felt that they were going away from a sad and awful scene, soon night settled upon them among the mountain solitudes. As they shivered amid the snow and strove to look down through tears of burning anguish toward the mutilated forms of dear ones and upon desolated homes, what tongue could tell, what pen depict the poignancy of their grief?

CHAPTER FIVE

Reminiscences by Maj. J. G. Trimble, United States Army, (Retired)

I. The Kind of Country They Marched Over

SHOULD an officer stationed in Oregon receive an order about the 25th of December to march his company three hundred miles to take part in an Indian war, both he and his men would, most likely, consider the same a very cool proceeding. And they did. Now, this is about the distance from Camp Harney to the Modoc country. Our instructions were "light marching order," instead of comfortable wagons where one could stow a tent and numberless blankets. However, what comforts or necessaries could be taken along were piled upon those unfortunate mules and off we went.

The snow lay pretty deep at home, but we launched out into the great prairie, which resembled one huge, fleecy cloud, and in imagination the effect was the same as riding on the unsubstantial sky which possessed almost as much sustaining power. We plodded on through the virgin whiteness, never before disturbed by foot or hoof, and at the day's end dismounted to sleep in its folds. The old campaigner does not, however, take such a desolate view of the situation.

On the Lookout for an Attack at a Picket The Modoc Stronghold after its Capture
Station

From the collection of General C. P. Egan

Instantly, on halting, the great sage-brush plant is lighted; no shivering over a few green boughs or saturated logs dug from the wet, but a veritable can of kerosene. This great source of comfort in the winter wilderness grows to the height of six feet or more, bearing branches some inches in thickness and a stock fully half a foot in diameter, all oily and odorous. One bush is sufficient to thaw the benumbed feet and limber the aching joints. Then a pile can be gathered for the cooks and the fire by night. And in the same dreary neighborhood grows the red willow fringing the springs; this adds an intensity to the heat more than enough for all purposes.

Thus we moved on day by day, varying the monotony by an occasional dousing in slightly frozen streams, climbing the rugged bluffs, skirting the shallow lakes, winding over the great alkali plains that are even in summer white as snow. At the end of one hundred and fifty miles we ascended the mountain ridge that incloses old Camp Warner.

Now we quitted the sage-brush and the wind-swept valley for the somber solitude of the forest. Here the snow lies deeper, and our tired and panting animals must be lightened and shown the way. Here our spare grain sacks of "chicken gunny" are brought into service for foot-covering; and unlucky is he who fails to secure a supply of these air-letting stockings, the coarseness of the texture preventing the melting of the snow on the foot.

Now is our camp cheered by the fires from the pine, fir and juniper, and we linger long at night beside the fragrant heat. The hungry horses champ the scanty supper from the canvas nose-bag, threshing their icy tails and glancing with knowing looks at the accustomed blaze. The isolated sentinel moves cautiously among them or seeks shelter beside the convenient tree. The storm rages far overhead, and the air is filled with glistening diamond-like particles. The great forest monarchs bend and crack in the blast, ever and anon with a shiver discharging their overladen tops. At last fatigue claims rest. So, scooping the snow from the frozen ground on which we scatter a few hemlock boughs, all stretch themselves beside the smoldering logs in chilly slumber. This is the oft-repeated picture of our bivouac.

In the dark, cold morning after rather superficial ablutions, the frozen lash-ropes are thawed, the packs adjusted and we move out, but do not mount; horses will wade through snow two feet deep by alternating the lead, but beyond that man must break the way. So on we go, up and down the mountain, plunging sometimes armpit deep, dragging our unwilling beasts and often stopping to rescue a comrade or his horse from total submersion. The blazes on the trees are quite indistinct, the storm battening the snow far up on the weather side. The fairy-like track of the snowshoer can be sometimes sighted through the timber. He is our mail-carrier in these parts. Lightly equipped with letter-bag and staff, he skims quietly past the pine openings, up and over the ridge, and disappears. He is seldom met by the weary traveler blundering along the heavy trail, who casts envious glances at the beautiful mark which impresses him as the sign of some subtle, hidden motor. Still on we trudged and finally descended the long mountain side into Goose Lake Valley. Now we embarked upon the ice, and a full day's journey was made over the bosom of this beautiful lake.

Again our route took us through the sage-covered

knolls and into a valley where the snow lay even deeper than before. A cabin was spied on the hillside like a black blur on the snowscape. Here the cattle-men were hibernating through the cold snap, their nearest neighbor being fifty miles away. Thence on through the sleet and storm, until at the end of two long weeks we halted beside the Agency of the Klamath. After a short rest at this point, we again mounted and plunged into the forest-covered spurs of the Sierras. And so we went on for fifty more miles till Lost River was found. The main command joined and the campaign began.

II. The Kind of Country They Fought In

The great lava-bed where the desperate Modoc Indians took refuge is situated in northeastern California, on the extreme verge of the State. In extent it is about five miles by three and a half and covers an area of fifteen hundred acres, where the lava plain is well defined, although the lava country extends for many miles farther, even to Pitt River and Goose Lake. The McLeod range of mountains bound the upper or southern side, a beautiful timbered range, on the highest peaks of which the snow remains throughout the year. Directly at the base of these mountains stand the rows of Lava Buttes or extinct craters, red, grimy, and uncanny to behold.

The plain from these descends by gentle inclination to the lake, a body of water some twenty miles in length by a mile or two in width, varying in extent and depth as the conformation of the land gives scope. The general side of approach is bounded by a line of almost precipitous bluffs covered with grass, except where rough overhanging ledges of rock crop out, barring all passage or confining the trail to one particular route. The eastern side presents an apparently open way through slightly undulating knolls; but the country is so broken and strewn with boulders and blocks of stone that no very easy access is to be had even on that side.

Standing on the highest eminence, the eye can scarcely traverse or take in the whole area of this blighted region. An elevated ridge, or series of upheavals, extends completely through the center from lake to mountain, and in the center of this ridge are located the caves or strongholds selected as the best defense by the Indians. Into these the animals which provided subsistence during the siege were driven and slaughtered.

Notwithstanding the sterility of this section as a whole, abundant and luxurious grass is to be found struggling through the cracks and crannies of the rock; sage-brush and greasewood abound which would supply the needs of many men for many months. The one thing lacking, when the lake is guarded by an army, is water; and this it was that practically caused the abandonment or change of quarters by the Modocs as the warm weather approached.

The troops marched for the first time into the lava-bed from a distance of about ten miles and descended the bluffs by a trail a mile or more in length through a dense fog. Very few of the soldiers knew what such a spot resembled or what it was. No wonder then that they should be defeated where every step was obstructed by blocks of slippery lava the size of houses, and pits or pot-holes the depth of mining-shafts; where the foe could fire from the right, the left, above and below. Even subterranean passages, leading from cave to cave, facilitated attack and rendered retreat a certainty. The only counterpart to such a battle-ground in the annals of our Indian fighting was the Everglades of Florida, and there the forces were equally stubborn and alert.

The dead victims of the effort to dislodge them were bestowed in five different graveyards; and so uncertain was life throughout the campaign that many reflected only upon what part of the sulphurous domain their bones would be cast. Four and five separate and distinct days of battle were expended against the rocky fortresses; but the general ignorance of the country, the lack of woodcraft and knowledge of Indians, as well as bad management of troops due to inexperience brought only disaster, discouragement and humiliation. Finally superstition, the want of cohesion, and treachery among themselves scattered the savages and made them an easy prey to the constantly increasing command surrounding them. The soldiers worked hard and withstood much exposure, tramping through the snow and lava with bandaged feet quite often, as the glassy lava and scoria beds cut through shoe and leather as through paper; sleeping at night on the bare rock, and frequently this latter comfort was denied, when anticipated alarm or the night of travel required many of their number to be afoot. A long dreary winter! And for what? To drive a couple of hundred miserable aborigines from a desolate natural shelter in the wilderness, that a few thriving cattle-men might ranch their wild steers in a scope of isolated country, the dimensions of some several reasonable-sized counties.

CHAPTER SIX

The Killing of the Commissioners

By Major Trimble

THERE were a great many tragical and pathetic happenings in the lava-beds during the Modoc War in 1873. In fact, all occurrences were tinged more or less with diabolism. Now these matters acquired in the minds of every one the feeling just expressed by reason of the hesitancy with which the campaign was prosecuted. At least, that is my own humble opinion. The mail-carriers were kept busy and the wires were kept warm conveying every word spoken and every movement undertaken in the vicinity of the seat of war to Washington, and from Washington to the Peace Commissioners; and everything that leaked out from their deliberations found its way to eager newspapers, and was there rehashed, recolored and fed to the community at large. So each and every actor felt as though a great drama in many acts was being played, each one startling the audience more than the one previously. First it was war, then peace, then council, then murder, then war again. Such veering and hauling was never before experienced by landsman or sailor.

General Canby and his colleagues had twice before

put their lives in jeopardy; but on the fateful morning of their last attempt the very sky was ominous of impending disaster. Talk had been going on the night before, and very early in the morning an occasional swarthy Modoc could be seen flitting through the uncomfortable camp, while men and officers gathered into little groups discussing the possibilities. When the commissioners emerged from the General's tent the snow was falling, and the wind swept dismally across the rocky fastnesses. One experienced officer remarked to me that the party was wrong in going to meet the Indians on that day. His utterance struck me with prophetic force. So another and myself repaired at once to the signal-station to watch, if possible, anything occurring at the council ground.

To retrace a little, when the commissioners were fully prepared to start for the council tent, situated by the lake side and distant but half a mile, it was noticeable that General Canby was dressed in his full uniform, wearing his high black felt hat with gold cord. His appearance was both handsome and dignified. He doubtless expected this to be a culminating assembly, when the Modocs would either submit to the will of the authorities or become outlaws in reality. Rev. Dr. Thomas walked by the General's side, a position he always held both in conference and in camp. Mr. Meacham was mounted on the fleet old race horse belonging to John Fairchild and he seemed very proud of his mount. Agent Dyer followed with his particular charge, the Indian woman Toby, and "her man," a white man by the way. This Indian woman had exhibited throughout the morning great perturbation, as, from hints dropped by hostile visitors on the night before, she feared the very treachery that followed. In fact, she had given a solemn warning of what would happen. However, the General, who was chief, had passed his word that the meeting would take place at the hour appointed; and he intended to keep it at all hazards, fondly hoping that the vexatious matter would be ended to the credit of the Government and in justice to the savage. General Canby was a man of the highest personal honor and courage.

After the departure of the commission, Dr. McEldery and I immediately climbed up the steep bluff overlooking the distant scene and took a stand quite near the signal-officer, Lieutenant I. Q. Adams, First Cavalry, who, with his sergeant, had been keeping watch since early dawn. After observing a little desultory flagging from Colonel Mason's camp, distant four miles across the lava-beds, Lieutenant Adams sprang up in great excitement, and gave the glass to the Doctor, with strict injunctions to keep it on the council tent while he read a most important message from Mason. Then, seizing the flag from the soldier, he began an energetic series of wig-wag motions. Then he told us the result of his communication with the station at Colonel Mason's camp.

He said that Lieutenant Sherwood had been shot by the Modocs, and that Major Boyle had narrowly escaped being shot also! It happened that these officers had left their camp but a few moments before to hold a parley with the Indians, though at long range, and as the latter had no doubt decided to begin war that day, they selected these two as the first and most convenient victims. Well, after this sad message had been confirmed by a few more signals, the Lieutenant resumed the glass. We were naturally filled with foreboding for the General and his brave companions.

Almost in a moment he announced an unusual stir

at the tent. I will mention here that Adams was a most expert signal-officer, having been quite prominent in that capacity during the War of the Rebellion. Keen of eye and very attentive to duty, he rendered most important service throughout this war from the very beginning.

The words just referred to were scarcely uttered when we all heard firing at the tent, though very faintly, and in a moment the Doctor, who was very keen-sighted, saw the tall form of the General stagger out into the open and fall. Lieutenant Adams jumped to the edge of the bluff and called out to the camp below:

"They are firing on the commission!"

All were astir in a moment. I ran down and assembled my troop, dismounted, and started without further order for the scene. Others were as quick to form and move at double time, but alas, the distance of half a mile in the lava-beds was as hard to traverse as five times that on ordinary ground. When the troops, consisting of nearly the whole force, arrived on the scene the massacre had been accomplished.

The General and his faithful friend and co-laborer, Dr. Thomas, lay dead some little distance in the rear or toward our camp. Mr. Meacham was discovered bleeding from several wounds, though alive. He had made a strong effort to escape, though his horse, which I presume he intended should aid him if required, had been taken off by the murderers. The arrangement of the council caused him to be separated from this resource. Agent Dyer escaped by the aid of his little pistol, a ruse he had practised in violating the treaty or obligation that all parties should meet unarmed. I do not believe there will ever be another such covenant. The woman Toby and "her man" Riddle were unhurt, though at the fatal moment at hearing the watchword of Jack, "At-tux" (all ready), she sprang to avert the demon's will, but in vain. For her faithful service during this war, through peril and in hardship endured, a pension was given her which she enjoyed until her death some years later.

Our large camp under the great cragged bluffs was that night a house of mourning. Officers took turns in watching the dead form of their commander day by day, until his honored remains were carried on the shoulders of some twenty or more stalwart veterans up the rocky, winding trail, and deposited in the ambulance which conveyed them away to other friends and civilization. Thereafter several other bodies traversed the same dismal journey, conveyed in the same manner and equally the victims of the Modocs' wrath.

MEMORANDUM OF THE ASSASSINATION MADE BY MAJOR BIDDLE,
ANOTHER EYE-WITNESS.

I was sitting in the signal-station with the signal-officer when the firing commenced on the other side of the lake. The signal-officer ran down to report it and asked me to watch the tent where the meeting took place. I saw a commotion and the commissioners and General Canby try to escape, and two Indians pursuing him and firing at him till he fell. I saw them go up to him, I thought to scalp him, but they did not; just took his clothes — a portion of them. I could not identify the Indians through the glass, so could not be a witness at the trial.

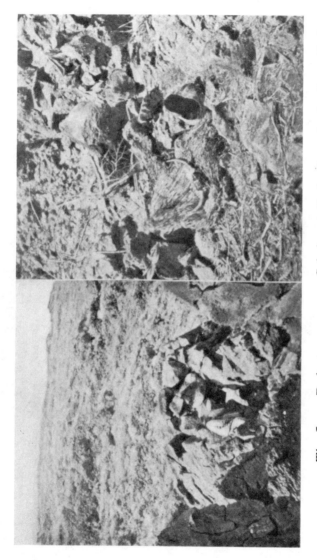

The Lava Beds   Schaknast Jim's Camp in the Lava Beds

CHAPTER SEVEN

The First and Second Battles in the Lava-Beds, and the Capture of Captain Jack

By Brig.-Gen. David Perry, United States Army
(Retired)

THE Modocs were a small band of Indians, located on Lost River, Oregon. Lost River empties into Tule Lake, which lies partly in California and partly in Oregon. These Indians, numbering about seventy-five or eighty adult men capable of bearing arms, were camped near the mouth of the river, and bordering on the lake. They traded back and forth to Yreka, California, and many could speak a little broken English. So far as I could learn they were entirely peaceful, and, according to tradition, their ancestors for many generations had inhabited that region. This, however, was not included in the Indian Reservation; therefore this small band of Indians must be removed from the home of their childhood, the land of their ancestors, that the white man might possess it. To this the red men demurred and it was, therefore, decided to send Jackson's troop of the First Cavalry from Fort Klamath, Oregon, by a sudden and stealthy march at night, surround them at daylight, and move them forcibly on to the reservation they hated.

To the Indian Department this apparently seemed an easy matter. How easy subsequent events show.

Jackson made the attempt and appeared before the astonished Indians on the morning of November 29, 1872. The latter, evidently considering this treatment a declaration of war, opened fire upon the troops and then fled to the lava-beds. They had undoubtedly considered this emergency and were prepared for it.

The lava-bed was of irregular shape, estimated roughly to be thirty-five miles north to south and twenty-five east to west, and washed by Tule Lake on northeast and east side. In the lava-bed were a number of extinct volcanoes, all of which had at some time assisted in distributing this enormous amount of lava. Most of it was of a dark color about the same as the Indians, and appeared like a solid molten mass suddenly cooled. There were many caverns and fissures, undoubtedly known to the Modocs, as I shall hereafter designate these Indians. There was only one trail over which animals could be taken, traversing the lava-bed from northwest to southeast, but animals might be taken around the edge of the lake, although exceedingly rough. This scoria, or lava, had hardened in undulations or waves, some of them reminding one of the waves of the Atlantic on the Jersey coast, could they be caught and held rigidly as you observe them coming in, one after the other. These, as can readily be seen, formed admirable natural defenses, the Modocs retiring from one crest to another as the troops advanced, and invariably, from their concealed position, inflicting loss.

At this time I was stationed at Camp Warner, Oregon, about one hundred and fifty miles from the lava-beds. The news of Jackson's fight and orders to proceed at once with my troop to his camp reached me by courier about December 2, 1872. Upon my arrival, I found Bernard with his troop First Cavalry already there, he having gone from Britwell, California. And Major John Green (affectionately designated by his younger officers as Uncle Johnnie), than whom no braver man ever wore the uniform.

By this time it became certain that we were confronted with no easy task, and troops were ordered in from all near-by garrisons, including about one hundred Oregon militia, reinforced by a major and a brigadier-general from the same State, who looked upon the whole affair as a sort of picnic. In the meantime, Bernard, with his own and Jackson's troop, had been ordered to the south end of the lake to prevent the Modocs leaving the lava-beds by that route. Lieutenant-Colonel Wheaton (brevet Major-General) had arrived from Warner and assumed command and moved our camp from the mouth of Lost River to Van Bremmer's Ranch, about ten miles farther west, as being more accessible, both as a rendezvous for troops and for supplying them, as everything had to be shipped via Yreka, California.

All being in readiness, it was decided to attack the Modocs on the 17th of January, 1873. Bernard was to move up the trail along the lake, leaving his horses in camp, and traveling at night, capture the Indian stock (ponies) grazing on the lake front. In this he was successful. After that and simultaneously with our attack of the Modoc position on the west, he was ordered to strike them from the east. What was afterward known as "Jack's Stronghold" was near the lake and about midway between the east and west attacking points.

We moved out the afternoon of the 16th and made a dry camp that night about one mile from the bluff at the north end of the lava-bed. This bluff was very steep and high, undoubtedly putting a stop to the further flow of lava in that direction; but by erosion there was quite a space grass-covered at the bottom, large enough to enable us later to put our whole command, much increased, in camp there. The command on the north side consisted of a battalion of infantry under command of Major Mason, my troop of cavalry, and the Oregon militia, the whole under command of Colonel Wheaton. We moved soon after daylight, the infantry taking the head of the column, the cavalry following, and the Oregon militia bringing up the rear.

Before the fight it had been a joke around camp-that "there wouldn't be enough Indians to go round." As I stood on the bluff and gazed out above the lava-bed that morning, it conveyed the impression of an immense lake. A mist or fog hung over it, so dense that nothing transpiring therein was visible, while about us at the top of the bluff all was clear. To see the column go half way down and then disappear from view entirely was, to say the least, uncanny and might have suggested the words of Dante's "Inferno," "All hope abandon, ye who enter here."

But I did not have time to indulge in fancies inspired by the sight of disappearing troops, as my turn to move soon came, closely following the infantry which deployed so soon as the descent was accomplished, their left vesting on the lake. I deployed my troop on the right of the infantry, and the militia in turn took position on my right. These dispositions had not been completed when the Modocs opened fire upon us, and the first man hit was a militiaman who was on the way to his position, passing in rear of my line. At the same time we could hear the reports from Bernard's guns, showing that he was attacking as directed.

In this way we pushed or worked along for perhaps a mile, the men screening themselves as well as possible. No Indians could be seen; they, of course, were much scattered in order to contest the advance of our whole front, the troops being much more numerous than the Modocs. The Indians would lie behind the crest of the waves, before mentioned, their black faces just the color of the lava; and, after firing, retreat to some other crest, where the same thing was repeated. They never exposed themselves for an instant, and the first warning the troops would have of their proximity would be the cracking of rifles and the groan of a comrade, with perhaps a glimpse of curling smoke as the fog lightened.

Knowing as they did every crevice and fissure through which to escape detection after each shot, it can readily be seen what obstacles the troops had to overcome in order to make any progress at all. These conditions continued, with the exception of the fog, which gradually lightened and finally disappeared throughout all the fighting of that day in the lava-beds.

We made but little further progress, and being much annoyed by the fire directly in my front, I ordered a charge by that portion of my line most exposed to it, when greatly to my surprise I found running along my entire front an enormous chasm absolutely impassable, so far as I could ascertain. Just then some of my men called out that they had found a way down into the chasm, at which the men nearest broke to the right and left and entered this gorge. On joining them, I found that the Modocs had evidently anticipated this very move and prepared for it. They had it completely covered by their rifles, and had it not been for the fact that at the mouth of the gorge stood an enormous boulder, I and my party must have been annihilated.

To get out of our predicament I called to one of my men, who had been stopped at the entrance, to hurry to Colonel Green, explain the situation, and ask him to order the infantry to make a demonstration in front of the Indians, in hopes that it would relieve the pressure on my position. This was done and I got back to my line with comparatively small loss.

We were now close enough to Bernard's right to call him, and found that he had made no greater progress on that side than we had on ours. By this time it must have been between one and two o'clock in the afternoon, and I heard Colonel Green, who was in command of the firing-line, call to Bernard that he was going to connect with his (Bernard's) right. This meant moving by our left flank along the lake and in front of Jack's Stronghold, which, of course, the Modocs would resist desperately as, in the event of our seizing it, they would be cut off from water. And this they did, and with such effect that our line, moving by the flank, was cut in two, part of my troop and the militia remaining on the west side. At this time the firing by the Modocs was so fierce and deadly that the whole command was forced to lie prone. I don't remember any order to that effect. None was needed. And the Modocs held us there until darkness permitted our escape.

During all this day's fighting I did not see an Indian, and I don't recall that any one else did, though they called to us frequently, applying to us all sorts of derisive epithets. It was at this point that our greatest number of casualties occurred. I was wounded about four P.M., having raised myself upon my left elbow to look at a man who had just been killed. A shot at my head missed that, passed through my left arm and into my side.

That night we retreated to Bernard's camp on the

south side of the lake, about twenty miles from the scene
of the fight, over a rough trail through the lava. General
Wheaton, with the remnant of the command on the
west side, returned to the main camp at Van Bremmer's
Ranch. Colonel Green was obliged to march around
the east side of the lake, in order to join General Wheaton, and this he did with as little delay as possible. We
who were wounded were sent to Fort Klamath, about a
hundred miles distant, which we reached at the end of
the third day.

It was now realized that to subdue the Modocs a much
larger force would be necessary, and troops were rushed
to the scene from all available points; but, before anything more could be done by the military powers, the
Washington authorities decided upon a peace commission to treat with these Indians, a great mistake at
this time, as any one should have realized the utter
futility of attempting such a thing with a savage foe
flushed with victory. After hostilities have actually begun, the only way to treat with an Indian is to first
"thrash" him soundly, which usually has the effect of
rendering him amenable to reason.

While these negotiations were being conducted my
wounds healed, and I was permitted to rejoin my command at Van Bremmer's Ranch, the date I am unable
to state. Shortly after this General Canby, the Department Commander and President of the Peace Commission, concluded that it might have a better effect upon
the Indians to inject a little display of force into their
deliberations, so he moved his whole command into the
lava-beds, Bernard taking up his old position on the
east side, from where he made his attack January 17th,
and we with all the other troops camping at the foot of
the bluff heretofore described. Our signal-station was

far enough up the bluff to command a view of everything in our front and communicate with Bernard.

It was no unusual thing, when flagging to the other command, to see an Indian appear on the top of Jack's Stronghold and mimic with an old shirt or petticoat the motions of our flags. From the signal-station close watch was kept on the tent where the Peace Commissioners were to meet Captain Jack and the other Modocs on that 11th of April, 1873. I neglected to state that, in the meantime, the command on the east side had been much strengthened and Major Mason given command.

Two or three days previous I had been detached to escort the body of a brother officer to Yreka, and returned the afternoon of the 11th, and at the top of the bluff heard the sad details of the massacre of the Peace Commission. . . . I have always thought, as these Indians could have had no animosity against General Canby, nor hoped to kill off all the soldiers, that they believed, if they could kill the Big Chief and incidentally as many of the lesser lights as possible, that, like a savage force whose leader had been killed, the balance would become demoralized, disintegrate and disappear. On no other theory can I account for such base treachery.

Of course all hopes or wishes for peace were now abandoned and preparations made for the coming struggle. The exact date I cannot recall, but think it was the 14th of April. I left camp at two A.M. with two troops of dismounted cavalry and three days' cooked rations. I marched about half-way to Jack's Stronghold and waited for the balance of the command, infantry and artillery, the latter as infantry, except a detachment that had a section of cohorn mortars. This command did not leave camp until eight A.M., and soon as they arrived were put into position much the same as January 17th, but this time, owing to our numerical superiority, we were able to make greater progress and by night had them closely pressed, though unable to dislodge them.

Then our cohorn mortars were put into position and dropped shells into their camp all night long at fifteen minute intervals. The firing by the Indians continued all night, and several times they tried to stampede our lines by fierce assaults; but in every instance without success, though their firing was incessant. The next day we succeeded in closing in a little more, and that night the mortars continued the same as the night before, viz: throwing shells into Jack's camp every fifteen minutes, while the Indians continued firing more furiously than ever, accompanied by demoniacal yells which made the scene one never to be forgotten by those who heard it.

Just before daylight the firing by the Indians slackened, and about the same time some of our advanced lines were enabled to gain ground, and about ten o'clock we discovered that the stronghold had been abandoned. One reason was that we had cut them off from water, and, also, the mortars rendered their stronghold untenable. As I remember, by noon of the third day not a trace of an Indian could be discovered. They had vanished completely and were lost to us among the vast caverns of the lava-beds which they knew so well. During the three days just described our men were killed going back and forth to our camp, so that if anything was needed a large escort had to be sent.

The following extract from a letter of mine, written April 17, 1873, well describes our condition:

"The great event of the campaign has been accomplished, viz: the driving of Jack from his stronghold. The fact of our remaining on the line day and night convinced him that we had come to stay. The infantry and artillery are camped in the stronghold. Bernard and Jackson have gone around on the east side, while I go the west side of the lava-beds, so that in the event of the Modocs trying to get out, we can cut them off. I can't write more to-night as I am very tired and have to be in the saddle at daylight. I have not washed nor combed my hair for three days. It's no pleasant thing to live in the rocks for three days and two nights with now and then a bite of cold food, and an incessant fire on the line all the time."

The cavalry as indicated above made the entire circuit of the lava-beds without finding any trace of the Indians, and close watch was kept in every direction to prevent their escape. No further fighting occurred until the 26th of April, but during the intervening time speculation was rife in camp as to the exact locality of the Modocs. That they had not left the lava-bed was certain. How they procured water was a mystery never solved satisfactorily. Once in a while a moccasin track would be reported and the locality closely watched, but no reappearance was ever reported.

On the 25th of April it was decided to make a reconnaissance into the lava-beds in an effort to locate the Indians. The command was to be composed of foot troops, infantry and artillery. Captain Thomas of the latter arm sought and obtained the command, consisting of sixty or seventy men and six officers, including the doctor, as follows: Captain Thomas, Lieutenants Howe, Cranston, Wright, Harris, and Dr. Semig. The command left camp at seven A.M., and about noon signaled back that they had struck the Indians. We could distinctly hear firing, and with a glass make out a portion of the troops. There did not appear to be any

Schonschis Rock; Tule Lake in the   Bluff to West of Tule Lake
Distance

From the collection of General C. P. Egan

LOCATION OF JACKS CAVE
IN THE LAVA BEDS
FROM SKETCH BY CAPT. A.J. LYDECKER, U.S.A.
— CREVICES – NATURAL RIFLE PITS
⸺ ROCK BREASTWORKS PUT UP BY INDIANS

hard fighting, and everybody in camp supposed that Thomas could easily take care of himself, if unable to inflict any punishment upon the Indians.

About three P.M. some stragglers and wounded men made their way into camp and said the command had been ambushed and cut off. Colonel Gillem immediately despatched all the available men in camp under command of Colonel Green to the assistance of Thomas. I did not accompany the command, owing to trouble with my wound that interfered with my walking. We did not anticipate anything serious, but supposed Thomas had probably taken up a strong position, and waiting for darkness, would make his way back to camp. During that night quite a number of stragglers came in, and in the morning Colonel Green signaled that they had found the bodies of Thomas, Howe and Wright, Harris and Semig, the last two both wounded. Cranston they were unable to find. Colonel Green returned the morning of the 28th with the dead and wounded. They had been without sleep or rest for two nights and a day, part of the time in a pelting rain.

It now seemed that the only thing to do was to wait until, compelled by starvation, the Indians would be obliged to leave the lava-beds. There was no more fighting until the Indians struck Jackson's command as they were leaving the lava, but of this I can give no account as to date or particulars of fight.

The events above narrated bring me to the capture of Captain Jack. When the Indians left the lava-beds, Colonel Green took up the pursuit with all the cavalry that he could quickly get together. My squadron being too far away, I did not participate. However, General Davis, who had succeeded General Canby in command of the Department, decided to move his headquarters to Applegate's Ranch on the east side and in the direction the Modocs had taken. We had just gotten into camp at Applegate's when the General sent me word that the Modocs had surrendered, but that Captain Jack and his family and a few followers had escaped, and for me to take my squadron and endeavor to effect his capture. I started at once and taking a few Warm Spring Indians, whom I knew to be good trailers, started to cut the main trail. This was some time after noon, and about sundown I struck one trail of Colonel Green's command, and knowing that I could accomplish nothing by following that went into camp.

During the night I made up my mind that Jack intended going back to the lava-beds where he could conceal himself indefinitely, so at daylight I took the back track and before noon my scouts reported squaw tracks traveling in the same direction as ourselves. I have neglected to state that my squadron consisted of my own and Captain Trimble's troop of the First Cavalry. About the time that these tracks were reported we were marching parallel to a deep gorge that lay on our right and impassable for animals except at a few crossings, and, coming upon one of these, directed Trimble to cross to the opposite bank. Soon after my scouts sent me word that the tracks led into the ravine. I then deployed my company, under my lieutenant, and went ahead with my interpreter and found that the ravine turned to a sharp angle to the left.

I had reached the bank and stood on a ledge projecting well out, watching my scouts who had crossed and were intently discussing some signs they had discovered, when one of them suddenly ran back and said they had found squaw tracks that had gone out there and thence ran back to the ravine, probably had seen Trimble. Just at this time I saw on the opposite bank of the ravine and about a hundred yards to my left an Indian dog suddenly appear at the top of the ravine, and just as suddenly an arm appeared and snatched the dog out of sight. I then knew that the coveted prize was mine. In the meantime my men lined the bank.

Jack and his family were secreted in a little cave near the top of the ravine and within point blank range of the ledge on which I stood. I told my scouts to ask Jack if he would surrender, and to come out if he desired and give himself up. He replied that he would surrender, but requested time to put on a clean shirt before making his appearance. This I granted and sent word to Trimble to come up and receive him and conduct him back to the crossing where I would join him. I then took Jack and his family back to headquarters and turned him over to General Davis together with his rifles.*

Thus ended the terrible Modoc War where so many valuable lives were sacrificed, and which I always believed might have been avoided by a little judicious handling of these Indians at the outset.

For his gallantry in this campaign Captain Perry was recommended for a well-earned brevet.—C. T. B.

* It was quite pathetic, during the scout, to discover the means and maneuvers of this small band of fugitives to elude capture. They had with them the infant daughter of the chief, by whose tiny footprints, pattered on the earth, the trailers made sure of their game. While the small party took refuge in the cañon and sought to make preparations for further flight, one poor deformed henchman, with devoted loyalty, stood guard upon the height. A small white cloth on which was spread some freshly cured camas root, drying, claimed his attention for a moment, or it may be that the pangs of hunger overcame his watchfulness, for in his moment of inattention he was surprised and captured almost with gun in hand. Now, trembling with fright and unspeakable anguish, he was made to disclose the proximity of his master, who, upon his sentinel's repeated summons, returned the hail and came forth a captive, to return no more."— *Memorandum by Major Trimble.*

CHAPTER EIGHT

The Disaster to Thomas' Command

By Major Boutelle

I HAVE always considered the disaster to Major Thomas' command as one of the saddest in our military history. It was a small affair, but so senseless and unnecessary, and such a waste of a good life.

About a week or ten days after the last fighting in the lava-beds, which resulted in the expulsion of the Modocs and their retreat to a point near what was known as the Land Butte and Black Ledge, Major Mason's command, consisting in part of the troop with which I was serving, was in bivouac in "Jack's Stronghold." About eleven o'clock in the morning, as nearly as I can remember, my attention was attracted to men looking in a southerly direction, or toward the butte, soon to be made historic. I ran over to where Major Mason was standing, field-glass in hand, and asked him what was the excitement. He replied that he understood that General Gillem had sent out a party of about sixty under command of Major Thomas to ascertain if howitzers could be placed on the butte for the purpose of shelling Jack's camp located near by. I asked Mason if he thought General Gillem had believed that Thomas could reach the butte without a fight, and if he dreamed that he would be able, with a handful of inexperienced men, to make successful work against a party which had kept our whole command busy. The Major shook his head and replied, "Too bad."

Puffs of smoke from guns indicated that a fight was on.

About two in the afternoon a signal message from Gillem's camp, or headquarters of the expedition, conveyed the information that disaster had befallen Thomas and ordered out a relief party. At the same time a party was also ordered out from Gillem's camp. The several detachments joined *en route* and proceeded as fast as possible through the lava-bed, until it was thought we were in the vicinity of the place where Thomas was last seen. All firing had ceased several hours before. We found nothing and, darkness coming on, we went into camp, first piling rocks about the position we selected for defense from a night attack, and prepared to wait until dawn, when we could see to resume our search. It would have been suicidal to have gone blundering aimlessly through the lava-beds at night and our fate would have been worse than that of Thomas. Strong guards were posted and the rest of us tried to get some rest for the work of the next day.

Between eleven o'clock and midnight eight men, six of whom were wounded, stumbled into our line, bringing the appalling information that Thomas and nearly all of his officers were dead, and the enlisted men of his command nearly all dead or so badly wounded that they were helpless. The men said that they could guide us to the party. The troops were at once called to arms. The wounded men were directed the nearest way back to Mason's command, and with the two unhurt men from Thomas' command we moved forward.

About an hour before daylight the guides were obliged to admit that they were lost and they could not tell where to look for Thomas. Again we halted and began the work of throwing up rock breastworks against a possible attack. While this work was in progress the gray of the morning appeared, and I thought I would look around in front of our lines and see if I could find anything indicating that the troops we were looking for had been there before us. A similar idea seemed to have occurred to Sergeant Boyle of the command. As we were cautiously moving forward over the broken ground, the natural tendency caused us to approach each other, so that at the same time we came upon the most heartbreaking sight it has been my fate to behold.

The terrein was of irregular lava-rock ridges between which the decomposed rock had formed fertile soil, overgrown by very large sage-brush. In the bottom of one of these little depressions under the sage-brush, some little distance from our second halting-place, were Major Thomas, dead, Lieutenant Howe, dead, Lieutenant Harris, mortally wounded, and Acting-Assistant Surgeon Semig dangerously wounded, together with a number of enlisted men, all dead or wounded.

The fearful ordeal through which these poor fellows had passed — shot down in the morning, lying all day without food, water, attention, or protection from the cold, with the horrible fear of impending death at the hands of the Indians — had so thoroughly imbued them with the one idea, that while they heard us within a hundred yards of them, piling rocks and talking, they had no thought but that we were Indians preparing for their slaughter as soon as light should enable them to pick off their victims. Their relief when the survivors recognized us can scarcely be imagined.

I sent Boyle back to the command which was at once brought to the front, and the work of succor and search was begun. The Modocs were in plain sight while we were thus engaged; but made no demonstration, probably thinking that Mason's entire command was there.

The search for the survivors continued all day. Lieutenant Wright (Colonel Tom) was discovered with a few of his men some distance to the left of Thomas. All were dead. Cranston could not be found at first. His body, with the bodies of half a dozen enlisted men, was found some time after to the left and front.

This useless sacrifice was one of the most sickening errors of the whole Modoc fracas. General Gillem has been justly blamed for sending an inexperienced man in command of such an expedition. The experience of the past few weeks should have indicated to him that it was not proper to send any small party anywhere in the lava-beds. It is true that Thomas, a distinguished veteran of the war, had never seen any Indian service and lacked that kind of experience, but experience in hell, even with the fire out, was rare. Nobody on earth had ever had any such experience previous to our first attack with the Indians in the stronghold.

It was afterward learned that Thomas had found no signs of Indians up to the time of the attack, and was resting his command and taking luncheon when he was surprised by a withering fire coming from the rocks in almost every direction. He attempted to make disposition of his force, but, seeing his party rapidly falling and that there was no hope of escape, coolly remarked that he supposed that where they were was as good a place to die in as any other, and so fought out the losing battle to the end. He died, as did many other brave fellows, sacrificed to the blunders of Odeneal and others. A lovelier character or a braver heart probably never graced the army of the United States than Major Evan Thomas, Fourth Artillery, twice brevetted for gallantry, — at Gettysburg and, I think, at Fredericksburg.

The sight of dead men was not new to me. In my service during the Civil War I had seen them by the acre, but the sight of the poor fellows lying under the sagebrush dead or dying and known to have been uselessly slaughtered was simply revolting.

In the midst of all the horrors, I recall something awfully ludicrous. As I discovered that Semig was living I exclaimed:

"Hello, Doctor, how are you?"

"Oh," he replied, "I am all right, Captain, but I am so d——d dirty."

I asked him if he was hard hit. He replied that he guessed that he was. With one hand, not disabled, he pointed to his shoulder and exclaimed:

"My shoulder here is busted and my heel down there is all split to hell."

I opened his shirt, and seeing the track of the bullet across his chest, I told him that he was as good as three quarters of a man at least, that his shoulder was not dangerous, though serious, and that with the loss of a few inches of his leg, he would be able to go on all right. He looked up with a half credulous grin and said:

"Boutelle, do you think I'm a d——d fool? I'm a doctor."

I was right. He lived for years, having had that heel amputated.

All that day we were engaged in our search and making preparations for going out as soon as darkness would conceal our movements. Meanwhile, signal communications had been established with Gillem's headquarters, and Assistant-Surgeon McEldery, with a dressing-case and such articles of comfort as he could carry upon his splendid shoulders, had made his way out and was administering to the wounded, upon whom, knowing that they were comparatively safe, the dreadful reaction had set in. Added to the horrors of the day was an absence of water. There was none nearer than Tule Lake, except a spring supposed to be in the possession of the Indians. The pleadings of some suffering from peritonitis, the result of intestinal wounds, were dreadful and continuous. When it ceased we knew what had occurred. They were dead.

As soon as it was dark the command was put in motion for a return to Gillem's camp about four or five miles distant — mark the distance! I was placed in charge of the stretchers to carry the wounded. I had three reliefs, one to carry on the stretcher, one to carry the guns of those bearing the wounded, and one resting. I hardly know how to describe what followed. The command was a good one, as good as any in existence, well-officered, ready to fight and fight well, but what they had seen and endured was too much for human endurance. Added to the horrors of the situation, a bitter storm of sleet and rain came down in torrents, freezing as it fell. In a short time an overcoat would stand alone.

You write me that you purpose writing history. The history of this night's work would not be complete without an account of the entire demoralization of good men. The night was as black as a wolf's mouth. Very little of the time could you see your hand before your face. As soon as darkness fell most of the enlisted men of the command were in a state of complete demoralization. My stretcher party, knowing that they could not be detected, joined the mob working its weary way toward a beacon kept burning for our guidance on a bluff near Gillem's camp, with the one idea of getting back! Officers stormed, commanded and pleaded. Do not understand that there was any insubordination, for there was not. As a stretcher party became exhausted, anybody — nobody knew whom, for no one could see — was seized and placed on the handles. I firmly believe that a few shots from the Indians would have caused the entire abandonment of the wounded in a wild race to camp.

After several hours of this kind I concluded that my muscle was worth more than my authority and I dropped beside the moving mass. As I caught the outlines of faces against an occasional glimpse of light in the sky, I called aside three men of my troop. When I had my third man, I said to them:

"You see the utter demoralization here! I want you to stay with me and we four will carry off one wounded man."

This they cheerfully did, and we happened to get hold of the stretcher bearing Lieutenant Harris of the Fourth Artillery, whom we carried the remainder of the night and until we reached Gillem's camp, about an hour after sunrise. We were from about seven o'clock in the evening until half-past six in the morning making four or five miles!

Such looking faces as the dawn revealed are seldom seen. Eyes seemed to have receded a half inch and around all were dark circles. Several times I heard one man say to another:

"I wonder if I look as you do!"

As you need embellishment for your book perhaps a relief from the gruesome tale will be in order.

During the War of the Rebellion a young Irishman by the name of Geoghegan enlisted in the army and soon won his way to a commission and was assigned to a sword with the Tenth Infantry, in which Lieutenant Harris was at that time serving. The two soon became friends. Geoghegan's heart was light, strong and good. His habits were convivial and he in time found that he had become addicted to too great use of whisky. Rather than bring disgrace upon himself or the army, he resigned. Hearing of the Modoc outbreak he enlisted under the name of Sutherland and was assigned to the troop with which I was serving. He was one of the men selected to assist in carrying on a stretcher and in so doing helped carry off Harris, his old-time and dearest friend, who died without knowing whose tender hand had been so careful to keep him tucked up on his shoulders. Years after, when Sutherland (Geoghegan) had been discharged, and had reëstablished himself as one of the first citizens of the State of Washington, a member of the Legislature, Receiver of the Land Office, and so on, he told me that part of the story which I had not known.

Before blaming the men for the demoralization described, one should consider that the command rested in Jack's Stronghold, which afforded no comfortable resting-place, the night before the movement. All the night following it was searching for the Thomas party, all the next day engaged in collecting the dead and wounded and caring for the latter, and that night carrying off the wounded in one of the worst storms I have ever seen. The nervous strain was too great for ordinary endurance.

It is often remarked that army and navy officers frequently appear much older than they are. The unthinking and the ignorant sometimes charge it to idle or dissolute habits. They are probably much like other men in their habits, but the others seldom have such experiences.

It may be thought that such accounts of demoralization as I have given you might well be omitted. I do not think so. Under too trying circumstances the best of men may fail, and it may help a little in their chagrin that others have done the same, and that it was not cowardice or a lack of enduring nerve.

The foregoing you will have to edit.* You have facts for a good chapter. I have just read what I have written, and told my wife what I had been doing and that I did not like my work. She suggested that she would read it to me and perhaps it would sound better. I told her I could not stand it, but would send it to you.

I inclose a rough outline of the scene of the Thomas massacre. It is probably quite a good bit out on directions. The meanderings of the lake shore are not attempted.

If anybody again writes me if I know anything of our Indian campaigns, I'll tell them I don't. I have never written for publication and am too old to learn.

---

* I would not think of altering the Major's graphic and thrilling description. No imagination could better describe that ghastly midnight retreat in the bitter storm with the helpless wounded. No wonder the old soldier looks old after such an experience as this and the others set forth in this volume.— C. T. B.

CHAPTER NINE

Carrying a Stretcher through the Lava-Beds

Major Trimble's Account of the Return of the Thomas Relief Party

ABOUT the most saddening, as well as the most fatiguing, experience which happened in my career as a soldier in connection with the above, took place at the lava-beds during the Modoc Indian War, 1873. The brave Capt. Evan Thomas, Fourth Artillery, and his small command had just been massacred or dispersed, and the relief under the command of Col. John Green, having arrived on the ground late in the evening, drove off the few remaining hostiles, and wearily awaited the approach of day to commence the search for the bodies of the slain and wounded.

Early in the morning these were found, presenting different forms of anguish and distortion, some in the position of desperate defense, others prostrate in figures of dire helplessness, and quite a number yet alive, but in the agony of painful wounds. All were soon gathered in, some to be informally interred, others attended with the means at hand and prepared for transit to the camp.

As the sun disappeared from sight on this sorrowful

day, and the dusk was thickening over us, the order of march was announced, carrying parties told off, and the nine stretchers with their bleeding occupants placed in column. Only a few miles of journey lay before us, but these were miles of rock, precipice and chasm; and as we took up the march, black and swiftly gathering clouds began to discharge their bucketfuls of wrath, and with short notice all were soon drenched and shivering in our thinly covered pelts. The Warm Spring Indians in charge of the famous scout, Donald McKay, took the lead, and in the order by file we moved forward.

The hostiles, who had been confronting us all day, toward evening showed in considerable numbers on the ridge near by, apparently close, but from the nature of the country far beyond reach. They lit their signal fires, and danced about them in glee; and some, suspecting a movement on our part, had posted themselves between us and our destination, there to intercept and annoy.

Our movements were slow, the head of the column frequently halting, and those at the stretchers calling often for relief, as the poor sufferers had to be lifted over high rocks and across gulches. They were jarred and shaken terribly and frequently had to be adjusted in position. Not a sound was heard except those made by the fall and shifting of the great black boulders, as they were displaced to clear the trail, and the occasional groans from the wounded.

We had progressed about half a mile when the wild braying of our two released pack-mules, stumbling past, disclosed our movements to the wily Modocs. Quickly some two or more rifle shots broke the stillness, and as before arranged, all on our side promptly took the position of squat. This was the only demonstration from the Indians, and we soon resumed the march.

The darkness had now become so intense that each man had constantly to tap the shoulder of his comrade in front in order to keep the direction and avoid being left entirely behind. Soon the halts became so frequent as to give rise to the fear among many of our being discovered at daylight weary, unprepared and struggling with our helpless burdens. About midnight the rain changed to snow, and the wind from a gentle breeze to keen and cutting storm. All had now served many times at the stretchers and ready volunteers were sought in vain; details were made by orders, and repeated and vociferated orders at that; many, from a slight feeling of panic and uncertainty, slyly shifting the labor to those more resolute and manly.

The peculiar state of feeling of the whole had been very much wrought upon of late by the numerous disasters and doleful events just transpired; such as the treacherous killing of our esteemed commander, General Canby, and his colleague, Rev. Mr. Thomas. Would that I could command language to describe these two great characters — martyrs to duty in the strictest sense. After gentle remonstrance from loving subordinates, they went forth, their lives in their hands and the cause of humanity uppermost in their hearts. Besides, we had the three days of hard and unsuccessful battle, and the several murders and killing in the region adjacent to the lava-beds. Each stretcher required the work of six strong and feeling men, and in this duty the officer fully shared the labor imposed upon the soldier; none more willingly than our veteran colonel.

After climbing, stumbling and tramping, until the first rays of the coming day appeared, we reckoned our journey but half accomplished, and the sun had mounted high as we halted across the famous stronghold of

Captain Jack, luckily for us then deserted. Now was the extent of the great lava-bed disclosed to us under these circumstances, the row of black lava buttes towering grimly in the distance, resembling huge red ovens gone out of business. Aided by the storm in the air and our own abject feelings, amidst this chaos of nature one could almost discover in imagination a resemblance to a scene in the drama of the "Inferno," substituting the misery of cold for the torture of heat. There were only lacking the little black Modocs to represent the demons; and again in imagination I think these were supplied.

What a weird and woebegone sight we presented! The want of proper water for the past thirty-six hours, the scant food and scantier clothing, and the chilling storm had blanched every cheek. Add to this the heavy coating of snow on the head and shoulders of each, the many bandaged heads and limbs, and sadder than all else, our racked and tortured charges, whose pallid faces now became visible as they lay resigned to any event, and you have a picture none could forget. We reached the main camp all alive at eight o'clock A.M., thus consuming thirteen honest hours in traversing a distance of five miles. The wounded comrades were quickly placed under skilful treatment, and all but three finally recovered.

One circumstance, in my opinion, contributed not a little to this disaster; that was the certain knowledge by the Indians of the approach of the command, even from the beginning of the march. From the high sand butte behind which they were intrenched the glistening gun-barrels, reflected on the black vitreous lava, distinctly marked each movement. Some of us, who took post at the signal-station, easily traced the troops up to the very moment of contact, and afterward almost each individual movement, though no firing could be heard. A reconnaissance to find the enemy had to be made in daylight, and the hostiles with knowing, snake-like maneuvers and clinging moccasins could always anticipate the soldiers.

Lieut. George Harris, Fourth Artillery, was one of the wounded found upon the field and carried across the lava-beds. The Lieutenant bore his great suffering manfully, being one of the least complaining. His wound was through the body, very severe, and as it transpired, mortal. He was tenderly cared for in a good wall tent pitched for the purpose, and his mother telegraphed for, — at least informed as quickly as possible of his condition.

This refined and delicate lady, past middle age, lost not a moment after getting the painful despatch, but taking train to San Francisco from her home in Philadelphia journeyed day and night until reaching the terminus of railroad transportation at Redding, California; thence she came on without rest by stage-coach, ambulance or spring wagon to the vicinity of the high bluffs which bound the lava country; thence by saddle mule down the boulder strewn trail until the camp was reached and her darling boy clasped in tender embrace.

I was on duty some distance from the main camp when my attention was called to a strange object traveling down the trail, and which could not be made out properly until a gray lace streamer floating behind established the fact that it was a lady's veil! Only a mother's devotion could have withstood such a journey, and the good Lord seemed to have held the ebbing life of her son in His own powerful keeping until her arrival. She was thus enabled to soothe his dying moments, to be recognized by him and remain by his cot side until the last. His death occurred just twenty-four hours after she arrived. The body was inclosed as fittingly as the circumstances would allow and carried to the hilltop, where it was placed, I believe, in the same conveyance that had brought the dear lady from the frontier to the Modoc stronghold, and borne thence to its last resting-place near his native city. I was told that Mrs. Harris was a sister or relative of Bishop McIlvaine, the once eminent Bishop of Ohio.

CHAPTER TEN

The Last Fight of the Campaign

From the Report of Brig.-Gen. H. C. Hasbrouck,
United States Army (Retired)

I MARCHED from Redding, California, my Battery B, Fourth Artillery, being equipped as cavalry, under the command of Captain John Mendenhall, Fourth Artillery, April 19, 1873, and arrived at Promontory Point, April 28th. April 29th marched under Captain Mendenhall to Captain Jack's old stronghold in the lava-beds. May 7th I left the stronghold in command of my own battery and Troops B and G, First Cavalry, and arrived at Peninsula Camp, May 8th. May 9th, under verbal instructions of the Department Commander, marched to Sorass Lake in command of my battery, Captain Jackson's Troop B, Lieutenant Kyle's Troop G, First Cavalry, and Warm Spring Indian scouts under Donald McKay, Act.-Asst.-Surg. J. S. Skinner, medical officer. Camped at the lake with the cavalry and Indians, and sent the battery to camp in the timber about one mile to the southeast. May 10th was attacked by the Modocs just before daylight. Their main line occupied a line of bluffs about four hundred yards distant, and a smaller party soon took possession of a lower line about two

Colonel H. C. Hasbrouck

Colonel James Jackson,
U. S. A., retired

Captain O. C. Applegate

General Jeff C. Davis, U. S. A.

Group of Officers who Fought in the Modoc War

hundred yards nearer. Outposts had been established the night before upon the higher bluffs, but the Modocs succeeded in getting possession without their knowledge. The horses were stampeded by the first volley and Indian yells and ran through the camp in every direction. Under the personal supervision of Captain Jackson, the men who were asleep in their blankets got their arms with steadiness and alacrity. I directed Lieutenant Kyle to take a portion of his Troop G and recover the herd, and Lieutenant Boutelle to order the battery up at once.

A few minutes after the first shot was fired I ordered a charge, and the nearer line of bluffs was quickly carried. Capt. James Jackson, First Cavalry, led the right, and First Lieut. H. M. Moss, First Cavalry, the left of the charging party which was dismounted and composed of B Troop and part of G Troop. After a short pause the high bluffs were carried and the Modocs pursued with as much rapidity as possible for about four miles, when further pursuit was abandoned.

At the commencement of the action I directed Donald McKay to send his Indians, who were mounted, one half to the right and one half to the left. They were soon on the flanks and endeavored to gain the rear of the enemy, but his retreat was so rapid that they were unable to do so. When the battery arrived at the foot of the bluffs, the men were dismounted and sent forward through the rough lava rocks, but our line had advanced so quickly that they did not arrive on the firing-line until after the fighting was over.

Lieut. F. A. Boutelle, having delivered his message to the battery, joined the charging party just as the higher bluffs were taken. I would have continued the pursuit but for the want of water. It was expected to find some at the lake, but it had dried up and none could be obtained, though wells had been dug the night before. The officers and men had no water issued to them this day. I had but twenty gallons and that was reserved for the use of the wounded of whom there were twelve. The horses were all recovered by night.

For list of officers and men who particularly distinguished themselves, I respectfully refer to my report to the Cavalry Command, Modoc Expedition; and for the list of killed and wounded, to the report of Act.-Asst.-Surg. J. S. Skinner to Chief Medical Officer, Modoc Expedition.

The Modocs left one warrior dead on the field. They abandoned a number of ponies, a lot of blankets, fixed ammunition, and loose powder and bullets which I turned over to the Warm Spring Indians. Just after sundown, the wagons sent for having arrived, the wounded were transported to Peninsula Camp with Lieutenant Boutelle in charge of escort, and the rest of the command marched to Promontory Point, the nearest place to water and the supposed position of the Modocs.

May 11th. Sent despatch to Department Headquarters that I believed the Modocs were near Sandy Butte in the lava-beds, and as the country in that direction was impracticable for mounted troops, asked authority to turn in horses at Peninsula Camp.

May 12th. Turned in horses to Peninsula Camp and marched on foot to Sandy Butte and found Modocs in strong position there. Donald McKay was obliged this day to relinquish command of Warm Spring Indians and be sent back to go into hospital.

May 13th. Visited Major Mason, Twenty-first Infantry, whose command had camped the night before about three miles north of the butte.

May 14th. Arranged with Major Mason plan of attack for the next day. In the afternoon of the 14th an Indian scout reported to me that he thought the Modocs had fled. First Lieut. J. B. Hazleton, Fourth Artillery, with twenty-six men, all of whom had volunteered for the purpose, advanced through the stronghold and confirmed the report.

May 15th. Followed the trail about eight miles and found that it led in a southwest direction; returned to Sandy Butte that evening.

May 16th. The horses for the command came up just after sundown. Act.-Asst.-Surg. J. E. Fallon reported to-day.

May 17th. Followed trail with command mounted and found it led along the Ticknor road and afterward branched off toward Antelope Springs. Met Captain Perry, First Cavalry, with his squadron half-way to Van Bremmer's. My men who had had no water all day received a small supply from him. Went into camp at Van Bremmer's.

May 18th. Captain Perry marched to Antelope Springs. I was to march to ford on Butte Creek, and the next day the two commands were to march toward each other in the valley of the creek until they united. While on the march to the ford I found the trail of Indians going up the hill opposite Van Bremmer's. I sent Captain Jackson to follow it with a troop of cavalry while I moved slowly down the road with the rest of the command. Very soon some shots were heard and I ordered B Troop and the Warm Spring Indians to join Captain Jackson at a gallop. When we joined Captain Jackson, I found him in hot pursuit of the Modocs who were the Cottonwood or Hot Creek branch of that tribe. They were pursued along the top of the hills opposite Van

Bremmer's Mountain about eight miles, to a point near Fairchild's Ranch and at as fast a gait as the very difficult ground permitted. Two bucks and three squaws were killed, the latter through mistake, and a number of squaws, children, ponies, blankets, etc., were captured.

Beside the rocks there were many juniper trees which afforded good places for hiding. Had the ground been more open many more would have been killed or taken. The Indians were now so much scattered and the horses so exhausted that the pursuit was stopped and the command camped at Van Bremmer's. Captain Jackson was distinguished in this affair for his gallantry and sound judgment. Lieutenants Moss, Boutelle, and Kyle led their men ably and gallantly. Acting Assistant-Surgeon Skinner, the efficient medical officer of the command, rode in advance with the line officers. All the men, as in the previous affair at Sorass Lake, did their duty. A message to Lieutenant Hazleton, commanding Battery B to remain in the road with the pack-train, until he should receive further orders, was incorrectly delivered by the orderly to whom it was intrusted, and the Battery continued its march to Butty Creek and did not return to Van Bremmer's until the 19th.

May 19th. Marched to Fairchild's Ranch and sent twenty men under Lieutenant Boutelle to escort mail-carrier, who reported to me he had been fired on while making his way to Tule Lake and forced back.

May 20th. Command was saddled and about to resume march in search of the Modocs, when Mr. Fairchild told me that he had learned from one of the captured squaws in our possession that the Modocs were tired of fighting and wanted to surrender unconditionally, and that they were on their way to give themselves up when we attacked them on the 18th. I sent out the squaw to tell the Indians to come in and give themselves up, and made her distinctly understand that the surrender was to be unconditional.

APPENDIX

APPENDIX

I

GENERAL CUSTER AGAIN

My discussion of the Little Big Horn Campaign * called forth a number of interesting comments. Most of the critics who have written to me have agreed with my conclusions. The other day there came to me from Fort William McKinley in the Philippine Islands a letter and an article on Custer's last fight. The letter corrects some minor errors in my account, and I therefore insert it in full. I also insert, with the permission of the distinguished author, the complete account of the battle which he has prepared with so much care, and which was verified in every particular by so eminent an officer as Colonel Benteen and others who participated.

Any and every contribution to the literature of this the most disastrous and most famous of the Indian battles of the United States Army is of great value and certain of a welcome. Hence the propriety of inserting it here.

It is followed by a memorandum by Colonel Ewert, with comment by General Godfrey on the fight of August 11th on the Yellowstone, in which Ewert makes the point that Custer intended to disobey orders on this occasion also. Both Godfrey and Varnum deny this, and I think it is probable that Colonel Ewert is confusing a camp rumor with a positive order.

One of the most famous of Indian fighters, civilians, that is, known as Yellowstone Kelly has furnished me with a brief sketch of one of the skirmishes in Miles' final campaign against Crazy Horse, that of Wolf Mountain. It is also appended not only from its intrinsic interest, but because it is typical of hundreds of little affairs which took place every day during these Indian wars. — C. T. B.

* In the preceding volume of this series, " Indian Fights and Fighters."

Headquarters, Thirteenth Infantry,
Fort William McKinley, Rizal, P. I.
October 8, 1906.

My dear Doctor:

I have read with much interest your "Indian Fights and Fighters," especially that portion of it which relates to the Custer Fight, and "Miles' Great Campaigning," as I was one of the junior 2nd Lieutenants of that grand organization, the Fifth Infantry, during those stirring days, 1876-80.

I first saw the "Custer Field" in the spring of 1877, visiting it with some of the officers of the Second Cavalry, who had been with Gibbon's command. For years thereafter I collected material, pictures, notes, etc., with a view to writing a history of the fight, but it was not until 1893 that I got down to actual work. My account is a "mosaic," a compilation, pruned down again and again. My first paper was over 100 type-written pages.

In 1894 it was my great good fortune to be ordered to Fort McPherson, Ga., near Atlanta. Colonel Benteen was then living near there, and every Sunday for over three months he and I would go over my work, until it reached its present form, when he pronounced it "the best paper extant on the Custer Fight." This was in 1895. That winter I read the paper to the regiment, as an illustrated lecture, presenting the views, 150 of them. Afterward the lecture was delivered twice in Atlanta — many times in Buffalo, N. Y. — at Wheeling, W. Va., and at other places. (Copy forwarded herewith which please return, remembering that it was completed in 1895.)

My original papers have been lost in one of my boxes which disappeared from my "plunder" during the moves which came to us in 1898 and subsequent years.

In your book you fail to mention having received any assistance from Gen. Chas. F. Roe, now Maj. Gen. N. G. of New York. Lieutenant Roe was with Gibbon's command at the time of the fight, and always claimed to "have something up his sleeve" pertaining to the campaign.

Mayhap *he* was the mysterious person of the affidavit referred to by General Miles. I *say* "mayhap." I *know* nothing. It is hardly conceivable that General Miles would refuse to state who his informant was unless he desired to protect him, and in the case of an enlisted man or interpreter or scout, he would hardly have kept silence so long. I merely mention this as a possible contingency.

Now a few remarks regarding your article in "The Last of Custer," page 243, II: "Benteen moved off westward." This is misleading. The general tendency of the Little Big Horn is northwesterly at that portion near the battle-field, and from there to its mouth. Benteen was ordered to the "left," which would carry him more to the east or south. (See map of Montana.) Near the bottom of the page you say "he . . . struck into the valley of the Big Horn." He never got near the "Big Horn." The whole operation was in the valley of the "Little Big Horn," or "Greasy Grass."

Of course these points are not material, but as a matter of history should be made as correct as possible.

In 1886, at the reunion of the survivors of the Seventh Cavalry on the Custer Battle-field, when Gall gave his version of the story, standing at the foot of the Custer monument, facing up the Little Big Horn River, I was present, and heard his description. I made copious notes at the time, but these notes were lost with the rest of my original papers pertaining to the fight.

On page 233 you speak of Reno as moving down a creek called "Reno's Creek." This is wrong. The creek is called "Benteen" or "Sundance" Creek. (See map opposite page 230.)

The country between the line on map "Custer's Route" and the river is impassable for horses, and *almost* so for footmen, therefore Custer had to either go forward before striking the village, or else turn back and cross where Reno did. Notice on the map that he never got within rifle distance of the Indian village.

Again on page 230 I think your "time" is wrong. Gall stated, by pointing, that the sun was nearly overhead when Custer and his immediate command was annihilated, and that this particular part of the fight lasted *much less than an hour*, probably not over half an hour. Another thing the Indians say is that many of the soldiers were pulled from their horses, that the horses were unmanageable, and that the soldiers had to use both hands to hold them in, pulling and jerking the reins, and sawing the horses' mouths from side to side.

Another story they tell is that some of the men with gray horses tried to get away, and that the dismounted soldiers on the hill fired into them to try and make them come back. Of course this latter story was never told in public.

Now, my dear sir, having bored you enough I will close — but I have one request to make, and that is, if you ever find out the truth of the "Affidavit" spoken of by General Miles that you let me know. I agree with you perfectly, as you will see from my manuscript written in 1895, that Custer disobeyed his orders in spirit and in fact; but one thing I disagree with, and that is that in my opinion Reno and his whole command would have been wiped out if he had ever pushed his first attack "home" as the saying is. The village extended full three miles down the valley teeming with warriors, young boys and young women. Few old people and few children were in the village, and if Reno had charged into this mass no one man would have lived to either get through or to get back.

One of Custer's men, so the Indians say, got away on his horse down the Little Big Horn, and the chase was given up, but the Indians chasing him watched to see where he would go. After a little he stopped, placed his revolver to his head, and blew his brains out. The Indians then caught his horse.

Very truly yours,

WM. H. C. BOWEN,
Lieut. Col. 13th Inf.

II

CUSTER'S LAST FIGHT

Compiled by Lieut. Col. Wm. H. C. Bowen, U. S. A.

Gen. George A. Custer graduated from the Military Academy in 1861, going immediately to the front. He was a young man of indomitable pluck, and although of the lowest military rank, he soon proved himself so able and willing that within a year he was a captain and aide-de-camp; and within another year he had raised himself to the rank of Brigadier General of Volunteers. In 1865 he was promoted Major General, and served as such until mustered out early in 1866. At the reorganization of the Army in 1866 four cavalry regiments were added to it, the Seventh, Eighth, Ninth, and Tenth, and Custer was gazetted to the Seventh, as Lieutenant Colonel.

The regiment, under Custer's command, saw much active service against Indians in Nebraska, Kansas, and Indian Territory during the next two years; after which it went South until 1873, when a part of it was moved to Dakota, taking station at Fort Abraham Lincoln (opposite Bismarck, North Dakota). A part was at Fort Rice, Dakota, and a part did not come from the South until just before the expedition started.

For some years previous to this there had been troubles of various kinds with the Sioux Indians and kindred tribes. In 1866 Forts C. F. Smith, on the Big Horn River, Montana, and Phil Kearney, on the Little Piney, Wyoming, had been established to open and protect a wagon-road from a point near the then western limit of civilization, to the rich mines and splendid grazing lands of western Montana. The Indians, owning the country through which the road ran, protested. They did not care to have *any* white men in their country; they did not wish to have *any* soldiers near there. They had no wish for civilization. Game was plenty; the great plains were covered with buffalo, elk, deer and antelope. The climate was suited to their habits, and they were contented. Who can blame them ? That whole section of country was a "Garden Spot," and to one who knew it in those days the love of the Indian for it is no wonder. If the "white man" could have been kept out, it would still be a paradise for the hunter; but Providence had other ends in view. The adventurous white man could not be kept back for long; gold was discovered in the "Black Hills," and what can keep a white man from gold ? Nothing. Indian protests and orders from the Government availed nothing. Adventurers *would* go into the forbidden country, and of course some of them were killed by the right-ful owners. These killings called for reprisals, and before long the Government found itself with an Indian war on its hands.

In 1874 and 1875 General Crook, from the Department of the Platte, with headquarters at Omaha, Nebraska, and troops, including the Seventh Cavalry from the Department of Dakota, made incursions into the Indian country, embracing Wyoming, Dakota, and Montana, and lost some men, but there was no general fight. The Indians hostile to the Government by this time amounted to thousands, and the President, Generals Sherman and Sheridan, and others in authority, had many consultations as to the best methods of bringing these Indians to terms. The question had passed beyond the power of moral suasion; nothing but force would do.

So, early in 1876, General Crook started against these disaffected Indians, composed of the different tribes of the Sioux, the Northern Cheyennes, etc. He struck them near the head waters of the Rosebud River, and suffered a severe check, if not a defeat. At any rate, he found that nothing short of several thousand troops would be sufficient to teach the Wards of the Nation the lesson needed. Placing his command in a strong camp he waited for reinforcements. General Terry, with the Seventh Cavalry and an infantry force, was to come in from the north and east. General Gibbon, with the Seventh Infantry and a battalion of the Second Cavalry, was to come from the west, while General

Crook's reinforced command was to close in from the south. If these several commands had moved in unison the Indians would have been hemmed in and surrounded without possibility of escape, but such was not to be the case.

The country in which all these movements were to take place was at this time absolutely a *terra incognita* — an unknown country. No white guides could be found, because white men had never been over the ground. For the same reason there were no reliable maps of this region. All was guesswork, consequently there could be no unity of movement.

On May 17th General Terry's command left Fort Lincoln for the hostile camp, wherever it might be found, situated somewhere in the West, hundreds of miles distant. In order to subsist this command in an uninhabited country, a large pack-train, a wagon-train of over one hundred wagons, besides ambulances, were required. This wagon-train carried thirty days' rations and forage, extra ammunition, tents, cooking utensils, bedding, hospital supplies, etc., etc. A steamboat had been sent up the Yellowstone River with extra supplies, and to act as a base of supplies.

A day's march covered from ten to forty miles, generally averaging perhaps twenty miles, and determined in great measure by the requirements of wood, water and grass; wood for fires, for of course no wood could be carried by the wagons; water for both men and animals; grass for the grazing of the animals.

There were approximately about 1,500 animals which had to be cared for, in addition to the men. A campaign against Indians meant something more than marching and fighting. It meant also providing against starvation and sickness, and required much forethought and preparation on the part of the commander and his staff-officers.

Reveille was generally sounded from 4:30 to 5 o'clock A.M., and by 6 o'clock the command was usually on the march. Camp was made about 2 o'clock P.M., sometimes a little earlier, seldom much later, for time was needed in which to give the animals their much-needed grazing.

On May 29th the command reached the Little Missouri. On the 30th General Custer and four troops scouted up this stream for twenty miles or more, but found no recent Indian signs. On the 31st the crossing of this stream took place. The command lay in camp June 1st and 2nd, on account of a snowstorm. On or near the Little Missouri was the place where it was expected that first signs of the hostiles would be found; but as the scout of Custer, just referred to, had been barren of results, the Indian village must be looked for farther south or west, somewhere in the region covered by the Big Horn, Little Big Horn, Rosebud, Tongue and Powder Rivers, all of these streams heading in the Big Horn range of mountains.

On June 8th Terry's and Gibbon's columns joined each other near the mouth of Powder River. Gibbon reported no recent "signs" north of the Yellowstone, which proved conclusively that the whole body of Indians *must* be within the country just referred to. Now, if all went well, they would be caught between two fires, Crook on the south, Terry and Gibbon combined on the north. They could not slip through to the west on account of the Yellowstone River. They might get away to the east and go back to their reservations, but this was not likely without a fight. Now as to their numbers.

About one third of the whole Sioux Nation, including the Northern Cheyennes and Arapahoes, were present at the battle, estimated, including women and children, at between twelve and fifteen thousand; one out of four is a low estimate in determining the number of warriors present. (Every male over fourteen years of age may be considered a warrior in a general fight, such as was the battle of the Little Big Horn.) Also, considering the extra hazards of the hunt and expected battle, fewer squaws would accompany the recruits from the agencies. The *minimum* strength of their fighting men may then be put down as between 2,500 and 3,000, with probabilities that they were nearer 4,000. Frank Grouard, General Crook's chief scout, estimated the fighting strength of the camp at 9,000—all armed with latest improved firearms, Winchesters mostly.

The principal warrior chiefs of the hostile Indians were: "Gall," "Crow King," and "Black Moon," Uncpapa Sioux; "Low Dog," "Crazy Horse," and "Big Road," Ogalalla Sioux; "Spotted Eagle," Sans-Arc-Sioux; "Hump" of the Minneconjous; and "White Bull," "Little Horse," and "Lame Deer," of the Cheyennes. To these belong the chief honors of conducting the battle, of whom, however, "Gall," "Crow King," and "Crazy Horse" were the ruling spirits in the fight.

But, you say, what of "Sitting Bull"? I thought he was the chief, the ruling spirit over all, the head man. I will tell you.

There were a number of Sioux Indians under Sitting Bull, known as hostiles, who never went to an Agency, except to visit friends and relatives (for the greater number of Indians at this time were collected at agencies, where they were partly fed and clothed by the Government, but were allowed to leave, on pass, for the purpose of hunting, visiting, etc.). They, the hostiles, camped in and roamed about the buffalo country. Their camp was the rendezvous for the Agency Indians, when they went out for their annual hunts for meat and robes. They comprised representatives from all the different tribes of the Sioux Nation. Many of them were renegade outlaws from the agencies. In their visits to the agencies they were usually arrogant and fomenters of discord. Depredations had been made upon the commerce to the Black Hills, and a number of lives taken by them or by others, for which they were blamed.

The authorities at Washington had determined to compel these Indians to reside at the agencies,— hence one reason for the Sioux War of 1875-76. This was also known as an Interior Department war. In 1875 the Interior Department sent runners to the hostiles; telling them to come in or "we will bring you in." The Indians, feeling themselves extremely strong, were very arrogant, and replied: "We know the way in; if we don't come in, you come out and fetch us; we'll be here when you come; we'll wait for you."

Sitting Bull (Ta-tan-ka I-yo-tan-ka), an Uncpapa Sioux Indian, was the chief of the hostile camp; he had about sixty lodges of followers on whom he could at all times depend. He was the host of the hostiles, and as such received and entertained their visitors. These visitors gave him many presents, and he was thus enabled to make many presents in return. All visitors paid tribute to him, so he gave liberally to the most influential, the chiefs, — i. e., he "put it where it would do the most good." In this way he became known as the chief of the hostile Indian camp, and the camp was generally known as "Sitting Bull's Camp."

Sitting Bull was a heavy-set, muscular man, about five feet eight inches in stature, and at the time of the battle of the Little Big Horn was forty-two years of age. In council his views had great weight, because he was known as a great medicine man. He was a chief, but not a warrior; he was a diplomat, but not a soldier. A short time previous to the battle he had "made medicine," and had predicted that the soldiers would attack the Indians, and that the soldiers would all be killed. He took no active part in the battle, but, as was his custom in time of danger, remained in the village, or on a hilltop near it, "making medicine." Personally, he was regarded as a great coward and a very great liar, "a man with a big head and a little heart." (Left the camp in such a hurry that he left one of his twins behind.) Frank Grouard, General Crook's chief scout, — a white man who was captured by the Sioux and who lived with them for six years, — says that Sitting Bull was a brave warrior, that he would not ask or order a man to go where he would not lead, etc. This may have been true, but the concensus of opinion seems to be as I first stated.

The command passed the remains of a lodge where a "Sun dance" had taken place, about June 5th. This was always a ceremony of great importance to the Indians.

On June 10th Major Reno, Seventh Cavalry, was detached from the command with six troops of the Seventh Cavalry, to scout up the Powder to the Little Powder, thence over to Mizpah Creek, from Mizpah to Pumpkin Creek, down the latter to the Tongue River, thence down the Tongue to the Yellowstone, where he would again join Terry with the balance of the command.

Now a few words in regard to the feelings, the personal feelings of the two senior officers of the Seventh Cavalry against their chief, General Terry. As early as May 8th, in St. Paul, Minnesota, and near the headquarters of the Department Commander, Custer said to a brother officer, referring to the coming campaign, in words to this effect: "It is my purpose to cut loose from Terry at the first opportunity, and make my operations independently of him. I got away from Stanley" (this referring to a campaign undertaken in a previous year, 1873), "and I will be able to swing clear of Terry." But unfortunately this remark of Custer's was not reported to Terry until after his return from the campaign. Wasn't this a breach of discipline? If Custer had these feelings it is possible that Reno shared them, for instead of carrying out his orders for the scout as just given, in direct violation of instructions he bolted straight for the Rosebud, which he struck near its mouth. He found a trail about three weeks old and followed it for a short distance, and then returned without having accomplished his mission, which was to ascertain whether there were any Indians on the head waters of Powder River, Tongue River, etc.

On June 19th General Terry received the news of Reno's discovery of the Indian trail. On the 21st he had a conference on board the steamboat "Far West," at which were present, besides himself, General Gibbon, General Custer, and several of the staff.

The Indian encampment was believed to lie to the north of the Big Horn Mountains, east of and near the Big Horn River, in the valley of the Little Big Horn River. The immense snow-fields of the Big Horn Mountains fill all these streams, and during the hot days of early summer a great volume of water pours down them. The incline of the bed of the Big Horn is so great that when the channel is full, as it usually is in the month of June, the stream is practically impassable. It is thus seen that the Indian position could only be approached from the north or east. If a concentrated attack was made from the north, a line of escape was left open to the eastward. General Terry's plan was for Custer's column, which was the strategic one of his command, to occupy this eastward line and so cut off escape in that direction before the Indians were disturbed, while Gibbon's column closed in from the north. In order to effect this "combined movement" and secure joint action as speedily as possible, it was very important that Gibbon should be informed of the situation from the head of Tulloch's Fork, and of Custer's discoveries and consequent movements.

General Custer was ordered with his regiment to follow the trail discovered by Reno *a certain distance*, then branch off toward the head waters of the Little Big Horn, locate the Indian village if possible, *and be in the valley of the Little Big Horn on June 26th*, when he would be joined by the rest of the command *as soon after that date as possible*. Terry with the balance of the command was to follow the Yellowstone to or near the mouth of the Big Horn, thence up its valley to the mouth of the Little Big Horn, where he would be not later than the night of the 26th. Note carefully the date, June 26th. Custer was also ordered to send scouts down Tulloch's Fork, and communicate with Terry, if possible. Special men, selected for the purpose, were detailed from Gibbon's command with this end in view, but were not used. Why? Because Custer had his own aims, intentions and objects to attain. He never intended to wait for Terry and Gibbon to come up; he hoped to strike the Indians and whip them without assistance. He wanted all the glory there was to be gotten out of it for himself alone; he even went so far as to refuse to take along the battalion of the Second Cavalry, which was a part of Gibbon's command. His desire was to get away by himself, to become his own master, to obey his own personal instincts only.

Noon of the 23rd General Custer mounted and started up the Rosebud, followed by the command. Eight miles out they came to the first of the Indian camping places. It certainly indicated a large village and numerous population. There were a great many "wickiups" (bushes stuck in the ground with the tops drawn together, over which they placed canvas or blankets). These were the temporary shelters of the transients from the agencies. During the day three of these camping places were passed through, and halts were made at each one. Everybody was busy studying the age of pony droppings and tracks and lodge trails, and endeavoring to determine the number of lodges. These points were the all-absorbing topics of conversation. Camp was made about 5 o'clock, having marched about fifteen miles.

June 24th the command passed a great many camping places, all appearing to be of nearly the same strength.

The march during the day was tedious; many long halts were made so as not to get ahead of the scouts, who seemed to be doing their work thoroughly in front, but giving no attention to the right, toward Tulloch's Fork, which was a great mistake and a direct violation of orders. About sundown camp was made; distance marched about thirty-five miles. Orders were given to be in readiness to move again at 11.30 P.M., and the march would be taken up, as Custer was anxious to get as near the divide as possible before daylight.

A little after 2 A.M., June 25th, the command was halted to await further tidings from the scouts; distance marched about ten miles. Part of the command unsaddled to rest the horses. After daylight some coffee was made, but it was almost impossible to drink it; the water was so alkaline that the horses refused to drink it. Some time before 8 o'clock, General Custer gave orders to be ready to march at 8 o'clock, and gave information that scouts had reported that they had discovered the locality of the Indian villages or camps in the valley of the Little Big Horn, about twelve or fifteen miles beyond the divide, but that he, Custer, didn't believe a word of it; that he had looked through their glasses and could see nothing. Just before setting out on the march, Custer, "Bloody Knife" (the Ree scout), and several other scouts, and a half-breed interpreter were squatted in a circle having a talk, after the Indian fashion. The scouts were doing the talking, and seemed nervous and disturbed. Finally "Bloody Knife" made a remark that Custer could not seem to understand, and he asked in his usual quick, brusque manner, "What's that he says?" The interpreter replied, "He says we'll find enough Sioux to keep us fighting two or three days." Custer smiled and remarked, "I guess we'll get through with them in one day."

The column started promptly at eight o'clock, and marched uninterruptedly until 10.30 A.M., when it halted in a ravine; distance marched about ten miles.

It will be noticed that from noon on the 23rd to 10.30 on the 25th about eighty-one miles had been covered.

Little sleep and no rest to speak of had been possible for either man or animals. Was this a fit condition with which to commence a desperate fight? No, a thousand times no. If a commander ever needs fresh men and fresh animals, it is at the beginning of an attack on an Indian village. No tired, sleepy, hungry, thirsty men are wanted at such a time.

Captain Varnum, Seventh Cavalry, has something to say about this march. I quote his own words:

"We got into camp about dark, and I was skirmishing for grub, being pretty well tired out. Custer came to our camp (the scouts') and sat down, holding a confab in the brush with the Crow scouts. Custer then explained to me that the Crows said that on the divide between the Little Big Horn and the Rosebud there was a high hill with a Crow's nest in it, where the Crows went when they tried to steal horses from the Sioux; that when it became daylight they could tell by the rising of the smoke whether there were Indians on the Little Big Horn or not. He wanted some intelligent white man to go with these Crows and get from them what they saw, and send word back to him. I told him I supposed that meant me, and it ended in my going. I took with me Charles Reynolds, Mick Bouyer, five Crows and eight or ten Rees. Custer said he would move at 11 o'clock at night; I was to go at 9. He would go to the base of the mountains where I was to be, and I was to send him a note as early as possible of what I learned. I got to the Crows' nest about 2.30 A.M. on the 25th, and about twenty-five miles from where I had left Custer. I threw myself down and fell asleep; but in about three-quarters of an hour I was waked up. It was then just day-light. The Indians (Crows) wanted me on the bluff above us. I scrambled up. I saw the two tepees, spoken of so often, on the branch down which we went to fight. The Indians tried to show me an immense pony herd in the valley of the Little Big Horn. I couldn't see it. They told me to 'look for worms.' In fact my eyes were pretty sore anyway. I had ridden about seventy miles without sleep, and my eyesight was not very good for long range. I sat down and wrote a despatch to Custer, and sent it off at about 4.45. Before the Rees left with the message, however, the smoke of some of Custer's camp-fires was seen about ten miles off, possibly not so far. The Crows were angry at Custer for allowing fires under the circumstances. Custer got my message at about 8 o'clock and started soon after, and the dust of his column could be plainly seen as soon as he did so, though not his troops."

It is seen that the most ordinary precautions against discovery were not taken, and indeed the advertisement of his approach was sufficient to excite the indignation of his scouts.

The Little Big Horn River, or the "Greasy Grass" as it is known to the Indians, is a rapid mountain stream, from 20 to 40 yards wide, with a pebbled bottom, but abrupt, soft banks. The water at the ordinary stage is from two to five feet in depth, depending upon the width of the channel. The general direction of its course is northeasterly down to the Little Big Horn battle-field, where it trends north-westerly to its confluence with the Big Horn River. The other topo-graphical features of the country which concern us may be briefly described as follows: Between the Little Big Horn and the Big Horn Rivers is a plateau of undulating prairie; between the Little Big Horn and the Rosebud are the Little Chetish or Wolf Mountains, a broken country of considerable elevation, of high precipitous hills and deep narrow gulches. The command had followed the trail up a branch of the Rosebud to within, say, a mile of the summit of these mountains which form the divide. Not many miles to the right was the divide between the Little Big Horn and Tulloch's Fork. The creek that drained the watershed to the right and front is now called Sundance, or Benteen's Creek. The trail, very tortuous, and sometimes danger-ous, followed down the bed and valley of this creek, which at that time was dry for the greater part of its length. It was from the divide between the Little Big Horn and the Rosebud that the scouts had dis-covered the smoke rising above the village, and the pony herds grazing in the valley of the Little Big Horn, somewhere about twelve or fif-teen miles away.

Here we find Custer and his command within sight of the Little Big Horn, and nowhere near so far to his left as he had been ordered to feel, thirty-six hours ahead of time. Not only this, but his presence had been discovered by the enemy. Why has he not communicated with Terry? Why has he not used the scouts sent for this purpose? Why has he made a night march, a march of torture to man and beast? I answer: "For his own personal and selfish ends." He had no wish, no desire to coöperate with the other commands. Of course he wished to whip the Indians, but his wish was to do it himself; to have assist-ance from no one. If there was to be any glory or reward to come from this affair, Custer, and Custer only, was to be benefitted.

Of course, if the plan had been carried out, Custer, at the expected time, — the 26th, not the 25th, — would have found himself nearly in contact with the enemy.

A well-matured plan, based on reasonable conclusions from known facts, contemplating the coöperative action of two bodies of troops, intending to bring them into joint action at a specific date and place, — the purpose explained not alone in the written orders, but in full con-ference of all the commanders, — is defeated by the failure of one column to carry out its assigned share, and this failure not caused by unforeseen conditions found to exist by its commander while in its execution, but because he followed the trail directly, which he was certainly "desired," if not actually forbidden, *NOT* to do, and arrived at the point of coöperation thirty-six hours in advance of the appointed time.

In this there was wilful and direct disobedience, and there was hardly less culpable neglect of duty in the fact that no attempt was made to send to Terry, whose position was known and easily reached, one word of information that the whole plan of the march of that column was changed and that it would be on the appointed ground on the morning of the 25th, instead of the afternoon of the 26th.

Before quitting this feature of the case, let us see how General Gibbon put himself on record on this subject. In transmitting the map of his itineraryist from Fort Shaw, M. T., November 6, 1876, he writes as follows:

"So great was my fear that Custer's zeal would carry him forward too rapidly, that the last thing I said to him when bidding him good-by, after his regiment had filed past you when starting on his march, was, 'Now, Custer, don't be greedy, but wait for us.' He replied gaily, as with a wave of his hand he dashed off to follow his regiment, 'No, I will not.' Poor fellow! Knowing what we do now, and what an effect a fresh Indian trail seemed to have had upon him, perhaps we were expecting too much to anticipate a forbearance on his part which would have rendered coöperation of the two columns practicable.

"Except so far as to draw profit from past experience, it is perhaps useless to speculate as to what would have been the result had your plan, as originally agreed upon, been carried out. But I cannot help reflecting that in that case my column, supposing the Indian camp to have remained where it was when Custer struck it, would have been the first to have reached it; that with our infantry and Gatling guns we should have been able to take care of ourselves, even though numbering about two thirds of Custer's force, and that with 600 cavalry in the neighborhood, led as only Custer could lead it, the result to the Indians would have been very different from what it was."

Crook had had a "check" but no massacre, and even the remainder of Custer's column was able to hold out against the victory-flushed Indians until Terry and Gibbon came up. Then, notwithstanding the fact that this latter force numbered but 400 men, and the Indian force was practically untouched, they incontinently fled. Is it not easily conceivable that, had Gibbon and Custer been acting together, as Terry had planned, the force would certainly have had no check, much less an overwhelming disaster, if indeed it failed of a signal victory? Even if Custer's whole body of troops had been together, it is most probable that no such disaster could have occurred. Indeed, it is well established that, at the inception of Custer's attack, the Indians began packing up and preparing to fly, some of them actually leaving the field; and possibly the signs of this purpose, which Custer could easily observe from the high hills he was on, led him to believe that the village was in full flight, and prompted his hasty and disastrous attack on the village from the north. Let us be charitable and think so, at any rate.

It may not be out of place here to quote what the late Lieut. Gen. P. H. Sheridan has said officially on this subject:

"Had the Seventh Cavalry been kept together it is my belief it would have been able to handle the Indians on the Little Big Horn, and under any circumstances it could have at least defended itself; but separated as it was into three detachments, the Indians had largely the advantage, in addition to their overwhelming numbers."

Custer made a forced march and held to the Indian trail instead of moving still southward, and this brought him on the night of the 24th near to the position he ought to have occupied on the morning of the 26th, and at least thirty-six hours before Gibbon could possibly be expected to be in place. The fact that Custer did not have any new information concerning the hostile Indians when he began forcing the pace is put beyond question by Captain Varnum, his chief of scouts.

We now come to the fight, and I take my account from Captain (then Lieutenant) Godfrey, who commanded Troop K, a part of Benteen's battalion; from Benteen himself; from Colonel Goldin, late a private in the Seventh Cavalry; from Gall, one of the principal Indians in the conflict; from Colonel Hughes, late aide-de-camp to eneral Terry; and from other sources.

It was well known to the Indians that the troops were in the field, and a battle was fully expected by them; but the close proximity of the column was not known to them until the morning of the day of the battle. Several young men had left the hostile camp on that morning to go to one of the agencies in Nebraska. They saw the dust made by the column of troops; some of their number returned to the village and gave warning that the troops were coming, so that the attack was not a surprise.

Just before starting on the last stage of the march which ended in the fight, troop commanders were ordered to make a detail of one non-commissioned officer and six men to accompany the packs; to inspect their troops and report as soon as they were ready to march;

that the troops would take their places in the column of march in the order in which reports of readiness were received, and that the last one to report would escort the pack-train. This was an order already in force, but was reiterated.

The inspections were quickly made and the column was soon *en route*, Benteen in advance, as he was first to report. The command passed the last dividing ridge between the Rosebud and Little Big Horn valleys a little before noon. The regiment had already been divided into battalions, 1 under Major Reno, 3 troops, 1 under Colonel Benteen, 3 troops, and Custer himself, 5 troops, and pack-train, 1 troop.

Benteen's column had already moved out and was several miles away when the rest of the regiment started.

Major Reno's battalion marched down a valley that developed into the small tributary to the Little Big Horn, now called Sundance, or Benteen's Creek. The Indian trail followed the meanderings of this valley. Custer's column followed Reno's closely and several hundred yards to the right, and the pack-train followed them about nine miles behind. Benteen's battalion was ordered to the left and front, to a line of high bluffs about three or four miles distant. Benteen was ordered to send word if he saw anything to Custer, but to pitch into anything he came across; if, when he arrived at the high bluffs, he could not see any enemy, he should continue his march to the next line of bluffs, and so on, until he could reach the Little Big Horn Valley. He marched over a succession of rough, steep hills and deep valleys. The view from the point where the regiment was organized into battalions did not discover the difficult nature of the country, but as it advanced farther the terrane became more and more difficult and more forbidding.

The horses were greatly jaded by the climbing and descending, some getting far to the rear of the column. Benteen very wisely determined to follow the general direction of the rest of the command, and he got into their trail just in advance of the pack-train. During this march on the left he could occasionally see the battalion under Custer, distinguished by the troop mounted on gray horses, marching at a rapid gait.

Some time before getting on the trail Benteen came to a water hole, or morass, at which a stream of running water had its source. He halted the battalion and watered the horses. Just as he was leaving the water hole the pack-train was arriving, and the poor thirsty mules plunged into the morass in spite of the efforts of the packers to prevent them, for they had not had water since the previous evening. A burning tepee was passed, fired presumably by the Indian scouts of the command, in which was the body of a warrior, who, as was afterward learned, had been killed in the battle with Crook's troops, on the Rosebud, on the 17th of June.

The battalions under Reno and Custer did not meet any Indians until Reno arrived at the burning tepee; here a few were seen. These Indians did not act as if surprised by the appearance of troops; they made no effort to delay the column, but simply kept far enough in advance to invite pursuit. Reno's command and the scouts followed them closely, after he received orders "to move forward at as rapid a gait as he thought prudent, and charge the village afterward, and the whole outfit would support him." This order was received when Reno was about five miles from the Little Big Horn River. His battalion moved at a trot to the river, where he delayed about ten or fifteen minutes, watering the horses and reforming the column on the left bank of the stream. Reno now sent word to Custer that he had everything in front of him and that the enemy was strong. Custer had moved off to the right, being separated from Reno by a line of high bluffs and the river. Reno moved forward in column of fours about half a mile, then formed the battalion in line of battle across the valley, with the Indian scouts on the left; after advancing about a mile farther, he deployed the battalion as skirmishers. In the meantime, the hostiles, continually reinforced, fell back, firing occasionally, but made no decided effort to check Reno's advance. The horses of two men became unmanageable and carried them into the Indian camp. The Indians now developed great force, opened a brisk fire, mounted, and made a dash toward the foot-hills on the left flank where the Ree scouts were. The scouts ignominiously fled, most of them abandoning the field altogether, and never stopped until they reached the supply camp at Powder River, nearly 170 miles to the rear.

Reno, not seeing the "whole outfit" within supporting distance, disobeyed his orders to charge the village; he dismounted his command to fight on foot. The movements of the Indians around the left flank and the flight of the scouts caused the left to fall back until the command was on the defensive in the timber, and covered by the bank of the old river-bed. Reno's loss thus far was one wounded, and the two who had been carried into the Indian camp by the runaway horses. The position was a strong one, well protected in front by the bank and fringe of timber, somewhat open in the rear, but sheltered by timber in the bottom. Those present differ in their estimates of the length of time the command remained in the bottom after they were attacked in force. Some say "A few minutes," others "about an hour." While Reno remained there his casualties were few. The hostiles had him nearly surrounded, and there was some firing from the rear of the position by Indians on the opposite bank of the river. One scout, "Bloody Knife," was killed close to where Reno was, and directly afterward Reno gave orders to those near him to "mount and get to the bluffs." This order was not generally heard or communicated; while those who did hear it were preparing to execute it, he countermanded the order, but soon after he repeated the same order, "to mount and get to the bluffs," and again it was not generally understood. Individuals, observing the preparations of those on the left, near Reno, informed their troop commanders, who then gave orders to mount. Owing to the noise of the firing and to the absorbed attention they were giving the enemy, many did not know of the order until too late to accompany the command. Some remained concealed until the Indians left, and then came out. Four others remained until night and then escaped. Reno's command left the bottom by troop organization in column. Reno was the foremost in this retreat or "charge" as he termed it in his report. The hostile strength pushed Reno's retreat to the left, so he could not get to the ford where he had entered the valley, but they were fortunate at striking the river at a fordable place; a pony trail led up a funnel-shaped ravine into the bluffs. Here the command got jammed and lost all semblance or organization. The Indians fired into them, but not very effectively. There does not appear to have been any resistance, certainly no organized resistance, during this retreat.

Lieut. Donald McIntosh was killed soon after leaving the timber. Dr. DeWolf was killed while climbing one of the bluffs a short distance from the command. Lieut. B. H. Hodgson was wounded in the leg, and his horse was killed. He took hold of a comrade's stirrup and was carried across the stream, but soon afterward was shot again and killed. During the retreat, Private Davern, Troop "F," had a hand-to-hand conflict with an Indian; his horse was killed; he then shot the Indian, caught the Indian's pony, and rode to the command.

Reno's casualties thus far were, 3 officers and 29 enlisted men and scouts killed; 7 enlisted men wounded; and 1 officer, 1 interpreter, and 14 soldiers and scouts missing. Nearly all the casualties occurred during the retreat and after leaving the timber. The Ree scouts, as already stated, continued their flight until they reached the supply camp at the mouth of the Powder; the Crow scouts remained with the command.

We will now go back to Benteen's battalion. Not long after leaving the water hole, a sergeant met him with an order from Custer to the commanding officer of the pack-train to hurry it up. The sergeant was sent back to the train with the message; as he passed the column he said to the men, "We've got 'em, boys." From this and other remarks it was inferred that Custer had attacked and captured the village.

Shortly afterward the command was met by an orderly, bearing this message, signed by Colonel Cooke, Adjutant: "Benteen, come on. Big village. Be quick. Bring packs," with the postscript, "Bring packs." The column had been marching at a trot and walk, according as the ground was smooth or broken. Firing was heard; the valley was full of horsemen riding to and fro in clouds of dust and smoke, for the grass had been fired by the Indians, to drive the troops out and cover their own movements. On the bluffs to the right was seen a body of troops, and they were engaged. But an engagement appeared to be going on in the valley, too. Owing to the distance, smoke, and dust, it was impossible to distinguish if those in the valley were friends or foes. Benteen ordered his battalion to dismount and deploy as skirmishers on the edge of the bluffs overlooking the valley, and his timely arrival probably saved Reno's command from annihilation, for very soon after this the Indians withdrew from the attack.

Benteen's battalion was ordered to divide its ammunition with Reno's men, who had apparently expended, but probably lost, nearly all in their personal possession.

While waiting for the ammunition pack-mules, Major Reno concluded to make an effort to recover and bury the body of Lieutenant Hodgson. At the same time he loaded up a few men with canteens to get water for the command; they were to accompany the rescuing party. The effort was futile; the party was ordered back after being fired upon by some Indians who doubtless were scalping the dead near the foot of the bluffs.

At this time there were a large number of horsemen, Indians, in the valley — at least 1,000, says Benteen. Suddenly they all started down the valley, and in a few minutes scarcely one was to be seen. During this time the questions were being asked: "What's the matter with Custer, that he doesn't send word what we shall do?" "Wonder what we are staying here for?" etc., thus showing some uneasiness; but still no one seemed to show great anxiety, nor did any one feel any serious apprehension but that Custer could and would take care of himself. Some of Reno's men had seen a party of Custer's command, including Custer himself, on the bluffs about the time the Indians began to develop in Reno's front. This party was heard to cheer, and seen to wave their hats as if to give encouragement, and then they disappeared behind the hills, or at any rate, escaped further attention from those below. It was about the time of this incident that Trumpeter Martini left Cooke with Custer's last orders to Benteen.

During a long time after the junction of Reno and Benteen, firing was heard down the river in the direction of Custer's command. All were satisfied that Custer was fighting the Indians somewhere, and the conviction was expressed that "our command ought to be doing something or Custer would be after Reno with a sharp stick."

Captain Weir and Lieutenant Edgerly, after driving the Indians away from Reno's command on their side, heard the firing, became impatient at the delay, and thought they would move down that way. Weir started in person, without orders and without permission, to take a survey from the high bluffs to the front. Edgerly seeing Weir going in the direction of the firing, supposed it was all right and started down the ravine with the troop. Weir from the high point saw Indians in large numbers start for Edgerly, and signaled for him to change his direction, and Edgerly went over to the high point, where they remained, not seriously molested, until the remainder of the troops marched down there. He was, however, soon attacked in force, and Benteen moved forward with the rest of his battalion and rescued him from his perilous position.

McDougall came up with the pack-train, and reported the firing when he reported his arrival to Reno. It was twenty minutes past four. It was about this time that thirteen men and a scout named Henderson rejoined the command; they had been missing since Reno's fight from the bottom; several of them were wounded. These men had lost their horses in the stampede from the bottom, and had remained in the timber; when leaving the timber to rejoin they were fired upon by five Indians, but they drove them away and were not again molested.

It was about half past two when Benteen joined Reno. About 5 o'clock the command moved a short distance down toward Custer's supposed whereabouts, intending to join him. The advance went as far as the high bluffs, where the command was halted. On the left of the valley a strange sight attracted their attention. Some one remarked that there had been a fire that scorched the leaves of the bushes, which caused the reddish brown appearance, but this appearance was changeable. Watching this intently for a short time with field-glasses, it was discovered that this strange sight was the immense pony herds of the Indians. The number of ponies in this camp at this time is estimated at from 30,000 to 50,000.

Looking toward Custer's field, on a hill two miles away was seen a large assemblage. At first the command did not appear to attract their attention, although there was some commotion observable among those nearer to its position. Occasional shots were heard, most of which seemed to be a great distance off, beyond the large group on the hill. While watching this group, the conclusion was arrived at that Custer had been repulsed, and the firing was the parting shots of the rear-guard. The firing ceased, the groups dispersed, clouds of dust rose from all parts of the field, and the horsemen converged toward Reno's position. The command was now dismounted to fight on foot.

Weir's and French's troops were posted on the high bluffs and to the front of them; Godfrey's troop along the crest of the bluffs next to the river; the rest of the command moved to the rear to occupy other points in the vicinity, and to take a good defensive position. At this time Weir's and French's troops were being attacked. The led horses were sent to the main command. The fire in a short time compelled the Indians to halt and take cover, but before this was accomplished a second order came to fall back as quickly as possible to the main command. Having checked the pursuit the retreat was begun, slowly at first, but keeping up the firing. After proceeding some distance the men began to group together and to move a little faster and faster, and the fire slackened. This was pretty good evidence that they were getting demoralized. The Indians were being heavily reinforced, and began to come from their cover, but kept up a heavy fire. The line was halted, the men were made to take their intervals, and again drove the Indians to cover; then once more began the retreat. The firing of the Indians was very heavy; the bullets struck the ground all about; but the "ping-ping" of the bullets overhead seemed to have a more terrifying influence than the "swish-thud" of the bullets that struck the ground near by.

The Indians, having taken possession of all the surrounding high points, opened a heavy fire; they had in the meantime sent a large force up the valley, and soon the troops were entirely surrounded by the enemy. It was now about 7 o'clock P.M. The firing continued until nearly dark (between nine and ten o'clock).

Of course everybody was wondering about Custer, why he did not communicate by courier or signal. But the general opinion seemed to prevail that he had been defeated and driven down the river, where he would probably join General Terry, and with whom he would return to Reno's relief. Quite frequently, too, the question, "What's the matter with Custer?" would evoke an impatient reply.

It has been previously noted that General Custer separated from Reno before the latter crossed the Little Big Horn under orders to charge the village. Custer's column bore to the right of the river. A ridge of high bluffs and the river separated the two commands, and they could not see each other. On this ridge, however, Custer and staff were seen to wave their hats, and heard to cheer just as Reno was beginning the attack; but Custer's troops were at that time two miles or more to his right. It was about this time that the trumpeter was sent back with Custer's last orders to Benteen, the last white man from Custer's column.

When Reno's advance was checked and his left began to fall back, Chief Gall started with some of his warriors to cut off Reno's retreat to the bluffs. On his way he was excitedly hailed by "Iron Cedar," one of his warriors, who was on the high point, to hurry to him, that more soldiers were coming. This was the first intimation the Indians had of Custer's immediate column; up to the time of this incident they had supposed that all the troops were in Reno's attack. Custer had then crossed the valley of the dry creek, and was marching along and well up the slope of the bluff forming the second ridge back from the river, and nearly parallel to it. The command was marching rapidly in column of fours, and there was some confusion in the ranks, due probably to the unmanageableness of some excited horses.

The accepted theory for many years after the battle, and still persisted in by some writers, was that Custer's column had turned the high bluffs near the river, moved down the dry (Reno's) creek, and attempted to ford the river at the lowest point of these bluffs; that he was there met by an overpowering force and driven back; that he then divided his battalion, moved down the river with the view of attacking the village, but met with such resistance from the enemy posted along the river-bank and ravines that he was compelled to fall back, fighting, to the position on the ridge. The numerous bodies found scattered between the river and ridge were supposed to be the first victims of the fight. I am now satisfied that these were the men who either survived those on the ridge, or attempted to escape the massacre.

The Indians state that Custer's column was never nearer the river or village than his final position on the ridge. On the battle-field, in 1886, Chief Gall indicated Custer's route to me, and it was on the high ridge east or back of the field.

The ford theory arose from the fact that there were found there numerous tracks of shod horses, but they evidently had been made after the Indians had possessed themselves of the cavalry horses, for they rode them after capturing them. No bodies of men or horses were found anywhere near the ford, and these facts are conclusive to my mind that Custer did not go to the ford with any body of men.

As soon as Gall had personally confirmed Iron Cedar's report, he sent word to the warriors battling against Reno, and to the people in the village. The greatest consternation prevailed among the families, and orders were given for them to leave at once. Before they could do so, the great bodies of warriors had left Reno and hastened to attack Custer. This explains how Reno was not pushed when so much confusion at the river crossing gave the Indians every opportunity of annihilating his command.

Not long after the Indians began to show a strong force in Custer's front, Custer turned his column to the left and advanced in the direction of the village to near a place marked as a spring, halted at the junction of the ravines just below it, and dismounted two troops, Keogh's and Calhoun's, to fight on foot. These two troops advanced at double time to a knoll, now marked by Crittenden's monument. The other three troops, mounted, followed them a short distance in their rear. The led horses remained where the troops dismounted. When Keogh and Calhoun got to the knoll the other troops marched rapidly to the right; Smith's troop deployed as skirmishers, mounted, and took position on a ridge, which, on Smith's left, ended in Keogh's position (now marked by Crittenden's monument), and, on Smith's right, ended at the hill on which Custer took position with Yates and Tom Custer's troops, now known as Custer's Hill, and marked by the monument erected to the command. Smith's skirmishers, holding their gray horses, remained in groups of fours.

The line occupied by Custer's battalion was the first considerable ridge back from the river, the nearest point being about a mile from it. His front was extended about three-fourths of a mile. The whole village was in full view. A hundred yards from his line was another but lower ridge, the farther slope of which was not commanded by this line. It was here that the Indians under Crazy Horse, from the lower part of the village, among whom were the Cheyennes, formed for the charge on Custer's hill. All bodies of Indians had now left Reno. Gall collected his warriors, and moved up a ravine south of Keogh and Calhoun. As they were turning this flank they discovered the led horses without any other guard than the horse holders. They opened fire upon the horse holders, and used the usual devices to stampede the horses — that is, yelling, waving blankets, etc.; in this they succeeded very soon, and the horses were caught up by the squaws. In this disaster Keogh and Calhoun probably lost their reserve ammunition, which was carried in the saddle-bags. Gall's warriors now moved to the foot of the knoll held by Calhoun. A large force dismounted and advanced up the slope far enough to be able to see the soldiers when standing erect, but were protected when squatting or lying down. By jumping up and firing quickly, they exposed themselves only for an instant, but drew the fire of the soldiers, causing a waste of ammunition. In the meantime Gall was massing his mounted warriors under the protection of the slope. When everything was in readiness, at a signal from Gall the dismounted warriors rose, fired, and every Indian gave voice to the war-whoop; the mounted Indians put whip to their ponies, and the whole mass rushed upon and crushed Calhoun. The maddened mass of Indians was carried forward by its own momentum over Calhoun and Crittenden down into the depression where Keogh was, with over thirty men, and all was over on that part of the field.

In the meantime the same tactics were being pursued and executed around Custer's Hill. The warriors, under the leadership of "Crow King," "Crazy Horse," "White Bull," "Hump," and others, moved up the ravine west of Custer's Hill, and concentrated under the shelter of the ridges on his right flank and back of his position. Gall's bloody work was finished in a few moments, and the annihilation of Custer was accomplished; the frightful massacre was completed.

Smith's men had disappeared from the ridge, but not without leaving enough dead bodies to mark their line. About twenty-eight bodies of men belonging to this troop and other organizations were found in one ravine near the river. Many corpses were found scattered over the field between Custer's line of defense, the river, and in the direction of Reno's Hill. These, doubtless, were of men who had attempted to escape; some of them may have been sent as couriers by Custer. This part of the fight only lasted thirty or thirty-five minutes. (One, however, escaped — blew out his own brains; sixteen escaped to the mountains, were followed and killed.)

There was a great deal of firing going on over the field after the fight, by the young men and boys riding about and shooting into the dead bodies; the heads of most of the dead were crushed in, and pounded almost to a jelly by the stone hammers in the hands of the squaws, who thronged to the scene of carnage as soon as the last soldier was dead, for the purpose of mutilating the dead bodies and of securing plunder, of which there was plenty.

This all happened on Sunday, June 25th. On Monday morning, long before light, the Indians began again their attack on Reno's position. During the night the troops had been busy throwing up intrenchments, securing water, attending to the wounded, etc., etc.; so when the attack was begun on Monday they were far better prepared for it than might have been supposed. The fighting was fast and furious, so far as the use of ammunition was concerned, but there were comparatively few casualties. The fighting lasted until nearly noon. In the meantime the Indians had fired the grass and the timber, and nothing could be seen at any distance on account of the smoke. Shortly after the firing ceased the smoke lifted sufficiently to show the whole camp filing past Reno's beleaguered hill, with strong bodies on flank and in rear, to protect the column from possible charges by the soldiers. It took the camp from five to eight hours to march past. One can well imagine from this the number of souls present in this, the largest camp known of on the American continent.

The rest of the day was given up by the troops to attending to exhausted nature, making better security for another possible attack, etc., for it seemed hardly possible that the victory-flushed host of hostiles would leave this handful of soldiers, after having made such a successful fight the day before.

Tuesday morning, June 27th, the command enjoyed the pleasure of a square meal, and had stock properly cared for. The commanding officer seemed to think the Indians had some "trap" set, and required the men to hold themselves in readiness to occupy the pits at a moment's notice. Nothing seemed determined, except to stay where they were. Not an Indian was in sight, but a few ponies were seen grazing down in the valley.

About 9.30 A.M. a cloud of dust was observed several miles down the river. A white man soon came up with a note from General Terry, addressed to General Custer, dated June 26th, stating that two of the Crow scouts had given information that Custer's column had been whipped and nearly all had been killed; that he did not believe their story, but was coming with medical assistance. The scout said that he could not get to the lines the night before, as the Indians were on the alert. Very soon after this Lieutenant Bradley, Seventh Infantry, came to the lines, and reported the death of Custer and 196 men. The shattered remnants of the command were simply dumfounded. This was the first intimation it had had of his fate. It was hard to realize; it did not seem possible.

General Terry and staff and officers of General Gibbon's column soon after approached, and their coming was greeted with prolonged cheers.

During the rest of that day all were busy collecting effects and destroying surplus property. The wounded were cared for and taken to the camp of the Montana column.

On the morning of the 28th, three days after the fight, the troops left the intrenchments to bury the dead of Custer's command. The morning was bright, and from the high bluffs they had a clear view of Custer's battle-field. They saw a large number of objects that looked like white boulders scattered over the field. Glasses were brought into requisition, and it was announced that these objects were dead bodies. Captain Weir exclaimed, "Oh, how white they look!"

All the bodies except a few were stripped of their clothing. Nearly all were scalped or mutilated, but there was one notable exception, that of General Custer, whose face and expression were natural; he had been shot in the temple and in the left side. Many faces had a pained, almost terrified expression. It is said that Rain-in-the-face, a Sioux warrior, has gloried that he had cut out and eaten the heart and liver of one of the officers. This I can hardly believe, for Benteen told me that when Rain-in-the-face saw Custer's body, he went to it, shook the right hand of the poor dead body, and said, "My poor friend." It was this same Rain-in-the-face that prevented Custer's body from being mutilated. Other bodies were mutilated in a disgusting manner. The bodies of Dr. Lord and Lieutenants Porter, Harrington and Sturgis were not found, at least not recognized. Afterward bodies taken for all but Harrington were recognized, for the Army Register of 1877 reports only his as missing.

The clothing of Porter and Sturgis was found in the village, and showed that they had been killed; 212 bodies were buried on the Custer field. The killed of the entire command was 270, including 5 civilians, relatives, newspaper reporters, and 1 scout, Charley Reynolds; and of wounded there were 52. The only living thing found on the Custer battle-field was Comanche, a troop horse, who was and still is cared for by the regiment. He is never ridden, but is always led out to all parades of the regiment.

Godfrey concludes his narrative thus:

"The question has often been asked, 'What were the causes of Custer's defeat ?' I should say:

"First: The overpowering numbers of the enemy and their unexpected cohesion.
"Second: Reno's panic rout from the valley.
"Third: The defective extraction of the empty cartridge shells from the carbines."

        Personally, I disagree entirely with the Captain in his conclusion, and give my own views as follows:

The causes of Custer's overwhelming defeat were:

First: Disobedience of orders in bringing on the fight thirty-six hours ahead of time.
Second: Separating his command into four columns, neither of which was within supporting distance of each other.
Third: His failure to believe that the Indians would make a bold attack.

Custer's force was abundant to have enabled him to obey his orders.

It was not ample, as Terry had foreseen, to meet a contingency not contemplated, and which could not have arisen had his orders been adhered to. We need go no farther than the story of what occurred after the annihilation of Custer to make it perfectly clear that his force was ample for all that he was instructed to do. This may be very briefly stated. Reno's attack was a miserable failure, ending in a disorderly rout and a scramble for the hills, where the cool head and noted courage of Benteen saved the two battalions from a disaster even greater than had occurred to Custer.

After sweeping Custer's five troops from the field, and encouraged by the victory over Reno in his attack on the upper part of the village, the Indians swarmed down upon the now assembled force in almost overwhelming numbers, evidently confident that it was a question of only a short time when it too would have to submit to the fate which had befallen the other. But it was not to be. Benteen was there; the remnant held its own, without water, without rest, without sleep, until

Gibbon's command came in sight, when the whole Indian force abandoned the field.

The gist of the plan for the campaign, as already stated, was to direct the movements of the two columns (Gibbon's and Custer's) in such a way that if the Indians fled they could not escape to the southeast without being driven upon Crook; they could not go to westward because they were already near the eastern bank of the Big Horn River, and the eastern boundary of the territory of the Crow Nation, with whom they were in open hostility; northward they would be met by Gibbon, and the Big Horn Mountains lie to the southward, in which they could not have maintained themselves for any considerable time if they once permitted themselves to be cooped up in them.

If they made a stand, the purpose is clearly set forth in Terry's report; Custer was to keep on the southward (after determining where the trail led), for the double purpose of intercepting flight if it should be attempted, but above all so to maneuver his strategic column as to give time for Gibbon's column to come up. This plan was founded on the belief that the two columns might be brought into coöperating distance of each other. Or, as Gibbon states in his letter of November 6th, previously referred to:

"I saw Custer depart on the 22nd, with his fine regiment fully impressed with the conviction that our chief aim should be to so move that whatever force might be on the Little Big Horn should not escape us. And it was fully understood between us that to give my troops time to come up, and to guard against escape of the Indians to the south, he should keep constantly feeling to his left."

The Indians had given ample proof in the affairs with Crook that they would make a good, stand-up fight. They were in numbers, as Gaul expressed it in my hearing, "like the grass that comes up in the spring." They were well armed, and had plenty of ammunition. Fight they would, and fight they did, inflicting a defeat which our army will never forget.

I close with a remark made by Sitting Bull while in the British Possessions, and referring to Custer's attack: "They tell you I murdered Custer. It is a lie. I am not a war chief. I was not in the battle that day. His eyes were blinded that he could not see. He was a fool and rode to his death. He made the fight, not I."

Note by General Godfrey

In reading over the testimony of Interpreter Girard, I notice he makes the important statement that Custer's orders to the scouts were that they must follow any trail that led to the left, no matter how small. This was on the night march, June 24th. To show further care in this matter, Varnum states that at a halt on the march of the 24th, I reported to the General that I had seen a small trail leading to the left some miles back on the trail, but had only followed it far enough to see that it led up a ravine some distance. He was asked if the scouts had made any report of it. On learning that they had not, the General was angry at the neglect to investigate by the scouts and he ordered Varnum to go back and investigate and report at once. It was found that it led up the ravine some distance, then over the prairie and then down into the valley to the main trail again. The incident had escaped my memory. This shows that there was no intention of letting the Indians escape by the left flank.

III

LETTER FROM COLONEL EWERT REGARDING GENERAL CUSTER

Dear Dr. Brady:

I have read your articles in "Indian Fights and Fighters" with much interest, which may be expl ined by the fact that I served out West in the regular army 186 -70; 1871-76 and 1878-83; the first period in the Thirty-sixth and Seventh Infantry in Wyoming and Utah; the second in the Seventh Cavalry in Tennessee, Dakota and Montana, and the third in the Fifth Infantry (mounted on Indian ponies a part of the time), in Montana and Dakota.

The articles relating to the Seventh Cavalry are, of course, of paramount interest, as I was personally acquainted with nearly every officer and enlisted man in the regim nt, and was with the command in both 1873 and 1874 expeditions.

I write this letter to inquire why you elaborate the little skirmish of August 4, 1873, and fail to mention the all-day fight of August 11th on the Yellowstone three miles below the mouth of the Big Horn, in which Lieutenant Braden was severely wounded, and Tuttle, Troop E, killed? Custer left Stanley on the evening of August 8th, with ten troops of his regiment, to follow a large, well-defined trail of about 600 Sioux hostiles. We rode all night and (excepting two short rests) all day on the 9th. On the evening of the 9th we arrived on the north bank of the river and found the trail leading into the stream. Indian scouts, swimming across, established the fact that the hostiles had crossed to the south bank and thence, as General Custer believed, over into the Valley of the Big Horn.

On the morning of the 10th Custer forded a small branch of the river on to a good-sized sand bar with the entire command, and from there endeavored to float our rations and ammunition across on a raft built during the previous night. The swift current prevented the raft reaching the south bank, although every exertion was made to have it do so, so that finally Custer ordered the troops back to their camp of the previous night. Now, it was understood in the command that General Stanley had positively instructed General Custer not to cross the river under any circumstances, yet here, in spite of this positive order the subaltern, on August 10th, endeavored by all the means at his command to disobey the superior. I mention this to show that your deductions as to deliberate intent to disobey Terry in 1876 had a parallel in 1873, with General Stanley.

While trying to cross the Yellowstone on the 10th approximately 1,200 Indians were lying in the bluffs on the other side, no doubt imploring the Great Spirit to permit us to cross over, as the extermination of our command, thus hemmed in between the bluffs and the river, would have been mere play for the Reds. The Indians, believing that we had abandoned the plan of crossing, attacked us at daybreak on the morning of the 11th. We were now fighting on the defensive, all the men being hid under the face of the bluff, and in firing only required to expose head and shoulders, and yet, in spite of this advantage, we were kept busy and never out of danger of ultimate defeat, until about four o'clock P.M., when General Stanley arrived with his infantry and a 3-inch Rodman. Then the Indians ran for the Big Horn Valley and disappeared from our view for the remainder of the summer.

I was First Sergeant in H Troop (Captain Benteen's) and left the Seventh April 10th, 1876, my term having expired, so that I was not "in at the death" in June, 1876.

I have always believed that General Custer never mentioned the battle on August 11th very much on account of the narrow escape we had from the fate which later overtook the regiment on the Little Big Horn. If, as you say, you are writing history, the above statement of facts may be of assistance in correctly setting forth the occurrences during the Yellowstone Expedition of 1873.

Very respectfully,

THEO. EWERT.

GENERAL GODFREY'S COMMENT ON GENERAL EWERT'S LETTER

MY DEAR DR. BRADY:

As to Colonel Ewert's letter, I presume that he was there because he relates particulars that indicate he was present. But his troop was not there. He belonged to Benteen's troop which was left at the stockade near the Glendive. Major C. A. Varnum has just joined at this post, and I showed him Ewert's letter and asked if he remembered anything about the so-called order to Custer forbidding him to cross the Yellowstone under any circumstances as claimed by Ewert. We did make every effort to cross the river, but without avail. There were no Indians confronting us to hamper our efforts. They did not discover our presence until early the next m rning, when an Indian came to the river just opposite our bivouac to water his horse; almost at the same time one of our men went down to the river for water and saw the Indian. The Indian turned his horse quickly and rode away. It was some little time before any body of Indians came to make the attack. Neither Varnum nor myself has any remembrance of the order that Ewert mentions so positively, and we both think that it was a camp story. J. F. Weston, Commissary General U. S. A., then a lieutenant in the Seventh, made heroic efforts to carry a line to the opposite shore, but the current was too swift. The morning of the 11th the river had fallen very much. But the Indians coming to us made it unnecessary to cross, in fact kept us very busy. Lieutenant Braden was wounded on the 11th as you state, not on the 4th as in the record as published in the Journal.

We did not think that we were in any great danger of massacre on the 11th. It is true that one troop, French's, which was on the downstream side across the valley was being pushed pretty hard when Stanley's column came in sight and the Indians cleared his front. The center had pushed them back some distance. Dismounted skirmishers, then three troops charged and drove them about a mile, halted for a few minutes, did some firing across a narrow deep cañon and then we got orders to charge and pursue, which we did for about five miles; *i. e.*, above the mouth of the Big Horn. Our orders were not to cross the Yellowstone. and this may be the foundation of the camp story of Ewert.

E. S. GODFREY.

IV

MEMORANDA ON THE WOLF MOUNTAIN CAMPAIGN, MONTANA, 1877 *

About Jan. 3, 1877, the command went into camp near Wolf Mountain, Tongue River, close to a cañon. I was still in the saddle contemplating with a pained aspect the appearance of the army wagon that contained the scouts' plunder and bedding, which as usual had been overturned in one of the numerous crossings of Tongue River, when General Miles called to me and directed me to take my party of scouts and go up the river some distance and watch out for Indians.

We had passed, the day before, the freshly abandoned camp of a large force of Indians, who were still in the vicinity.

Proceeding a mile up the cañon of the Tongue, we turned to the left, and from a point of bluff found an excellent lookout that was sheltered by a large cedar tree.

From this point we presently observed some Indians traveling down the valley; on nearer approach observing them with glasses, they appeared to be squaws. It was evident to me that they were either ignorant of the recent removal of the Indian camps from that vicinity, and the proximity of the troops, or that the Indians were up to some scheme.

As they neared our place of concealment, I saw that there were several women and a boy. I at once turned to the Indian scouts and warned them not to touch them. We rode down a gulch and quietly approached them. They stopped and commenced to cry. We made signs to them not to be afraid and motioned them to move on in the direction of our camp. They appeared to be Cheyennes and could not or would not talk Sioux.

They were taken to headquarters, and there being shortly thereafter an alarm of Indians up the valley, we struck out again in that direction.

This time the Indian scouts did not follow us. The party numbered five, as follows: the three Johnsons, Tom LaForge and myself. The Indians were seen in the distance, and when we had attained the point where the squaws were found, ten or fifteen Indians showed themselves behind a little rise of ground awaiting our approach. We immediately charged them and that is where we made a mistake.

The Indians were resting their guns on their crossed gun sticks, and

* See page 326, et seq., " Indian Fights and Fighters."

when within some sixty yards, some forty or fifty of them who had been concealed, rose up and delivered their fire as we circled and returned the volley. The poor marksmanship of the Indians alone saved us from extermination. Tom LaForge's horse was shot under him, and for this reason we took position near by in a small clump of scrub oak.

The firing then became general, the hostiles soon enclosing us on three sides. Our Indian scouts who had followed us took position about three hundred yards below; one only, the "Bannock," riding coolly through the fire to join us. I remember that he joined me in scaling a bank that overlooked our position, and together we drove off five Indians who were crawling to reach the brow of the bank. They were not fifteen yards away, and disappeared before we could get in a shot. We fired at a party riding across the flat and had the satisfaction of knocking one off his horse.

They made it so hot for us here that I was forced to rejoin my companions in the oak grove. The "Bannock," however, concealed himself in the grass and did good execution during the engagement. This Indian did not know what fear was.

By this time the command had become aware of our predicament and a detachment under Lieutenant Hargous, of the Fifth, had been sent to help us out. The approach of this force and the fire of the field Napoleon gun which sent a shell directly over us drove the Indians or seemed to from our front, and about dusk we took advantage of the lull and "got out of there."

Over 100 Indians were opposed to us. At the first fire one Indian was knocked down, another was struck from his horse in the fight that followed; but from the peculiar tactics and mode of fighting of these people it is impossible to tell if others were hit. All of my party were good shots and trained frontiersmen.

The next morning the Indians were all around us and a very pretty fight followed which lasted all day.

L. S. KELLY.
(Yellowstone Kelly.)

INDEX

INDEX

A

ADAMS, Lieut. I.Q., First Cavalry, signal officer, 288

Antelope Springs, 323

Applegate, Ivan D., agent, 261; fails to persuade Modocs of futility in resisting U. S. authority, 262; orders military to enforce compliance and thus begins the Modoc War, 263; his story of first battle, 272–279; acts as guide and interpreter, 274

Applegate, O. C., makes forced march to intercept Modocs, 277

Applegate's Ranch, 303

Appendix, 329 *et seq.*

Army and Navy Journal, 76

"At-tux," watchword of Modoc chief to begin massacre, 290

B

BACON, Lieut., marches to seize Thacher's Pass, 29

Bailey, Maj. H. L., 141; his note on battle of Clearwater, 161–163.

Bancroft, Lieut., 141; wounded at Clearwater, 158

Bannocks, friendly Indians, 221

Barncho, imprisoned for life, 253

Battle of the Big Hole, 164–190; of Camas Meadows, 191–197; of Clearwater, 17–18; of the Lava-Beds, 291–304; of White Bird Cañon, 90–111; *N. Y. Herald's* account of, 108–110; Gen. Perry's account, 112–118

Bear's Paw Mountains, Chief Joseph meets his Waterloo at, 224

Benteen, Capt., at Canon Creek, 216; mentioned, 329

Bernard, Capt., 132; at the lavabeds, 293; captures Indians' ponies, 293

Bibliography, 365

Biddle, Maj., his note on murder of commissioners, 290

Big Hole, Battle of, 164–190

Black Jim, executed for murder of peace commissioners, 252

Bloody Point, massacre of, 230

Blow, the first, 258.

Boddy, Mrs., her ghastly find, 278; her escape and wanderings, 279

Bogus Charley, 242; turns State's evidence, 252; his ruse, 271

Bomus, Lieut., improvises a mule pack train, 152

Boston Charley, medicine man, 239; shoots Dr. Thomas, 245; hanged, 253

THE END